an early journey
home

Remembering your son—
pg 163

Discovery House Publishers

Books, music, and videos that feed the soul with the Word of God

Box 3566 Grand Rapids, MI 49501

an early journey home

helping families work through the loss of a child

MARY ANN FROEHLICH

Library of Congress Cataloging-in-Publication Data

Froehlich, Mary Ann, 1955-
   An early journey home : helping families work through the loss of a child
     p. cm.
   ISBN 1-57293-061-6
   1. Church work with terminally ill children. 2. Church work with the bereaved. I. Title.

BV4460.6 .F76 2000
259'.6--dc21

                         00-034625

Cover Design: Stephanie Milanowski
Book Design: TypeRight Graphics, Grand Rapids, MI

Printed in the United States of America

    1 2 3 4 5 6 7 / CHG / 06 05 04 03 02 01 00

*Dedicated to all those children
who have taken an early journey home
and the families
who remained behind.*

*With deep appreciation to the families
who have shared their experiences.
Names have often been changed
to protect their privacy.*

Acknowledgments

I want to thank those who shared the vision for this book and offered their expertise to bring it to completion: Steve Fretwell and David Wiersbe for their spiritual insights; John Froehlich for his constant love, support, and computer expertise; PeggySue Wells for her tangible support and generosity of spirit; Robert DeVries, Carol Holquist, Tim Gustafson, and their team at Discovery House; and dear friends who have walked the road of grief with me.

I am especially grateful to those families who shared their grief experiences: Barbara, Max, and Marquis Garwood, Victoria and Mike Haskins, Virginia Hiramatsu, Bethany Homeyer, Hayley and Karen Horn, Don Matlock, Doral and Diana Matlock, Carol and Fred Patterson, Keith and PeggySue Wells and their children, Kathy and David Werum, and many families who chose to remain anonymous.

Contents

P A R T 3
Helping Grieving Families: Sudden Loss and Complicated Grief

Introductory Note

Many writers come to their craft only after they have been shattered by life in some way. —*Christopher Vogler*

Saying good-bye to one's own child is the most painful of human experiences. Parents travel the hardest journey. This book is not written for them. It is written for helpers who desire to minister effectively to terminally ill children and grieving families. Sharing their burden of loss will exhaust you physically, emotionally, mentally, and spiritually.

Death and grief are well-studied topics in secular and Christian circles. Yet the loss of a child is an area that some Christians still shy away from. Could this happen to us? It strikes too close to the core of our faith. It terrifies us and brings too many questions. Yet I believe that the majority of today's Christians want to deal with this tougher issue. You are one of them or you would not be reading this book. If we can learn to minister to persons who suffer this deepest, painful loss, we will be better equipped to help anyone grieving a loss. This book is written for pastors, chaplains, Christian health-care professionals, lay ministers, and friends of suffering families.

An Early Journey Home: Helping Dying Children and Their Families began fifteen years ago as my personal struggle to reconcile my faith as I watched terminally ill children suffer and die, leaving behind devastated families. I naively assumed that when I left my job in a children's hospital to pursue other opportunities and raise my own family, I would leave that world of suffering behind. But the professional wall came down only to allow me to walk more closely beside grieving friends, family, and others that God brought into my life. *An Early Journey Home: Helping Dying Children and Their Families* is a revised and expanded version of the original book.

While the focus of the original *Early Journey Home* was helping dying children and their families, this second book offers a more balanced treatment of sudden catastrophic loss and complex grief. I thank my friends at Discovery House for the privilege of continuing the journey.

*C*hapter 1

An Early Journey Home

"Kim expired. Sunday 10:45 AM."

Expired? I stared at the message posted at the therapist's center. It was Monday morning, and Kim had died almost a full twenty-four hours before.

Expired? What an odd word to use. Was the technical aspect of *expiration* supposed to distance us from the intense pain of Kim's death?

Expired? No, Kim had died and gone before us to take an early journey home.

I had been working at Children's Hospital only a couple of months when Kim became my first "favorite patient." She was a shy, blonde, blue-eyed, seven-year-old girl with leukemia, who was afraid of most of the hospital staff. She had opened up to me easily during our music therapy sessions and began to ask for me daily whenever she was hospitalized. It was easy for me to become attached to her; ours was a mutual love affair.

Medically, Kim was not supposed to die. She had a type of leukemia that was treatable, and she had been doing well at home in remission. But that Sunday morning she came to the hospital slumped over her father's shoulder and could not be revived.

Kim's funeral was the first child's funeral I had ever attended. The strongest memory that remains with me is the mental picture of her thirteen-old-sister, who had been inseparable from Kim, crying uncontrollably at the graveside and her parents trying to comfort her in the midst of their own grief. I knew that their pain would always be with them.

And so began my journey of working with dying children. I am not an expert on the death of a child. An expert is someone who has walked the road before. I am not expert, because I have not personally lost one of my own children. People like Kim's parents are experts.

I have been privileged to stand by many dying children and share the grief of the families who have lost them. Yet I know now that my deep pain and loss could not even come close to their suffering.

My dear friend and co-worker warned me that I was getting too close to Julie. Julie was a fragile six-year-old girl dying of cystic fibrosis. Struggling to make ends meet financially, her parents could rarely visit her. I spent every minute possible with Julie when she was hospitalized. She was usually found sitting on my lap or being carried by me through the hospital. I even attended her birthday party at the family's mobile home park and I recall that we couldn't light the candles on her birthday cake because of her oxygen tank. I had never been so attached to a patient. Her slow, lingering death hit me very hard. I accepted her death, but I would constantly ask God why she had to suffer so terribly.

My greatest weakness as a therapist was that I could not distance myself from the patients the way my co-workers could. Not yet having children of my own, the patients became "my" children. This intimacy forced me to take my own journey of pain, doubts, and questions. If you commit yourself to helping dying children and their families, you, too, will have to take a personal journey in the process.

As the months passed into years, the deaths of patients began to blur together in my mind, but the memories still haunted me.

Tina was bright, talented, pretty, and dying. She was a spunky six-year-old who was dying of leukemia and fighting it all the way. Tina was also a ham, and our music sessions were a great delight. We made tapes together singing her original compositions. We even taped a video in the hospital filming department. She played every instrument and sang every song that we could think of. We then had a screening in her hospital room, attended by her doctors, nurses, family, and friends. She had always dreamed of being a TV star and now she was one.

At her memorial service, to my shock, the minister played one of our tapes. It was too painful to hear that small voice singing again, after her death.

Tony was an eighteen-year-old Down syndrome young man who went into a coma and died following heart surgery. His mother, who never left his side, was devastated. Not only did she need to deal with her own grief but she found a lack of sincere empathy from those around her. As I later related this experience to friends, they suggested that perhaps "his death was a blessing since he was disabled." Anyone who has known or worked with Down syndrome individuals knows that they are some of the most precious, giving people God has placed on this earth. Tony was his mother's son and had been the focus of her life for eighteen years. His death left a gaping hole. Her pain was no less than any other mother.

Erin was a two-year-old dying of a brain tumor. Her mother didn't want to miss one minute with her, so they slept together at night. I always wondered what that first night after Erin's death was like without that little body beside her.

Charlie's mom was a single parent who had devoted her entire life to caring for her only child. I remember her coming often to the hospital after his death, bringing his toys and games to donate to the playroom. When she lost Charlie, she lost her role in life as well. She had nowhere to go.

Though never documented in any textbook, I have observed one common characteristic in the dying children I've known.

They seem to have a maturity and compassion for others far beyond their years. They are happy, giving, resilient, and courageous children. It is as if God has "grown them up" early for their special calling. You may be surprised to learn that a children's hospital can be a joyous place with more laughter than tears. Children are better equipped than adults to face death for one reason: children know how to seize the moment, live life to the fullest today, and not focus on the lost future. Entering into this last celebration of life is the key to effectively helping dying children and their families. They teach us how to help them die, embracing the life they have left.

There will be no way to diminish our grief upon the child's death. The price of intimacy is pain. Whenever we involve ourselves deeply in a relationship, we risk the pain of losing that loved one. That person has become a part of us, and it hurts when that part is cut away. It is no wonder that the most intimate of human relationships—parent to child—causes the greatest pain when it is severed. The process is major surgery and leaves a deep scar. Scratches heal and disappear. Scars heal and remain for life as reminders of past wounds. The initial pain may be gone, but the memory stays. The helper's scars are not as deep as the parents', but they certainly exist.

The greatest struggle on my journey to becoming an effective helper surprisingly did not come from the dying children and their families but from fellow Christians.

Sometimes Christians, who are otherwise solidly grounded in their faith, are uncomfortable discussing or even thinking about dying children. Most doctrinal positions and theological beliefs do not prepare us for this most tender aspect of human suffering.

One Sunday morning many years ago, I was lost in thought over a patient who had died the preceding Friday. In stark contrast, the head of the women's Bible group announced their next activity would be a tea where women could have "their fashion style and colors done."

It struck me with searing intensity that people were hurting and dying while the church was giving fashion classes. Where had the church lost sight of its real purpose, to be in the trenches of life with hurting people? The fact that the Christian life never was intended to be comfortable became undeniably real to me that Sunday morning.

Another experience occurred years before when I was a new Christian in college. With some dear friends, I became involved with the "God-intends-success-for-his-people" movement. We were all healthy, vibrant young people interested in professional ministry as we embarked on life's adventure. We were confident that God protected us daily. I was seduced by the attractive philosophy, mentally listing numerous mini-miracles a day. It wasn't that death and suffering were foreign to me. On the contrary, I had lost my share of dear loved ones to heart attacks, cancer, and accidents. But since these tragedies happened to our family of non-Christians, it occurred to me that a life with God's care prevented such painful experiences.

It wasn't long before my friend's husband lay dying in the hospital with a serious intestinal condition. The members of the group did not come to the hospital to visit, did not offer financial help, did not bring meals to his wife, or help in any other way. She specifically asked them to drive her to the hospital when she was exhausted, but they responded that the hospital was too far away. Instead they questioned the couple's faith, thereby adding guilt to their burden, and abandoned them. These Christians did not know how to suffer; therefore, they did not know how to help the suffering. It scared them, paralyzed them, and incapacitated them for ministry. If the essence of the gospel was to equip the saints for ministry, then it became clear to me that this view of Christianity was distorted and dangerous. It was a theology of spiritual immaturity and untested faith.

My journey of experiences forced me to carefully study Scripture to grasp God's biblical answers about suffering and death and to stop being afraid. Fear is our greatest obstacle to helping:

> *God is our shelter and our refuge,*
> *a timely help in trouble;*
> *so we are not afraid when the earth heaves*
> *and the mountains are hurled into the sea,*
> *when its waters seethe in tumult*
> *and the mountains quake before his majesty.*
>   —*Psalm 46:1–3* NEB

Those biblical discoveries I share with you in part 1 of this book. Part 2 prepares you to help dying children and their families. Part 3 covers the unique circumstances of sudden loss and complicated grief. You will meet grievers at varying stages of grief from the first year to the fortieth year of the process. Losing a child is a lifetime journey of grief.

God wrote this book through many special families who courageously shared their stories with me, some through interviews and some through writing and personal journals. Each did so with great anguish and tears. We often cried together. And why did these families endure this pain? For *you*. Their answer was always the same, "If this can help someone, I want to share it." Some grievers requested to remain anonymous. All grievers said it was a painful but healing, therapeutic process to relive their stories, bringing further closure to the most devastating experience of their lives.

I am indebted to a seminary professor, who later died a painful death due to brain cancer, who said, "We should close the textbooks and theological treatises and simply ask people how they survived their life challenges." How did God carry them through their pain? This volume is not intended to be a textbook but a window into the griever's heart. Fully experience their loss.

No human being escapes facing one's own death and the death of one's loved ones. It is life's eventual certainty. We must all take the journey.

$\mathcal{P}$art 1

The Biblical Journey: Preparing the Helper

Do not be far from me, for trouble is near and I have no one to help.

—*Psalm 22:11*

God is the ultimate expert. Other grieving parents are experts. But we are not experts: we are helpers. We stand by to love and uphold the grieving heart. For us to try to give advice to the dying child and the family is analogous to the nonswimmer standing on the shore yelling instructions at the swimmer caught in a riptide out in the ocean. If you can't dive into the water yourself to help the drowning swimmer, then you are not the person to help. Helpers must be willing to enter the grieving process *with* the sufferers, not stand on the sidelines giving advice to the sufferers or imposing what they think best. Not only is advice-giving not helpful; it can actually do harm. Jesus Christ calls us to be comforters, those who come alongside (paracletes). We are his ambassadors.

The purpose of this section is to offer a spiritual perspective on suffering and death to help you solidify your own spiritual foundation and relationship with God for the crises ahead. The death of a child shakes one's faith to the core. If you are floundering in your own sea of doubts and questions when a child dies, you will be paralyzed and unable to help. This section is not intended as advice to be given to grievers. Down the road you will be able to explore these biblical truths as fellow grievers searching for answers together, but that process is one of supporting each other and bearing one another's burdens, not of giving advice.

*C*hapter 2

Helpers Without Answers

Look by reason of his power God is supreme,
    what teacher can be compared with him?
Who has ever told him which course to take, or
    dared to say to him, "You have done wrong"?
                                    —Job 36:22–23 *JB*

This was the answer Job gave to Yahweh;
I know that you are all-powerful:
    what you conceive, you can perform.
I am the man who obscured your designs with my
    empty-headed words.
I have been holding forth on matters I cannot
    understand, on marvels beyond me and my
    knowledge.   —Job 42:1–3 *JB*

Theologians have been battling for centuries over the question—How does a good, all-powerful God allow human suffering and evil? If he is all-good, then is he not all-powerful? If he is all-powerful, then is he not all-good? No matter your own theological bent—whether you say that God "causes" or "allows" suffering—the undeniable truth is that God is at the end of all the arguments and ultimately in control. Either God has his hand in its purpose or he does not intervene to stop it. He is all-powerful.

We parents are painfully aware that we cannot guarantee our children's earthly safety. Three-year-old Kari is dying of a brain tumor. Often, more devastating than the death is the horror of watching one's terminally ill child suffer and deteriorate. Sandy, the teenage daughter of a leading Christian couple in their church, is brutally raped and murdered. Six-year-old Ryan is dying of AIDS resulting from a blood transfusion. Teenagers attending a youth service at a Baptist church in Fort Worth, Texas, are killed by an intruding gunman. Twelve-year-old Kevin is killed by a drunk driver. Many of the victims at the Columbine High School shooting were committed Christians.

Does God protect his children? "His eye is on the sparrow, and I know He watches me," a favorite hymn tells us. "Do not worry about your life . . . Consider the ravens: They do not sow or reap, they have no storeroom or barn; yet God feeds them. And how much more valuable you are than birds!" Jesus tells us in Luke 12:22–24. We read Psalm 91 to calm us, while waiting for a teenager to come home late at night: "No harm will befall you, no disaster will come near your tent. For he will command his angels concerning you to guard you in all your ways; they will lift you up in their hands, so that you will not strike your foot against a stone" (vv. 10–12).

Some Christians say that God has his purpose in all human events. Others say that God never has a hand in evil, but then they must admit that God does not choose to stop the evil either. The arguments go round and round and are pointless when you are looking into the face of a parent whose child lies on a hospital bed, covered by a sheet. Nothing wreaks havoc with our faith like the death of a child. "Where is God?" grievers ask. This is not a time for theological debate.

One grieving mother, whose three children were in an auto accident, profoundly sums up our incongruous struggle, "God was so good. He constantly sent people to stay with my surviving son in ICU so that my husband and I could make funeral arrangements for our other two teenagers." She was grateful for God's daily care, fully realizing that her oldest son and only daughter were in the hospital morgue.

Effective helpers have not "figured it all out" nor do they have all the answers. Effective helpers put their arms around hurting people and say, "I don't understand either. But I love you and I'm here to go through it with you." True faith is trusting God when we least understand his ways.

This is the model that our master helper, Jesus, gives us. He never promised us a life without suffering. He did promise his continuous love and presence:

> *I am convinced that neither death nor life, neither angels nor*
> *demons, neither the present nor the future, nor any powers,*
> *neither height nor depth, nor anything else in all creation, will*
> *be able to separate us from the love of God that is in Christ Jesus*
> *our Lord.*   —Romans 8:38–39

I have observed one distinct pattern in developing Christians. As they gain in maturity, they try to "figure God out" less, simply trust him, and put their effort into helping other people more. Trying to figure God out by analyzing the whys of his ways is very different from being solidly grounded in the scriptural truth of love and salvation that he gives us. These biblical Christians have learned how to "fly by the instruments."

Flying by the instruments is one of the most comforting concepts I learned in seminary. It compares a person living the Christian life to a pilot flying into battle taking risks. The pilot can capably fly by his own sight when the weather is beautiful, but when the severe storms come, he has a choice. He can crash and be destroyed, or he can fly by the instruments—even when his instincts tell him to do otherwise—and survive. Flying by the instruments is trusting the truth of God's Word when the storms of life are upon us and we don't have time to figure it all out.

Eight scriptural truths follow. They are God's promises, to keep you steady and focused—instruments to fly by—during your battles.

Scriptural Truth 1: We are loved. We have salvation and eternal life.

For God so loved the world that he gave his only begotten Son, that whosoever believeth in him should not perish, but have everlasting life. —John 3:16 KJV

The loss of a child, who brought us redemption, is the foundation of our Christian faith. God lost his Son, Jesus Christ, to death to save sinners. The reason for this tremendous sacrifice was that he loves us. God knows the parent's ache in watching a beloved child suffer and die. The comfort he offers us is solidly founded on empathy and compassion. Focusing on this fact has been the life preserver for many grieving Christian parents who have moved past anger and blaming God to surviving and effectively coping with their child's death. God does not ask us to go through what he has not gone through himself.

Scriptural Truth 2: Jesus understands our grief and isolation.

[Jesus] began to be deeply distressed and troubled. "My soul is overwhelmed with sorrow to the point of death," he said to them. "Stay here and keep watch."

Going a little farther, he fell to the ground and prayed that if possible the hour might pass from him. "Abba, Father," he said, "everything is possible for you. Take this cup from me. Yet not what I will, but what you will." Then he returned to his disciples and found them sleeping. —Mark 14:33–37

For we do not have a high priest who is unable to sympathize with our weaknesses . . . . —Hebrews 4:15

Our Savior—the man of sorrows, acquainted with grief—knows our pain. He knew devastating sorrow while on earth. He fell to the ground and with tears begged God to deliver him from the intense suffering he faced. He spoke this truth, "Everything is possible for you." But his next words were, "Yet not what I will, but what you will." This is the anguished prayer of every grieving parent, "Please heal my child, Lord. I know you can." And finally, "But your will, Lord, not mine."

Jesus felt so alone in his grief, even abandoned by his disciples. They had fallen asleep, exhausted from sorrow (Luke 22:45). May we as helpers not be so drained by our own grief that we cannot stand by the grieving family through their intense struggle.

Scriptural Truth 3: Our children are loved.

Jesus said, "Let the little children come to me, and do not hinder them, for the kingdom of heaven belongs to such as these." When he had placed his hands on them, he went on from there. —Matthew 19:14–15

God loves not only us but our children as well. He holds them in his tender care. Little children are special to God just as they were special to our Lord Jesus. Jesus genuinely enjoyed the company of children. The disciples thought that they would be a nuisance to him, not worthy to take up his time. But Jesus stood firm; he wanted the children to come to him and even held them up to adults as the best examples of trusting followers. The children came, and Jesus held them, loved them, talked to them, and played with them. Perhaps children truly are closer than adults to the gates of heaven. One of our beloved children's hymns holds profound truth in its simplicity:

Jesus loves me, this I know,
For the Bible tells me so.
Little ones to him belong.
They are weak, but he is strong.

Scriptural Truth 4: We have God's strength and guidance.

*Cast your cares on the LORD, and he will sustain you; he will
never let the righteous fall.*   —Psalm 55:22

The most painful of all human experiences—losing a child to
death—leaves families despaired, frail, weak, and without
future hope for their days on earth. Getting out of bed to face one
more day can be overwhelming. The pain never seems to numb
even a little. We have no human resources for persevering in the
face of this intense pain and devastation. But we do have God's
resources. We have his unending strength. He can face the day
when we can't face the next half-hour. He can carry us when we
can't take the first step toward a life without our child. God goes
before us to lead us and follows behind to protect and uphold us:

*The LORD will go before you, the God of Israel will be your
rear guard.*   —Isaiah 52:12

**Scriptural Truth 5: We have God's comforting presence.
   He will never abandon us.**

*"Be strong, stand firm, have no fear of them, no terror, for
Yahweh your God is going with you; he will not fail you or
desert you."*   —Deuteronomy 31:6 JB

There exists one fact in the Christian's life that cannot be
erased even in the most blinding of life's storms: God has
promised never to leave us. We may not feel his presence in the
consuming darkness, but he *is* there. He is our Father, and we are
his children. We can call him "Daddy" just as Jesus did when he
prayed "Abba Father." His constant love, care, and presence
never can be taken from us, no matter how shattering life's
circumstances may be.

Many grieving families have told me that in those moments

when the pain was unbearable they miraculously felt God's loving arms around them, holding them tightly. It was an undeniable reality. He was there.

Scriptural Truth 6: We have God's protection from evil.

We know that anyone born of God does not continue to sin; the one who was born of God keeps him safe, and the evil one cannot harm him. We know that we are children of God, and that the whole world is under the control of the evil one. We know also that the Son of God has come and has given us understanding, so that we may know him who is true. And we are in him who is true—even in his Son Jesus Christ. He is the true God and eternal life. —1 John 5:18–20

Pain touches us. Despair touches us. Suffering touches us. Death touches us. The whole range of human emotions and experiences touches us. But evil will *never* touch us. God promises to keep us safe and protect us from evil. We belong to God, and even in our weakest state, he builds a fortress wall around us to keep the evil one out. God will fight evil for us. We can rest assured that we are safe. Never confuse pain and suffering with evil.

Even though I walk through the valley of the shadow of death, I will fear no evil. —Psalm 23:4

The LORD will keep you from all evil; he will watch over your life; the LORD will watch over your coming and going both now and forevermore. —Psalm 121:7–8

Scriptural Truth 7: We can trust his purpose.

Praise be to the God and Father of our Lord Jesus Christ, the Father of compassion and the God of all comfort, who com-forts us in all our troubles, so that we can comfort those in any trouble with the comfort we ourselves have received from God. *For just as the sufferings of Christ flow over into our lives, so also through Christ our comfort overflows. If we are distressed, it is for your comfort and salvation; if we are comforted, it is for your comfort, which produces in you patient endurance of the same sufferings we suffer. And our hope for you is firm, because we know that just as you share in our sufferings, so also you share in our comfort.*   —2 Corinthians 1:3–7

We mere mortals do not like to suffer. We would never choose to suffer. But we cannot deny that suffering often brings great good and has ultimate purpose. Suffering of any kind—physical, spiritual, mental, or emotional—forces us to feel pain personally, to know it firsthand. No amount of intellectual input or professional training can substitute for personal experience. Those who have suffered greatly exhibit the most compassion, empathy, and desire to help others in similar situations. They are also the most effective helpers, because fellow sufferers know that their empathy is genuine and their expertise is proven.

God's purpose for us is to love others as he loves us and to mirror Jesus Christ. Grieving families who have reached out to love and support other grieving families know that their lives have great purpose.

Scriptural Truth 8: We will grieve for months, years, perhaps a lifetime. But we will not grieve forever.

Listen, I tell you a mystery: We will not all sleep, but we will all be changed—in a flash, in the twinkling of an eye, at the last trumpet. For the trumpet will sound, the dead will be raised imperishable, and we will be changed.
                    —1 Corinthians 15:51–52

"God himself will be with them and be their God. He will wipe every tear from their eyes. There will be no more death

or mourning or crying or pain, for the old order of things has
passed away."   —Revelation 21:3–4

This is the most important truth to which grievers cling. *Sweet reunion is coming.* The resurrection of the dead insures that we will see our dear loved ones on the other side of eternity when we live in a new heaven and a new earth. God will wipe away every tear we've cried. We will not mourn forever. We can stake our lives on God's future hope.

Grievers often experience vivid dreams and visions which comfort them that their loved one is safe with God for eternity. A reviewer once said that I should not publish such unbiblical ideas. I wrestled with this, unable to ignore the numerous similar accounts shared by grievers. Unbiblical? Throughout scripture, God reached out to communicate with and comfort his people through dreams and visions. Our God is the same yesterday, today, and tomorrow.

So it will be with the resurrection of the dead. The body that
is sown is perishable, it is raised imperishable.
                                  —1 Corinthians 15:42

Our light and momentary troubles are achieving for us an
eternal glory that far outweighs them all. So we fix our eyes
not on what is seen, but on what is unseen. For what is seen
is temporary, but what is unseen is eternal.
                                  —2 Corinthians 4:17–18

*C*hapter 3

Our Biblical Models: Fellow Grievers in Scripture

"Blessed are those who mourn, for they will be comforted."
—Matthew 5:4

The Bible is as much a book about suffering and grieving as it is about love and salvation. Throughout Scripture we see that the children of God suffered and grieved over the loss of their loved ones. David, Job, Paul, Mary, and our Lord Jesus were not exempt from the pain of loss; in fact, it was multiplied for them. Perhaps these fellow sufferers and the grievers of today have in common the higher calling.

Paul's Grief

When he had said this, he knelt down with all of them and prayed. They all wept as they embraced him and kissed him. What grieved them most was his statement that they would never see his face again. Then they accompanied him to the ship . After we had torn ourselves away from them, we put out to sea and sailed straight to Cos.

—Acts 20:36–38; 21:1

This treasure, tucked away in Acts, is a verse about relationship. It describes the essence of our Christian faith. God loves us deeply. He calls us out to love him deeply and to love others as an extension of that love. Because we love deeply, the pain will be intense when the relationship is severed. At some point every human relationship on this earth is severed. Death is the surest fact of our human existence.

The people at Ephesus were not losing Paul to death, but they felt the same intensity of pain, for they knew that they would not see him again in this life. The separation would be permanent. Paul had to tear himself away from his dear friends; the hurt of being torn apart was very real. There is nothing clean and easy in severing intimate relationships; it does feel like being ripped in two. Because God's people love deeply, they grieve deeply— in Paul's day as well as in ours. Later when Paul faced his own death, he asked Timothy to "come before winter" so that they could be together one last time to say good-bye. Paul was a man committed to relationships. He is our fellow griever.

David's Grief

David knew grief well. Could we have survived the following?

David mourned the loss of his dearest friend, Jonathan.

He lost the first son whom he and Bathsheba had conceived to grave illness. He understood this tragedy as a judgment on his sin. He had fasted and pleaded with God to spare his son and then accepted the finality of his death.

On returning to Ziklag to discover that the town had been burned and their families taken captive by the Amalekites, David and his men had "wept aloud till they had no strength left to weep" (1 Samuel 30:4).

David was to suffer one more grief, which was less bearable than any of the preceding ones—the brutal murder of his beloved son Absalom.

The king shuddered. He went up to the room over the gate and burst into tears, and weeping said, "My son Absalom! My son! My son Absalom! Would I had died in your place! Absalom, my son, my son!" Word was brought to Joab, "The king is now weeping and mourning for Absalom." And the day's victory was turned to mourning for all the troops, because they learned that the king was grieving for his son. And the troops returned stealthily that day to the town, as troops creep back ashamed when routed in battle. The king had veiled his face and was crying aloud, "My son Absalom! Absalom, my son, my son."   —2 Samuel 19:1–4 JB

David is our fellow griever.

Mary's Grief

Near the cross of Jesus stood his mother, his mother's sister, Mary the wife of Clopas, and Mary Magdalene. When Jesus saw his mother there, and the disciple whom he loved standing nearby, he said to his mother, "Dear woman, here is your son," and to the disciple, "Here is your mother." From that time on, this disciple took her into his home.
          —John 19:25–27

Can you imagine helplessly watching your child be tortured, mocked, and executed before your eyes? Mary watched the slaughter of her precious gift from God, knowing that her son had done nothing wrong. Her grief and rage must have been almost uncontrollable. Notice that Mary's sister and Mary of Magdala were by her side to comfort her through his hideous ordeal.

Jesus, God himself, knew her pain and asked his disciple to care for her, thereby creating a new family. Imagine how Mary and her "new son" must have supported one another through their grief. God does not intend for us to grieve alone—not during the ordeal of a loved one's death nor afterward.

Jesus' Grief

Jesus wept.
Then the Jews said, "See how he loved him!"
But some of them said, "Could not he who opened the
eyes of the blind man have kept this man from dying?"
—John 11:35–37

We of finite mind do not comprehend why Jesus would weep and grieve for Lazarus when he knew that he was about to raise him from the dead. Perhaps this is our greatest lesson in grief counseling. Jesus was moved by the pain of Lazarus's sisters and friends and immediately entered into their grief. He cried with them and felt their pain *first*, then went to raise Lazarus from the dead. Jesus put their relationship ahead of his power to solve their problem.

Jesus understood human grief, evidenced by the lengths he went to prepare his dearest friends, the disciples, for his death. He knew that the more the disciples understood about his coming death and were prepared for it, the better they could cope. Jesus needed to say good-bye and prepare for his own death. He told his friends that this would be a time for grief.

"I tell you the truth, you will weep and mourn while the world
rejoices. You will grieve, but your grief will turn to joy. A
woman giving birth to a child has pain because her time has
come; but when her baby is born she forgets the anguish because
of her joy that a child is born into the world. So with you: Now
is your time of grief, but I will see you again and you will
rejoice, and no one will take away your joy." —John 16:20–22

This is the relevant message for all of us. Now is a time of grief and earthly separation, but then we will know great joy in eternity. Jesus understands our grief.

Violent Death

Losing a loved one to violent death is the most painful of human griefs, and the early Christians were no strangers to that pain.

Some were tortured, refusing to accept release, that they might rise again to a better life. Others suffered mocking and scourging, and even chains and imprisonment. They were stoned, they were sawn in two, they were killed with the sword; they went about in skins of sheep and goats, destitute, afflicted, ill-treated—of whom the world was not worthy—wandering over deserts and mountains, and in dens and caves of the earth. And all these, though well attested by their faith, did not receive what was promised, since God had foreseen something better for us, that apart from us they should not be made perfect.
—Hebrews 11:35–40 RSV

What does this passage say? Does God break his promises to his faithful children? No! And here lies the key to understanding suffering. Note the preceding verses to this passage:

And what more shall I say? For time would fail me to tell of Gideon, Barak, Samson, Jephthah, of David and Samuel and the prophets—who through faith conquered kingdoms, enforced justice, received promises, stopped the mouths of lions, quenched raging fire, escaped the edge of the sword, won strength out of weakness, became mighty in war, put foreign armies to flight. Women received their dead by resurrection.
—Hebrews 11:32–35 RSV

These faithful men did receive God's promises. These victorious men (vv. 32–35) as well as the sufferers (vv. 35–39) and their grieving families who must have watched them die, had the *same faith* in God—the same salvation that you and I have. Yet their earthly outcomes were different.

The faith described in Hebrews 11:32–35 has been called "Noah faith." These men were spared from suffering; God delivered them *from* tribulation.

The faith described in Hebrews 11:35–39 has been called "Job faith." These men who were called to die for their faith were delivered through suffering, just as Job suffered for his unshakable faith in God.

God's promises stand firm. His faithful children are saved and delivered—sometimes from suffering and sometimes through suffering.

Grievers search for fellow journeyers to share their sorrow. The Scriptures offer an invaluable source of godly men and women, including our own precious Lord, who have known their path.

Fellow Grief Counselor: Isaiah

Isaiah is God's biblical model for a grief counselor. We know Isaiah as a prophet, but his role as pastoral grief counselor is less well known. In Isaiah's time, a counselor was defined as "one who knew God's plan." Counseling was an extension of prophecy.

Hezekiah lay ill and dying, Isaiah immediately communicated God's will to him: "Yahweh says this, 'Put your affairs in order, for you are going to die, you will not live'" (Isaiah 38:2 JB).

God is honest with Hezekiah through the prophet. He does not hide the fact of the king's coming death; instead he offers Hezekiah the opportunity to prepare for it. Grief counselors of our day have only recently discovered this important practice.

Hezekiah's response is to pray to God: "Ah, Yahweh, remember, I beg you, how I have behaved faithfully and with sincerity of heart in your presence and done what is right in your eyes" (Isaiah 38:3 JB).

Hezekiah does not ask God to change the circumstances. He simply asks to be remembered for his loyalty and focuses on his relationship with God. Then Hezekiah weeps. The king feels his grief deeply and does not hesitate to show his emotions. God hears his prayers and sees his tears (38:5) and adds fifteen years to Hezekiah's life. God clearly controls the length of our lives as he chooses. God entered into Hezekiah's circumstances and felt his emotions. As helpers, we must communicate the fact that God feels the griever's pain. Being in control, God intervened to change Hezekiah's situation. Isaiah asks for a fig poultice to be brought and applied to Hezekiah's ulcer as medicine. God does use his creation in accomplishing his purpose.

Hezekiah's Canticle

Following his recovery, Hezekiah composed a canticle (the combination of poetry and song) to express his journey of suffering. Note the stages of grief that he walked through.

38:10	Anger and desperation	Hezekiah faces the frustration of dying before his time on earth should be finished ("in the noon of my life"). He experiences angry despair.
38:11–13	Helplessness	Hezekiah imagines the actual experience of death ("like a weaver, you roll up my life to cut it from the loom"). He experiences helplessness.
38:14–15	Reconciliation with God	Hezekiah communicates with God, asking for protection. He understands

		that God is in control by causing his illness or removing it.
38:18–20	Deeper understanding of God's purposes	Hezekiah has a deeper understanding of death and life through God. He desires to share God's mercy with others ("Fathers tell their children about your faithfulness").

Composing this canticle was probably healing for Hezekiah, helping him to release his pain.

The key to Isaiah's effective counseling of Hezekiah was that they had a prior relationship rooted in God's principles. Isaiah's God-given role was to communicate the nature and will of God, and God consistently advised Hezekiah for many years. Isaiah was available to the king throughout his reign, in good times and bad. He stood by to support Hezekiah when the king ignored his advice and disobeyed God. Isaiah was committed to that cause. Hezekiah was a good king and worked for reform. His downfall lay in sometimes thinking that his plans (e.g., the siege of 701 BC) were an improvement on God's ways. Isaiah cultivated a consistent, unconditional, loving friendship with Hezekiah and was a mirror of God's love. Because he had earned Hezekiah's trust, Isaiah was able to counsel him effectively when he lay dying. He was honest with the king about his coming death and helped him prepare for it, while at the same time he offered God's message of hope. We helpers of today are called to do the same.

Fellow Griever Job

If Isaiah is our biblical model for a grief counselor, then Job is our model for a griever. Can you imagine losing everything that you hold dear—your home, your health, the support of your friends and spouse, and all of your children in a fatal accident? The pain is unimaginable. Job lost his entire estate, his health, the support of his wife and friends, and his ten children when severe wind crushed the house around them.

God allowed Job to be severely tested by Satan. Job suffered deep depression and despair. He wanted to die, but he did not sin. He did not turn away from God because they had an authentic relationship. Job knew to whom he belonged and the truth about his God.

> *The LORD gives and the LORD takes away;*
> *blessed be the name of the LORD.*   —Job 1:21

> *"If we take happiness from God's hand,*
> *must we not take sorrow too?"*
> *And in all this misfortune Job uttered no sinful word.*
>   —Job 2:10 JB

> *"For he wounds, but he also binds up;*
> *he injures, but his hands also heal."*   —Job 5:18

Yet Job was honest with God, expressing the full range of emotions, doubts, and questions common to grievers. As helpers, remember this critical point: to shake one's fist and cry out in anguish to God is not a sin. It is evidence of an active, communicating relationship. God is listening. Can we do any less? Many grievers have shared that God became very real to them for the first time when facing a loved one's death. Job knows that everything comes from God's hand. *He trusts God but he doesn't understand.* Don't grievers today take the same journey? Remember Job . . .

When grievers' worst fears come true . . .

> *"What I feared has come upon me,*
> *What I dreaded has happened to me.*

I have no peace, no quietness.
I have no rest but only turmoil." —Job 3:25–26

"The arrows of the Almighty are in me,
my spirit drinks in their poison;
God's terrors are marshaled against me." —Job 6:4

When grievers' hearts are broken and they are wasting away
with grief . . . .

My eyes have grown dim with grief;
my whole frame is but a shadow. —Job 17:7

My days have passed, my plans are shattered,,;
and so are the desires of my heart..
These men turn night into day;
in the face of darkness they say, "Light is near."
—Job 17:11–12

When grievers are resentful . . . .

Even today my complaint is bitter;
his hand is heavy in spite of my groaning.
If only I knew how to find him;
if only I could go to his dwelling.
—Job 23:1–2

When grievers feel abandoned by God . . .

I cry out to you, O God, but you do not answer;
I stand up, but you merely look at me.
—Job 30:20

When grievers feel abandoned by their friends . . . .

> *"Do I have any power to help myself,*
> *now that success has been driven from me?*
> *A despairing man should have the devotion of his friends,*
> *even though he forsakes the fear of the Almighty."*
>
> —Job 6:13–14

> *"Listen carefully to my works;*
> *let this be the consolation you give me."*
>
> —Job 21:1

When grievers do not understand God's ways . . .
There is no escape from the overwhelming pain and they no longer want to live.

> *But I will not hold my peace;*
> *I will speak out in the distress of my mind*
> *and complain in the bitterness of my soul.*
> *Am I the monster of the deep, am I the sea-serpent,*
> *that thou settest a watch over me?*
> *When I think that my bed will comfort me,*
> *that sleep will relieve my complaining,*
> *thou dost terrify me with dreams*
> *and affright me with visions.*
> *I would rather be choked outright;*
> *I would prefer death to all my sufferings.*
> *I am in despair, I would not go on living;*
> *leave me alone, for my life is but a vapour.*
> *What is man that thou makest much of him*
> *and turnest thy thoughts towards him,*
> *only to punish him morning by morning*
> *or to test him every hour of the day? . . .*
> *Why hast thou made me thy butt,*
> *and why have I become thy target?*
>
> —Job 7:11–18, 20

Job's friend called these words the "long-winded ramblings of an old man" (Job 8:2). May we as helpers never be so callous to a griever's anguish. Note God's anger with Job's friends (Job 42:7–8).

Job's pain was very real and intense. He may have accepted God's ways but he did not understand them. More important, he communicated honestly his rollercoaster emotions and complete despair to God. That was part of the grief work process. Job remained in a safe relationship with God, a God who answered back and challenged him, "Who is this whose ignorant words cloud my design in darkness?" (38:2).

Job replies, "I know that thou canst do all things and that no purpose is beyond thee. But I have spoken of great things which I have not undertsood . . ." (42:2). God richly blessed the end of Job's life, returning his wealth and giving him ten children. Yet anyone who has lost a child will tell you that this precious little one cannot be replaced. Job traveled the lifetime journey of grief.

Chapter 4

When Suffering Turns to Gold

Severe suffering breeds one of two responses in human beings: bitterness and anger, or love and compassion. It never breeds indifference. Sufferers turn to God or away from God. The key result is that whatever is the final response toward God will be the suffering person's response toward others. Sufferers who have survived crises either hate more or love more. I tell you two very different stories: one about a hater and one about a lover.

Mary often had arguments with her only son, Tom. He was as strong an individual as she was, and both had explosive tempers. At one family dinner at Tom's house, Mary vehemently opposed the way Tom was disciplining his children. She finally stormed out of the house and refused to speak to Tom for weeks. Then, Tom's family left on a vacation where Tom died in a tragic accident.

Mary was left broken. She not only had to grieve the loss of her only son but also the loss of any opportunity to reconcile their relationship. Her brokenness turned to hatred—hatred toward God, family, and friends. Paralyzed by anger, she lashed out at everyone around her. Her grief poisoned her.

Victoria and Mike Haskins, a dedicated Christian couple, were on vacation camping in the mountains with their family when their two-and-a-half-year-old daughter began to have severe respiratory problems. They rushed her to the hospital for tests, and a few days later they learned that she had the terminal illness cystic fibrosis.

Victoria and Mike were devastated. They experienced the struggles common to parents facing a child's death. They had marital struggles because of the intense pressure on their relationship, dealt with severe depression and thoughts of suicide, and suffered exhaustion because of the new routines of medical care required for their daughter. They also had to continue to care for their infant son.

Victoria told me that the most painful times came as she stroked her daughter's hair while she slept in the middle of the night and knew the child would die and her bed would be empty soon. The pain seemed unbearable. Victoria realized that she faced a decision. She could shake her fist in anger at God or she could praise and trust his purpose in this suffering.

Victoria and Mike chose to thank and trust God. They joined a support group for parents of dying children and reached out to the other members. They shared their testimony of peace with their daughter's doctors, nurses, and other hospital staff. Victoria was able to lead a non-Christian friend who was dying of cancer on a journey to faith in Jesus Christ. This friend would not share her struggles with death or anger toward God with anyone else. Victoria was the only one who understood, because she walked the same road with her daughter.

Victoria and Mike used their tragedy to reach out and minister to anyone God brought into their path. Their compassion and love increased daily. Their lives had purpose; their suffering had turned to gold.

The Question of Healing

Is any one of you sick? He should call the elders of the church to pray over him and anoint him with oil in the name of the Lord. And the prayer offered in faith will make the sick person well; the Lord will raise him up. If he has sinned, he will be forgiven.

—James 5:14–15

Sixteen-year-old Linda was dying of cancer. She and her family were strong evangelical Christians. Her pastor came to visit often. I was able to include spiritual songs in our music therapy sessions and discuss our common faith. Linda thought that her illness was the result of a sin she had committed recently and that since she had repented she would be healed. Her parents were unaware of that "particular sin" or that Linda felt responsible. She never told them. They, too, had faith that she would be healed.

The deacons of their church came to pray and put oil on Linda. But she was not healed and died soon after. The night of her death, Linda's family, friends, and deacons of their church surrounded her still body on the hospital bed. They lit candles in the hospital room. They believed that God could and would still heal her; they prayed that she would be raised from the dead. Linda had already gone home. Their faith was shattered and their grief unbearable.

Victoria and Mike's story had a different outcome. Shortly after Amanda's diagnosis, the deacons came to pray and anoint her with oil. Four years after Amanda's diagnosis and months of suffering, she was healed. To this day she never has had another symptom. On receiving news of her clean health, most of Amanda's doctors said that she must have been initially misdiagnosed. They could not account for the complete disappearance of her symptoms. The one Christian doctor on the team said, "Yes, she was healed." Today Amanda is married and a healthy mother of two children. Neither has cystic fibrosis.

A very sad but common phenomenon occurred to Victoria

and Mike following Amanda's healing. They lost their opportunity to minister to other families with terminally ill children. There was no reason for Victoria and Mike to continue to attend the support group meetings. Just their presence was a painful reminder to the other families that their children were not healed. "Why them and not us?" their faces said.

Victoria and Mike's best friends in the group, another Christian couple who had taken Victoria and Mike under their wing, lost their daughter to death the same month that Amanda was healed. It is a simple truth that human beings accept ministry more readily from fellow sufferers than from those who do not share their pain. This opportunity to care for other hurting people is the golden thread in the purpose of suffering.

Healing is a tough issue to grapple with. Amanda was healed. Linda was not healed. For every Amanda there are thousands of Lindas. God can and does heal people, but it is not the more frequent occurrence. Healing is the mystery of his ways. There is no magic formula to procure it, no particular "action of faith" in which the healed one engaged that the unhealed did not. God in his sovereignty knows best.

While working at the hospital I began to observe that often the patients most precious to me, with parents of the most sincere faith, were the unhealed. It occurred to me that perhaps there are two kinds of healing, two kinds of gold: temporary healing for life on this earth, and ultimate healing for life with God. When these families prayed for healing, God gave their children "ultimate healing" for eternity with him. Parents prayed for happy, pain-free, well lives for their children, and God bestowed it on them— never to be taken away again. It was not that God didn't answer their prayers or say no; his answer was a permanent yes.

A view of ultimate healing does not diminish the pain of the grievers, though. The helper's response of shared struggle must be the same: to support the family, never to analyze the circumstances. God's ways may be a mystery, but our job is not. The Scriptures clearly direct us to "rejoice with those who rejoice and mourn with those who mourn."

You will see in the chapters ahead that sometimes opposing beliefs about healing can cause strife between believers when faced with approaching death. I have never understood this conflict since earthly healing may delay death but never eliminates it. No one is permanently healed on this side of eternity. Death is unavoidable for each of us and our loved ones.

When our young daughter was diagnosed with terminal cancer, I knew that God could heal her and that he WOULD heal her. I never doubted him for one minute. As the year of hospitalizations and treatments passed and she grew worse, I remained confident that God was waiting to reveal his great power in our hour of greatest weakness. Our church and friends continued to pray for the miracle. Then my precious daughter began to suffer. I began to surrender completely to God, truly realizing that we cannot understand his ways. One day I prayed, "God, I do not understand. Please heal her or take her home and make her whole with you." She peacefully died at home during the night.

—A Grieving Mom

On Two Sides of Eternity

Summarizing our biblical journey, we can be secure in God's promises:

- God loves us and saves us for eternity. Nothing can separate us from his love and promises.
- God will carry us today and dry our tears in heaven's tomorrow. He will never abandon us.
- God will not allow evil to touch his children. Nothing

reaches us that is not first filtered through his hands of love and purpose.

- We have a Savior who understands our deepest grief and suffering. Jesus knew that God, his father, could do anything and begged to be spared his tortured death. Yet he trusted that God held the bigger picture of eternity in his hands.
- We live on two sides of eternity. Our resurrection hope is secure. God may not heal our children on this side but he does heal them permanently in eternity. We cannot see it yet. But that joyful reunion is coming . . . .

> *Christ came out of his tomb and so have they.*   *—Meg Woodson, who lost both her children to cystic fibrosis*

> *When my child was dying of cancer ten years ago, fellow Christians asked me if I had any unconfessed sin in my life. They questioned if I had enough faith. They only added to my pain and isolation. I realize today that these believers were scared. They wanted to find something wrong with me to assure them that they would never face this tragedy. Most people still don't understand. God did heal my child, just not on this side of heaven where I can see it yet.*
> *—A Grieving Father*

When we lose a dear loved one, eternity becomes very real to us, almost as if the curtain has come down for a season. God gives us the assurance that our beloved is safe, whole, well, and happy with him. This experience changes our entire life perspective, especially when we lose a child. Most parents dread their own death, saying good-bye to their children left behind. But grieving parents know a bittersweet joy as they age. They are going to their children. When they walk through that door to eternity, their child will be waiting to greet them. Sweet reunion.

$\mathcal{P}$art 2

Taking the Journey: Helping Dying Children and Their Families

If the Lord had not been my helper,
I should soon have slept in the silent grave.
When I felt that my foot was slipping,
thy love, O LORD, held me up.

                    Psalm 94:17–18

C *hapter 5*

Helping Through the Illness and Hospitalization

Our first priority as helpers is to help the child. We are involved in crisis intervention. The Chinese character for *crisis* means "danger" *and* "opportunity." Without intervention, the stress of a terminal illness is paralyzing and traumatic for a family's lifetime. To intervene is to come between. We can come between hurting families and this unbearable crisis to help them carry their overwhelming burden.

Pastoral care to sick children is often a neglected field in Christian ministry. Pastors and chaplains are comfortable offering pastoral care to adults. Youth workers are comfortable educating and discipling young people. Yet no specialization to bridge the gap exists that provides pastoral care to hurting children.

When a child is dying, most pastors and chaplains traditionally support the family. They know how to offer comfort to the adult parents, which is definitely needed, but this is the vicious circle. While it is true that supporting parents will enable them to comfort their child, in reality, the most effective way to help the parents is to help the child directly.

Finding the Right Hospital

Dying children must deal with medical procedures and hospitalization. Hospitalization ranks as one of the most stressful events that a child can experience. If not handled properly, it can be a most frightening and traumatic crisis. Your first task is to help the child and family cope with hospitalization. For most dying children, the hospital will become the world in which they live.

To begin, it is important to understand the difference between a children's hospital and a pediatric wing of a general hospital. A children's hospital focuses entirely on children. Most general hospitals cannot afford to do this. A children's hospital will have a Child Life program and philosophy committed to the total well-being of the child and family. The staff will do what is best for the child, not what is more convenient for him or her. Pre-admission tours are often available to familiarize patients with the hospital. Important questions to ask when investigating hospitals are:

Are there visiting hours? May siblings visit?

Children do not operate on adult clocks. Pediatric hospitals do not have visiting hours. Parents, siblings, and friends can come whenever it is convenient for the child. Some innovative hospitals even allow pets to visit.

Can parents remain with the child for the entire stay? Can parents sleep in the room at night?

The most serious part of a hospital stay for any child is the fear of being alone and separated from loved ones and familiar surroundings. Separation anxiety can be far more serious than a medical problem. Parents should choose a hospital where they are permitted to stay entire days or nights with their child.

Will parents be able to give input about their child and be part of the health care team?

The parents know their child better than anyone, and most doctors and nurses respect this. The staff should welcome parents' insights about their child and inform them about medical procedures at every stage of the illness. Caring doctors and nurses who take the time to talk with families are crucial.

Is there a Child Life program? Is there a playroom?

The Child Life program of a pediatric program is staffed by professional educators and therapists. Their sole purpose is to ensure the total well-being of the patient—emotionally, mentally, and physically. There should be a central playroom where group, as well as individual, activities are offered. The playroom is the "safe retreat" in the hospital. No painful procedures are allowed there. When children cannot visit the playroom, a therapist can work with them in their rooms.

The playroom is the natural setting to develop relationships. Patients make friends with other patients, parents meet with each other, and a common support base is built.

Teen retreat lounges can be found in adolescent units. Infant stimulation programs are available for babies. Be aware of appropriate programs for the patient's age.

Child Life Therapy Techniques

The hospital experience handled correctly can contribute positively to a child's development, while a negative experience can cause anxiety, fear, withdrawal, regression, defiance, and delay the physical healing process. The Child Life program provides "total person care" for each patient as well as for the family. It exists to minimize the trauma of hospitalization and is concerned with meeting the emotional and developmental needs of patients. The Child Life approach is not a frill. Happy and busy children get well faster.

Professional educators and therapists who work in the Child Life department are termed Child Life specialists and are certified by a national council. They plan therapeutic activities and interact with the pediatric health team composed of doctors, nurses, social workers, psychologists, dietitians, therapists, and chaplains. This team is committed to the physical and emotional well-being of the patient.

A myriad of backgrounds create an effective Child Life staff. Some Child Life specialists are certified teachers who continue the patient's educational program in the hospital during the absence from school. Some are recreational therapists. Others are child development specialists or have pediatric nursing backgrounds to deal with medical issues. Since creative expression is an effective way to cope with the stress of hospitalization and illness, others are creative arts therapists. Child Life specialists integrate a number of therapy methods to best help their patients. The helper can learn from them, do the same, and also teach parents how to help their children.

Medical Play Therapy and Preparation

Play therapy is the primary tool employed by Child Life specialists to help children cope with the stress of hospitalization. Play is the children's work; it is their medium of self-expression and the way they master anxiety. Through play, children gain control over real-life situations in which they feel helpless.

Play is the one activity that provides continuity between the hospital and the normal outside world and also serves as a diagnostic tool to observe the patient's reactions to hospitalization. Medical play therapy is a specialized area of play therapy.

The unknown is frightening. Hospitalized children should be told what will happen to them. From the smallest medical test (such as a blood test) to major surgery, every procedure should be fully explained to the child beforehand. This is medical preparation, achieved through education. Puppets, videotapes, and children's hospital books are examples of teaching tools to inform children. Medical play therapy offers patients the opportunity to have control as "doctor" and play out hospital procedures on dolls, stuffed animals, parents, or therapists with realistic medical equipment in a safe environment. The patient engages in medical play therapy before having an actual medical procedure to gain an understanding of what will take place; it gives the helper the opportunity to clear up any misconceptions. It is just as important for the patient to engage in medical play therapy after the procedure to work through any trauma and cope with the experience. This clues the therapist as to what the patient is feeling.

Bibliotherapy is the use of books in therapy. Children's books on hospitals and medical procedures are used to educate and prepare the patient as well as provide an opportunity to discuss the child's questions, fears, and concerns. It is the relationship of the helper reading to the child that is the key, not the book itself. The book is the tool. Bibliotherapy extends to reading books that bring up different emotions the child can relate to and discuss— books about other hurting children, or fantasies that distract patients from pain and help them leave the world of the hospital for a while. Christian helpers will want to use books about scriptural truth and God's love and care.

Verbalization

One primary goal in all therapy methods is to help children verbalize their feelings and discuss their fears and concerns about hospital experiences in a loving and accepting environment. Pediatric experts agree that a child needs to talk about the hospital experience to be able to cope with it. Verbalization precedes understanding and mastery of anxiety.

Listening to children open up about their concerns is not enough. Children are people of action; they are doers. They will talk to someone when they are involved in an activity—doing something—with that person. Traditional counseling approaches often result in the child's silence. Whether you the helper are playing a game, reading a book, "doctoring" a doll, or singing songs with the child, your task is to provide a safe environment where you can establish a relationship of trust with the patient and he or she can talk to you. Recreational activities provide that framework.

Creative Arts Therapies

Creative expression through artistic experience is an established method for coping with the trauma of hospitalization, especially when verbalization is difficult. The creative arts therapies are ideal for the hospitalized child because they offer: (1) an element of play; (2) an opportunity for creative expression and release; and (3) a safe environment for sharing concerns. Since the artistic medium is comforting, non-threatening, and not associated with medical procedures, the therapist can quickly establish a relationship of trust with the patient.

The creative arts therapies include art, music, dance, and drama/puppet therapy, with creative writing as an extension of these fields. Though the medium is different, the principles are the same in each process. The therapist employs his or her artistic medium as the tool in treating the patient's problem area.

Let us define music therapy as a specific example. Music making is an effective brain-compatible tool because it is one of the few processes that involve all of our modalities simultaneously—visual, auditory, motor, emotional, cognitive. It is the ideal cross-brain activity. While music therapy employs a strong developmental area that is comfortable for the child, a weak developmental area can simultaneously be treated. The child is distracted from his limitations and the disorder is more easily treated.

Music therapy in the clinical setting can help an accident victim regain the use of his hands through learning to play an instrument. It relieves pain and stress through imagery and relaxation techniques. Music therapy uses familiar songs to prompt terminally ill patients to discuss life experiences and prepare for death. It teaches children how to socialize through musical games, or helps a newborn infant discover his environment. Music therapy teaches individuals with respiratory or speech problems to sing. It implements group music activities to enhance self-esteem. Music therapy employs musical games and songs to encourage a child-abuse victim to discuss her experience or to distract a pediatric patient from the pain and trauma of hospitalization. The applications are endless. The need is identified first, and the musical experience is tailored to meet it.

In the hospital, music activities are a form of play for pediatric patients, offering normal avenues for growth and development and providing continuity between the hospital and the child's outside world. The medium of music meets the patient's need for creative expression and channeling of anxiety. Music therapy group activities conducted in the Child Life playroom allow patients to share with one another and offer mutual support. Music therapy provides the framework for verbalization. Original compositions, creating new lyrics for familiar songs, or fill-in-the-blank songs are opportunities for discussion of feelings.

Artistic processes are also diagnostic tools. Helpers learn what a patient feels and perceives through his or her creative expression. Like original music, artwork is an excellent clue to what children understand about their hospitalization. Drawing self-pictures shows how children view what is happening to their bodies.

In my work I guided patients in creating a large weaving. We worked on it together much as in an old-fashioned quilting bee. Each patient created one section and enjoyed explaining how his or her color choices reflected hospital life. Proud patients helped hang it on a hospital wall for all to see.

Creative dramatics and puppetry are other powerful mediums for children to communicate their fears. It is much easier to talk to a dog puppet named Floppy than a strange hospital worker. Movement therapists help patients adapt to their loss of mobility. Children become frustrated when they cannot move. Therapists focus on what patients can do, not what they cannot do. A bedridden patient may be able to move only one arm; she can create "arm dances" and imagine moving her entire body.

By writing poetry, painting pictures, creating group murals, composing music about hospitalization, or enacting their experiences through drama and movement, patients share their concerns with others and cope with the crisis of illness.

The most exciting aspect of the creative arts therapies is that their use is biblically based. What did David do when he struggled? He expressed his suffering through writing psalms. "The Lord is at hand to save me; so let us sound the music of our praises all our life long in the house of the Lord," Hezekiah completes his canticle of grief (Isaiah 38:20). It is a rare reference in Scripture where praise of God and communication through prayer is not linked with music-making. Song was a weapon in the spiritual life. Jesus understood the power of music in facing trial. The last event he and his disciples shared before departing the upper room for the Mount of Olives was to sing psalms together (Matthew 26:30). Paul and Silas sang hymns of praise with their feet in stocks in prison (Acts 16:25). David may have been the first known music therapist.

Now the Spirit of the Lord *departed from Saul, and an evil spirit from the* Lord *tormented him. And Saul's servants said to him, "Behold now, an evil spirit from God is tormenting you. Let our lord now command your servants, who are before you, to seek out a man who is skillful in playing the lyre; and when the evil spirit from God is upon you, he will play it, and you will be well."*
. . . And whenever the evil spirit from God was upon Saul, David took the lyre and played it with his hand; so Saul was refreshed, and was well, and the evil spirit departed from him.
—1 Samuel 16:14–16, 23 RSV

Music is inseparable from God's presence.

Respect for the Child

Respecting the patient and being his or her advocate is another important part of the helper's job. You must continually affirm that the child can trust you. In addition to helping patients cope with hospitalization through use of the above therapy techniques, you should also keep in mind the following:

1. Make sure that the patient is as comfortable and enjoying as normal an environment as possible. Encourage children to bring their favorite possessions from home. Help patients with continued schoolwork. Keep disruption of the normal lifestyle to a minimum.
2. Never surprise a child. No one should be allowed to perform a procedure on a child without fully explaining it first.
3. Always tell the truth. The rule is that if a procedure is going to hurt, tell the child it will hurt.
4. Do not "talk around" the child. Discourage others from talking about the child's medical problems as if the child were not present. Include the patient in the conversation.
5. Give the patient some control. For example, one cannot give the child the choice of whether or not he wants a shot, but one can ask him which arm he chooses to have it in. Children become frightened when they feel helpless in their situation.

Pastoral Care

Pastoral care to hospitalized children ideally is the integration of God's truth with effective therapy methods. It begins with the helper—the therapist/minister who reflects Jesus Christ and builds a relationship with the child that mirrors God's constant love and care. The child should "see Jesus" in you, the helper.

Your love and concern for the child overflow to his or her family. You care for them through helping their child and being available to support them through the trauma of hospitalization and the coming death. The key is an established relationship and bond of trust and love.

Each therapy process discussed above can be applied in a spiritual context. While acting out medical play therapy, you can discuss how God is in control, made our bodies, and will guide the doctors in procedures. You can assure patients that God never leaves them, even in the hospital. While everyone is unsure of the future, Christians can trust God to have carefully planned every step.

Bibliotherapy can include books about God's care for us and other biblical truths. The Bible, God's guidebook for life, is certainly the ultimate tool in bibliotherapy.

You can share Scripture passages that are presented to helpers in Part 1 of this book. You can help patients verbalize their feelings to you and to God through prayer, creative writing, composing songs, and singing hymns.

You are probably discovering that effective therapy methods are simply God's biblical methods for helping his children deal with pain "in secular language." When you help within a secular institution or support nonbelievers, you are still an ambassador of Jesus Christ. You communicate God's biblical truths of love and comfort in action. Even the most confirmed atheist when faced with his dying child will shake a fist angrily at God and say, "How could God do this to me?" It, too, is communication with God and an opportunity for ministry.

You can minister to hospitalized children by providing effective ways to cope that are rooted in God's love and care. Tangible skills for helping go hand-in-hand with your spiritual commitment.

In summary, your primary tasks are to directly help the child in these ways:

1. Support the family as they hospitalize their child. Be their advocate.
2. Educate parents about hospitals and the rights of pediatric patients.

3. Apply therapy techniques to help the child cope with the trauma of hospitalization. You should be familiar with play therapy, medical play therapy, creative arts therapies, pastoral care principles, and the use of Scripture.

4. Remember that helping children to verbalize their experiences is your goal. If you are uncomfortable with music and arts activities or play therapy/counseling techniques, you may enjoy playing board games, reading books, using puppets, or playing doctor.

5. The key is to help children talk to you. Listen carefully to learn their struggles and fears. Creative arts expression is especially important with patients who are not comfortable talking with you.

6. Most important, you are the mirror of Jesus Christ. Assure children of God's love and faithfulness. Help them communicate with God through prayer, Scripture, music, journaling, and creative writing.

7. Surrounding dying children with relationships of love and trust (with God, their families, and you the helper) is the foundation of their journey home.

Chapter 6

Living with Cystic Fibrosis

by Hayley Horn

Cystic Fibrosis

CF is a disease that affects the lung
It is not a lot of fun
I can't jump or run or play
That's why I'm at band for most of the day

I must take many pills a day
"You'll get better soon," they always say
This day hasn't yet come to my life
Until it does I live in strife

But the lungs are not the only effect
My liver is also scarred and wrecked
My skin is wrinkled and very dry
I can very easily die

This poem is for my parents
If they live longer than I
This poem is just to make sure
That I say goodbye

Now I lay me down to sleep
I pray the Lord my soul to keep
If I shall die before I wake
I pray the Lord my soul to take

by Hayley Horn

I am 13 years old, in the 8th grade, and I have cystic fibrosis. Cystic fibrosis affects many parts of my body—my lungs, intestines, sinuses, and liver. There is no cure for my disease but I hope that someday there will be one.

I was born with CF and I HATE having it! The doctors shaved my head when I was born to put IVs in my head. They stuck tubes down my nose and throat and hooked me up to all kinds of machines. I had surgery before I was twenty-four hours old. I didn't come home from the hospital until I was two months old.

I have to take about thirty pills a day, which cause many bad side effects. When I am healthy, I take at least seven breathing treatments a day. I have been in and out of the hospital many times for IV antibiotics, tests, procedures, and even surgeries. I hate all the needle pokes. I hate always going to doctor appointments.

CF makes it hard to breathe so I can't be physically active like my friends. I can't keep up with them, like when we go to an amusement park and they run on ahead. They don't mean to leave me in the dust. I just don't have the energy they have. I do like to go to the movies, play video games, play miniature golf, ride my jet ski, and play the piano and drums.

School is hard for me because I get tired walking on campus between classes, carrying my heavy backpack. I can't participate in PE like other kids. My teachers still try to involve me by asking me to referee or keep score. CF does not affect my learning. I have a 4.0 grade average and my goal is to be valedictorian of my class next year. I set high goals for myself and work hard despite numerous absences from school. My teachers are very supportive.

The best part about school is band. Music is one of the best things in my life. While my friends are involved in sports and cheerleading, I can participate in a group activity too. Band is fun and I feel that I am doing something productive that benefits my school. Band helps me keep going when I don't feel well and want to go home from school.

One good thing about having CF is that I get to eat anything I want (except for candy before dinner). My system doesn't absorb food properly so I need to eat a lot of high-calorie foods. I get a special pass at theme parks so my friends and I do not have to stand in those long lines. I have also met many wonderful people through Make-A-Wish Foundation. They gave me a professional drum set.

One of the hardest parts of having CF is that many people don't understand and they don't like me. They think that I'm weird or scary. Even people I thought were my friends turn on me when they find out. I explain that I'm not contagious but they stop listening. I lose a lot of friends that way. But I do have some good friends in band now. They understand my disease but don't think it's strange. They treat me like anyone else.

Friends

The joy, the fun, the laughter, the love
One said I came from up above
I don't know this, but maybe I did
But to you I'm just a normal kid

You're always there when I need you
You could have such good friends? I never knew

You are there in good times and bad
You are the best friends I've ever had

This is to my friends who seem to love me so much
These are the friends who never give up.
You guys will always be in my heart
Day after day, till death do us part

by Hayley Horn

CF is a disease which may shorten my life but I still have goals for the future. I want to go to a top college so I can have the best teachers. I want to be a surgeon (my grandpa was a doctor) or a lawyer. I want to be a surgeon so I can help people. I want to be a lawyer because I like to argue and I bring up good points. I also remember what people say and can throw it back at them. My parents and friends think I would be good at this career. My other goal is to open a Beatles theme park. All the restaurants, games, and rides would be named after Beatles songs. My one main goal is to always make my parents proud of me.

I do want to get married and have two children, a boy and a girl. But I am concerned that nobody will love me because I have CF. My biggest concern is that my kids will have the disease and I don't want them to go through all the trauma that I have gone through. They might be mad at me and then I would feel guilty.

Having cystic fibrosis is difficult but I try to be positive and do the best I can to enjoy my life.

A Mother's View

by Karen Horn

When Hayley was born with cystic fibrosis, life seemed so bleak. We couldn't imagine how our sick child would have any sort of happiness in her shortened life. I became dedicated to taking care of Hayley and her medical needs. I haven't slept through the night for thirteen years and am usually exhausted.

I knew grief early in life. My father died when I was seven years old.

He was an excellent musician, playing any instrument which was set before him. When he died, the music in our home left with him. I did not inherit his talent but I wanted music to be an important part of my child's life.

I exposed Hayley to music, like the Beatles and Motown, early in her life. It wasn't long before she began to display her own talent, beating on everything in sight with incredible rhythm to the music. I would sing to her and she would sing back. At two years of age, she was picking out familiar melodies on her small keyboard. She began taking piano lessons when she was five. She won a couple of awards for her compositions in elementary school.

In fifth grade, Hayley became involved in the public school music band program and this changed her life. She could not play any wind instrument because she did not have the lung capacity. But the teacher encouraged her to play the drums and she loved it. She has turned out to be an outstanding percussionist. After receiving a professional drum set from Make-A-Wish Foundation, she began taking private drum lessons and became the jazz band drummer in junior high school. Every afternoon after school, she attends rehearsals for jazz band, symphonic band, marching band, and drum line. My husband and I attend every music event to celebrate her and be there if she needs help. In addition to her homework, this is a rigorous schedule but I believe it is what has kept her going and hopeful about life. Music has given her the confidence and self-esteem which are often absent in children with cystic fibrosis. She can be part of a team even if she can't play sports.

The band has given her a purpose. Even when she doesn't feel well, she has told me, "I have to go to school today. The band needs me." Hayley has goals and dreams and can see a future, which is critical to her well-being. I could not be happier that my dad's talent jumped over me and landed on my daughter, where it was most needed, and that I have music in the house again.

Hayley and her mother teach us that it is not the number of years that we have together but how we spend those years that is more important. Children, living with terminal illness or not, long to belong to a group, make a contribution, develop their talents and skills, and envision their future. Not to guide sick children in this process is to rob them of living to the fullest the days they have left.

*C*hapter 7

Helping Patients and Families Through the Death

We now move from helping the child and family cope with hospitalization to preparing them for the death. The child will die in a hospital, hospice (health care facility for treatment of the terminally ill), or at home. Hospice means a team approach of total-person care to meet all needs of the patient and family and may include a separate location to die. It is an extension of Child Life care for the pediatric patient. Since most hospices do not have a Child Life specialization, the majority of pediatric patients die in a children's hospital. Others die at home. Home care of the dying, where the health-care team works with the family to treat patients in their home environment, is an option. Helpers bring the same skills to hospital, hospice, or home.

Who can best help the child die is the child's *own family*. Your task is to help them do that. It is no surprise that the family begins the grieving process when they first learn of the terminal illness. Often they become so lost in their own grief they fail to realize that they have an important job to do—to help their child die. That is hard work which requires full involvement, and is radically different from the natural human tendency to distance oneself from a patient in the final stages of illness to avoid further pain. The helper must realize that he or she can also fall into this trap.

If the parents begin pulling away before the death and do not grab on to the final opportunities to spend time with their child, their preparation will be less and their grief work will be that much harder after the death. The family must enter with the child into the *reality* of the dying process.

Help families build final memories—to take that last vacation trip, to fully celebrate that last Christmas or their child's last birthday. They celebrate these special, bittersweet days in a way we can never understand. Families know they must live these times to their fullest. Free them from any responsibilities that will stand in their way.

Siblings must be part of the process and not be shut out "for their own good." That will only intensify their pain and confuse them. The amount of involvement will, of course, depend on the ages of the siblings. The death should be talked about openly and honestly. Nothing should be hidden. There should be room for plenty of questions and no atmosphere of secrecy in the home. Siblings should be included, not excluded, from activities such as visiting the child in the hospital. The dying process needs to be a family matter that includes grandparents and other extended family members.

How much the patient or siblings understand about the coming death depends on their developmental concept of death as well as their faith in Jesus Christ. The preschooler who thinks that her brother will come back is not "denying death"; this is simply how young children view death—as a temporary and reversible happening. This is the age of active imagination, where fact and fantasy are interchanged. The preschooler's grief is intense with a wide range of emotions, and requires repeated explanations of the death. This is especially painful for parents. Rituals are helpful.

Preschoolers can view death as a punishment for breaking

rules or as a result of their wishing it. A young child who "wished his brother would die" when he was angry with him can think that he actually caused his death. You can assure preschoolers that God loves them unconditionally and this is not his punishment. Small children think that their deceased siblings will go on living in different circumstances. You can affirm that a brother or sister who trusted Jesus Christ now lives in heaven with him.

Preschoolers live in the present, not the future. The dying preschool patient will be more concerned about today's trauma of pain, what is happening to his or her body, and the family's reactions to the illness, than about the lost tomorrow. True grief comes from understanding that death is a lost future, but this loss is not a reality for the young child. You can promise preschoolers that you will help them live today and that God holds their futures in his hands.

By age seven the child is aware that dying means losing loved ones, and this realization of separation can cause fear. The middle-age child can see death as a person coming to take someone away. Depending on individual maturity, the child may still have some early preschool concepts of death, but he begins to understand that death is permanent and can conceive of an afterlife. You can assure these children that God wants only the best for them and is not a villain coming to take their loved one away.

Adolescents deal with death by employing adult coping mechanisms (such as denial, repression, and anger); they finally move into acceptance. They understand death is final. The teenage years can be the most difficult time to face one's own death. Two major focuses of this age are on physical appearance and social standing, and on setting goals and making future plans (living in the future). Death robs teens of both. Teenagers are often as traumatized by the way they look because of their illness, especially from radiation treatments for cancer and distance from their friends, as they are by their coming death. They lose the purpose for having dreams, planning, and achieving future goals. Grieving adolescent siblings will also need to enter adult grief work (as discussed in chapter 10).

Facing death with God's truth does make all the difference. It is the difference between death and life—an eternal life in Jesus Christ. Christian helpers can offer this unique facet of care to the dying and their families. You can offer hope and eternal healing. When dying children fear separation from their families, you can promise that their daddy, God, and their best friend, Jesus, will never leave them. When they fear an end to life, God promises them a better, unending life. When a grieving sibling says that her sister is alive somewhere else, you can say that she is right. When adolescents hate how they look, you can verify that they are beautiful to God and that he is planning heavenly goals for them. When patients fear the disease process in their bodies, you can tell them that God made their bodies, knows what he is doing, and will guide the doctor.

The same methods for helping the child cope with hospitalization remain the most effective methods for coping with death. Death must be an open topic. The coming death should never be hidden from the child.

Children cannot be fooled. They sense when talk about death makes adults uncomfortable. Children who were outgoing and expressive will become withdrawn and seem to experience a personality change when they face death. In reality, they have simply learned that their families cannot talk about the death or hear their concerns, so they keep them to themselves.

Preparation for medical procedures and education about what is happening to the patient's body in the disease process should be continued, with opportunity for play therapy. The use of books and the creative arts therapies will help the patient verbalize and express his or her feelings and concerns about death. Music is an excellent tool for providing safety and comfort in the final stages of death. Hearing is the last sense to leave the dying body.

Journaling is an especially effective way to cope with loss.

Interactive journaling, where family members write back and forth to each other, is a safe way to communicate when talking is uncomfortable and too painful. Parents often continue journaling after their child's death, sometimes in the form of letters to their deceased child.

The actual activities need to be tailored for the child's individual age. Medical preparation, books, and creative arts activities will be different for the three-year-old than the fifteen-year-old. This requires the helper to research a variety of resources for different ages and to know the individual likes and dislikes of each child.

No matter the method, your first goal is to provide an accepting atmosphere where the patient can talk about and understand death and help the family to do the same. Be familiar with local organizations, support groups, and literature you can recommend.

A second goal is to create as normal an environment as possible with short-term goals and projects. This is why dying young children learn to read, older children do their homework up to the week of their death, and parents still discipline disobedient behavior. This helps patients have hope and purpose for today. The worst thing is to encourage them to give up living the life that they do have left.

Your role as helper is twofold: (1) to fully enter the grief process and share the patient's and family's present pain; and (2) offer them a foundation and future hope in Jesus Christ. This integration of God's message with our human lives of suffering is the essence of the gospel.

To summarize, remember to do the following:

1. Help the family help their child die. Help parents and siblings to be wholly involved in their child's dying process. Encourage open, honest communication, with no secrets.
2. Be aware of the children's concepts of death that correspond to their age. Help siblings to grieve at their

levels of maturity. Discuss topics that may be too painful for the parents.

3. Discuss death as a coming reality. Help dying children grieve their own deaths. Affirm God's constant love and care and eternal life in Jesus Christ.
4. Maintain a normal environment with short-term goals for the dying child.
5. Be familiar with resource organizations, support groups, and literature to advise the family.
6. Prepare yourself to grieve.

*C*hapter 8

Zain's Journey: Advice from the Experts

This chapter is an account of the journey of a young man who knew how to die and the parents, Kathy and David Werum, who knew how to help him.

In his family's eyes, December 4, 1985, is Zain's "birthday." It is the day that twelve-year-old Zain died of a brain tumor and was born into the presence of God. One week before Zain's death, a family friend died of a heart attack. Zain's family was comforted because they believed that this dear friend had gone before to wait for Zain. Zain was not without plenty of friends on earth; he would not be without friends in heaven. He loved God as his parents did. He was bright, friendly, loving, and enjoyed life to the fullest.

During the summer of 1984, Zain's family was traveling up the California coast when Zain began to have recurring stomach sickness. A few weeks later, he began to have terrible headaches. The first doctor who saw Zain said that Zain's problem was psychosomatic. Zain's parents, Kathy and David, persevered, and a series of doctors and tests revealed that Zain had a rapidly growing brain tumor. There was little hope for his survival. It would be a matter of months before his death.

The doctors were honest: chemotherapy and radiation could prolong his life a little, but the treatments would cause Zain great misery and never cure him. Zain's parents decided not to pursue those treatments. They opted for alternative medicines that had no side effects. Kathy and David prayed for Zain's healing. They also prayed that if God still chose to take him, Zain would be as healthy as possible for their last few months together.

God did not heal Zain on earth, but he did protect him from great pain and suffering and allow him to lead a relatively normal, healthy life. Zain graduated with honors from sixth grade in June. He was an excellent student and up until the night before he died was concerned about finishing his homework. Kathy and David felt that God was very tender with them. Their last months together were wonderful and provided them with memories that would last a lifetime. Zain continued to love and trust his Lord, and he and his family thanked God for every "one more day" that they were allowed to spend together. Zain and his family believed strongly in the purpose of his illness and the special job that Zain had been given. And then one Sunday morning in December, Zain got up in church and gave hugs to each of the older women in the congregation. He made "appointments" with his best friends to spend time with them.

Zain never told anyone, but he knew that it was time for saying good-bye and tying up loose ends. Monday morning he had a seizure. The CAT scan revealed that the tumor had grown so massively that it was a matter of days until his death.

Kathy's hip had been recently broken, which caused her to be home constantly during those last weeks with Zain. Tuesday night she slept in a bed in another room in an attempt to keep her leg more comfortable. Zain asked if he could sleep with her. It was their last night together. They prayed, read, talked, slept, reminisced, laughed, and held each other through the night. It was God's gift to them. The next day Zain died in his parents' arms.

Several weeks after Zain's funeral, a dear eighty-four-year-old friend of Kathy asked her to come for lunch. She wanted to tell Kathy something that she never had told her before. She said that she had lost her four-year-old son in a drowning accident fifty years before, and that her grief hurt as much that day as it had the day it happened. She wanted Kathy to know that her pain would never stop—it would never "be over"—and that it was all right to hurt today, next year, or thirty years from now. Kathy was relieved and comforted. She would not have to feel guilty for carrying that pain with her when friends thought that she should be through grieving and go on with her life. There was no timetable for this deep grief. Kathy also knew that if she let that wound become calloused, her compassion for other hurting people would become calloused, too, and that would be the greatest tragedy of all.

One of the most helpful things that Kathy and David did through their last year together was to write letters to Zain in a journal. Kathy continued writing to him after his death. Zain was not dead but simply living in a new heavenly home. They have graciously allowed some of their journal entries to be printed here to teach helpers about the pain of grieving parents.

Dear Zain,

It's so strange—this strong feeling we all have that you lived your full life span. Too short for me but not for the Lord. He numbered your days before you were born, and you lived your complete life.

How can a boy twelve years old live a full life? But you did, and you did your job so well.

Love,
Mom

Dear Zain,

I admit I don't understand the "why" of what happened. But I don't have to, because I know our Lord, and I can accept it as part of his plan. He doesn't make mistakes. I trust him to know what he is doing and that it will serve a purpose (Romans 8:28).

Too often we are so overwhelmed by the problem that we cannot see the purpose.

Love,
Mom

Dear Zain,

You love God and understand him in a more mature way than any other eleven-year-old I know. (And others see this in you as well.) God says he never gives us more than we can handle, and he's asked you to handle a lot . . . it's kind of like God saying, "Zain I trust you . . . with a very important job that I want you to do."

Zain, I believe that the important job God has trusted to you (and us with you) is to be a witness that will bring a lot of people to be saved.

There are so many who know you and are praying for you and you have a special place in their coming to know Jesus or growing stronger in their relationship with him. *What an important job*; what a special confidence God has in you. All because you (as all of our family) have put your confidence in him.

This is the day that the Lord has made, let us rejoice and be glad in Him.

Love,
Dad

Dear Zain,

One week ago we came home from spending the night at the hospital. Again they told us that the tumor had grown and that you had maybe a day, maybe a few months to live—just what they told us last year. Only this time, we knew in a different way that the end was truly near.

We called Grandpa, Grandma, and Sister and told them but said too that life would go on. We made plans to get our Christmas tree and take you shopping in a wheelchair. You were so brave—you knew the tumor had grown, yet you didn't want to quit taking your medicines.

One week ago you came down about midnight and said you weren't real tired. One week ago you climbed in bed with me to spend your last night on earth.

It was such a special night. I knew that even then. I felt so gentle towards you and was so happy just to have you near. We talked for just a little while and then we both dozed off to sleep.

We awoke about 2 A.M. and talked some more. You were restless and I just talked to keep you calm. I asked if you wanted me to read to you as we always had, and you said yes. We read and talked for hours about so many special memories.

As morning dawned, we thanked God for another day of being together. You asked me to get your school work. I turned and said, "Zain, I don't know why you have this tumor and I don't know why God is allowing it to grow again, but we won't give up. Right?"

And you beamed at me. "Right!"

A week ago Koran left for school. You started to have a headache and throw up. I had a doctor's appointment in Vallejo and decided to go. Daddy was here to be with you. John called and said Lawrence had died of a heart attack about one o'clock in the morning. I left for the appointment; everything took so long but I felt so calm. When I was finally there it was about 11:20, and I called Daddy to see what was happening. He said simply that he thought I had better come home, for you might not be with us much longer—that your time might have come.

Merr and I were calm. We went to the car, and I thanked God that Lawrence had died that day. It was such a comfort to know that he was there if you needed him. We prayed for you and cried a little. I remember telling Merr it was okay if she speeded a bit.

We got home, and you were on our bed. John had been here and prayed and cried and read Scripture with Dad.

We sat beside you and told you how we loved you and how proud we were of you. The hour passed quickly with lots of people calling. It seemed the phone never stopped ringing, but it wasn't an intrusion; instead it was like everyone was sending their love.

You always knew what we were saying to you. Oh, Babe, I miss you.

You had a kind of seizure. We held you and helped you to get comfortable. We told you to relax, and you did—more and more, until suddenly I knew you were no longer with us, even though you still breathed a few more times. I started to pray and asked Jesus to open the gates wide, and when I said *wide*, that was it—you were gone.

Then Dad prayed, then Merr. We sang and held you. Sandy, your dog, had her head on your leg. We cried—Daddy just like when Sarah died.

It didn't take long for you to cool down, and then I kissed you one last time. Sandy, your dog, had already left. It was strange and neat, too, for she knew you—the person that she loved—was no longer in the world, and there was no reason for her to be there either.

All of our family came. We hummed "Alleluia" together while they took you out. That was hard on us.

We were all calm; somehow it was supposed to be. Like Koran had said a year ago, "I don't know what's going to happen, but it will be okay." It was okay. The Lord had made it okay. He didn't solve our problem the way we wanted, but he surely did take away your tumor, and he had answered my prayers that you be as well as possible for as long as possible.

Here it is nine days later. . . . Christmas is ten days away, and we are leaving in a few hours to spend the weekend in Placerville like we'd planned. That was what was important to Koran—that we continue to do all the things we had planned on doing.

Your memorial service was beautiful, as you know. And it was so neat to feel like the Lord was giving me the words that each person needed to hear. I pray that that continues. We are going to plant the Zain Werum Memorial Forest at church. Right now we have three trees—Colorado blue spruces.

Beautiful trees made for boys.

Love,
Mom

Dear Zain,

This actually starts one week ago tonight. Thursday we were taking off for L.A., so Wednesday I had been up late finishing things. I went to bed, and the dull ache was here. I started to cry—the empty sob—just wanting you to be there to fill the void. Suddenly, before I really began, you were there. I wish I could remember exactly what you said, but the gist was that there was no need for me to feel lonely. You would always be near, and we would be together again.

I stopped crying—there was no need—and the feeling of you do "love-me-more" for you came back to comfort me. I know that was a selfless thing for you to do.

Throughout our trip I have felt you close. I only cried once, and that was at Disneyland watching the circus show (you loved it) and looking up at the beautiful cloudy sky and the two birds flying free overhead and thinking that you are free. I don't want to keep you shackled to me because I miss you so, for I love you more, too. I love you, Babe.

The joy of the Christian life is to be able to truly know that, whatever happens, we can truly be happy, for somehow it will fit into the Lord's plan.

Love,
Mom

Dear Zain,

It's been two months. . . . .
Today I listened to the tape of the funeral for the first time. So good, and the quality is excellent, too.

This grief thing is strange; I *miss* you. I was conscious, this weekend in S.F., of just wanting to share with you, and feeling cheated because I can't. Also, I feel that it's unfair that you will always be "only" twelve years old in my mind. Thank goodness for our resurrection bodies.

Your sister got straight A's. I'm so proud. It's hard not to wonder how you would have done as a freshman.

I cried today and I feel better for it. I went through your room remembering how much you loved the things in it—the rocks, the marten on the rocks, each thing you placed there. You made the job so easy, because you had gone through so much already. Thank you.

I look at the places I failed you because of my own sin, and I'm sorry. I hope I didn't lead to your death. Lord forgive me.

Love,
Mom

Dear Zain,

I dreamed of you again—so vividly that you are still with me—walking and talking with you in the dream. You were taller and older looking, yet still the same Zain. I'm not sure if you were trying to reassure me or yourself that you could still enjoy birthdays and holidays. . . .

I miss you.

Love,
Mom

(Written two-and-one-half years after Zain's death.)

Chapter 9

Helping After the Death

A young girl was very late in coming home from school. Her mother became frantic. Finally her daughter arrived. "Where were you? What took you so long? Where have you been?" the mother demanded. "I was at Mary's house," the girl replied. "Her favorite doll got broken." "That was so important? Did you break the doll? Did you fix it? What took so long?" Tears began to well up in the little girl's eyes and stream down her face under her mother's inquisition. "I helped her cry," she said softly.

—God's Little Devotion Book for Moms

Now we come to the long journey after death. The most effective helpers during bereavement are those who have supported the family through the diagnosis, hospitalization, and dying process. They have walked the entire road with them, and this sharing of their pain extends past the death into grief work. You, the helper, will be grieving, too. To cry with mourners is one of the most therapeutic gifts you can offer them. Yet friends sometimes friends distance themselves from the dying person and grieving family to protect themselves from pain. Helpers can experience the same isolation if viewed as being too involved with the family.

Sudden loss due to a catastrophic accident causes the most difficult grief to bear. Parents of terminally ill children begin grieving when they learn of the illness. They have time to prepare and say good-bye to their child. They have already moved through some of the beginning stages of grief work and are nearer to acceptance when the death arrives. When a child dies suddenly, the parents have no preparation and are enveloped in shock. It will take them years to move through grief work. The most painful part of the ordeal is never having had a chance to say good-bye or create those needed last memories to last a lifetime. Again the most effective helper will be one who has a close relationship with the family and knew the child well. They can mourn together.

The following "letter" is an integration of interviews with numerous grieving families experiencing loss due to illness or sudden accident, current research on grief and death, and my personal experience. It is designed to show what effectively helps the griever.

Dear Helper,

I have never known pain like this before. In losing my child, I have lost not only my dear loved one, I have lost a part of myself. As her mother, I carried that child inside of me for nine months. She will always be a part of me. Holding her in my arms for the first time was a time of joy. Holding her for the last time is a time of grief and sorrow. As his father, I cherished this child as my heritage and future hope.

Being responsible for raising a child gives one such purpose in life. I've lost that now. I poured my life into my child and I will not see the fruit of my labors. I will never see her graduate from high school or college, hold a first job, get married, or have children of her own.

No one can be prepared for this devastating loss. We know that we will lose our dear loved ones—parents, siblings, friends, and even spouses—but no one expects to lose their child. If this was my only child, who will take care of me when I am old? I'm scared. The future is so bleak and empty.

I am physically and emotionally exhausted from caring for my dying child. It was a full-time job that consumed me. There was room for nothing else in our lives—not even our marriage. Our relationship has deteriorated. Our savings are gone. Our careers have suffered; how could we concentrate? We had to take excessive time off work. Financially we are struggling.

Then there was the guilt. When I was at home with my other children, I felt guilty for not being at the hospital. When I was at the hospital with my dying child, I felt guilty for leaving my other children. I couldn't win. It tore me apart. Now I feel guilty for all the times I wasn't the perfect parent.

The hospital was my lifeline. The staff became my friends. I relied on being with other families going through the same ordeal. I became attached to other patients—my child's friends. Now I no longer belong there. Where do I belong? My job was caring for my sick child. I have lost my life's role.

There is a good reason for the term *grief work*. Grieving a loved one is hard, agonizing work. When the shock wears off, my grief work will require every ounce of concentration and energy that I have. You cannot do it for me, but you can stand by to grieve with me. I must fully embrace this grief or I will never be healed from it. I cannot walk around it; I must walk *through* it. Physically I will struggle; not feel well, not eat, sleep, or care for my physical body. Those tasks seem very petty now. Do bring me meals so that I have the chance to eat. I do need nourishment and strength, though I don't enjoy eating. I am just numb.

Please do not advise me, impose what you think best for me, or judge how I am grieving. Everyone grieves differently, in different time frames in different ways. Remember that I am still the "same person." My temperament has not changed. If I have always been an extrovert, socially active, and gained strength from being with groups of people, I will need my friends around me now more than ever. But if I have been a private, introverted person who gained perspective in solitude, please don't decide that I shouldn't be alone now. I will need my privacy to work through this. Of course, I will still need people, just as the extrovert will need some time alone. But take your cue from me. Ask me what I want and respect it. Don't try to distract me from my pain or "keep me busy." You are not taking my grief away, but only delaying it. Putting it on the shelf prolongs my grief. I will do this in my own way and my own time.

When you are with me, love me, hold me, cry with me. Feel my hurt in your heart. Pray for me with tears. Let me feel God's love and care for me through you, and Jesus' arms around me through yours. Understand that I must move through the stages of grief: shock, denial, anger, guilt, hopelessness, and depression. But everyone is different; I will not go through them in some predictable textbook order. I want to go to bed, pull the covers over my head, and never come out. I may cry without stopping or I may completely shut down, beyond tears. It may take a few weeks or a few years for me to go through this. Most parents enter this grief process when they first learn of their child's terminal illness. Those who lose children suddenly have the longest road.

I may have disturbing dreams. I may have very real, comforting visions. Listen to me talk about them and please do not judge my mental state. God truly works in mysterious ways. I am consumed with eternity and the hope of reunion with my child. You cannot relate because the people you love are here on earth.

Above all, *listen to me*. Let me tell you that "this isn't happening to me"; let me be angry at God, blaming him and everyone around me; allow me to wonder aloud if the death is my fault. I have a roller-coaster relationship with God right now. One minute I feel safe in his loving arms and the next moment I am flooded with doubts and questions, feeling totally abandoned by him. He can handle it. I hope that you can too. Be my safe place to talk, cry, and feel totally accepted. I need my lifeline of friends now. I know that I scare you. You are wondering if this can happen to me, then it can happen to you. You may even try to find some reason for our loss to ease your own mind.

Please do not make packaged, insensitive statements such as: "Time heals all wounds," "I know how you feel," "Everything will be all right," "God will not give you more than you can bear," "At least you have three other children," "All things work together for good . . . ." Please do not tell me about someone else's story that is sadder than mine or send me books on grief. Don't say or do anything to minimize my grief or try to fix me. This only says that you have no idea how deeply I am hurting.

Please do come and share a relevant passage of Scripture with me as part of our relationship based in unconditional love. But do not quote Scripture out of context at me without making an effort to love me first. This is the "Scripture wall" used by Christians who need to feel that they have done their duty without having invested time in a relationship. Jesus never did that, and I need to see Jesus now. Gently help me remember that this intense love I have for my child is a tiny glimpse into how much God loves me.

Help me to be fully involved in the funeral. I want to celebrate my child's life. It was short, but worth living. Let me plan this as my last gift for my child. Understand that the funeral is not really for my child; it is for us who have been left behind. It is a time for tribute, for good-byes. I need to be active in this. It is an event I will always cherish. Well-meaning friends sometimes take over every detail of the funeral to spare the griever's pain. Sometimes they even clean out the room of the deceased so that the griever will not have to face it. You cannot spare me this pain, so do not try. I have to walk through every memory and relive our life together. I must look at every picture in every scrapbook, touch every toy, see the half-done homework, hear her favorite songs. I want to hold my child's things and do activities he enjoyed so I can feel close to him.

Let me be immersed in my grief. I must create something out of this grief—keep a journal, compile a scrapbook of bereavement cards, compose a song, write poetry, paint, or whatever God puts in my heart to do. I must have an outlet. That's what David did in the Psalms. Please do not think it is strange or morbid when I write letters to my deceased child. My loving relationship with him or her hasn't died.

Encourage me to walk this road of reviewing the life we had with our child. Precious memories are all I have. You have the present and future with your child. I have only the past. Take over the practical chores for me (washing, cleaning, cooking, transporting our other children) so that I have time to grieve.

Realize that our marriage is struggling now. It is not true that "crisis brings people together" when a dying child is involved. One partner (often the wife) wants to talk about the death, while the other (often the husband) wants to avoid the topic. The pain is too deep. Marriages are strained. We are probably grieving in different ways, in different time frames, and this is ripping us apart. Do not expect us to be the same couple you knew.

We are each drowning in sorrow and two drowning people cannot save each other. Intense pain is incredibly stressful. Divorce is not uncommon . . . relationships with friends, extended family, and churches can be strained. I understand why grievers use addictions to ease their pain. One will think of anything to stop the unending pain, even suicide.

Put me in touch with other people who have lost their children—when I am ready. There is no empathy like that of other grieving parents. I may want to attend a bereavement support group in a local hospital, seek grief counseling, or share with only one fellow sufferer. You can research local resources that I do not have the energy to call.

Don't tell me that "God is preparing me for a great ministry" or "my faith is being tested and disciplined through fire." Even if true, I am not ready to hear it. I can barely get out of bed, much less help someone else. This also is not a time for a theological discussion of God's sovereign purpose. Doctrine will not comfort me. My survival will come from completely focusing on my relationship with God through Jesus Christ. Help me focus on his tender, fatherly care of me and on Jesus' victory even in death. Don't distract me with figuring out God's plan. The most comforting thing you can say is, "I don't understand, but I love you and I'll be here." His love and presence—those are the promises of God. Reflect them to me.

Talk about my child. Don't avoid his name in conversation as if he never existed. That is very painful to me. Don't you like to talk about your children? You can say, "Tommy would have liked that," "That would have made Jenny laugh," "That was Sally's favorite ice cream." I am already thinking it, so give me an opening to talk about it. Remember her with me. You can't take my hurt away. Every little reminder hurts. But sharing the pain with me helps it hurt less.

We may need to take a vacation break as a family before returning to reality. Stand by me when I try to reenter the mainstream of life. Go with me on that first supermarket trip. Be there when I see my child's favorite cereal. Hold me when I try to return to church. When I see acquaintances in town, it hurts to watch them walk the other direction to avoid me. I know it's awkward and they don't know what to say. But I feel so alone. There are no magic words; just a hug would help.

You must understand that the hardest part of my grief comes after the funeral and the initial few months have passed. This is when the support of people around me will begin to diminish. Your life goes on but mine will never be the same. My life has been split into two parts—before and after my child's death. Please remember us on the following days:
- our child's birthday,
- the date of his/her death,
- major holidays (especially Christmas, Mother's/ Father's Day),
- any days or vacation times that you know were special to us as a family.

Holidays that once brought the most joy will now bring the most pain. I always see the empty chair at the table. The first year's anniversaries are the hardest to bear. I will need to recognize these anniversaries, especially the annual date of the death, with significant ceremony. Share these times with us. As the years go on, the pain will decrease, but it will always be there. Help me fill the emptiness with new rituals and traditions, like giving a donation to the cancer society or putting flowers in the church on my child's birthday.

Please remember my other children. Do special things for them now. Talk with them; love them; listen to their fears. They are falling through the cracks of my grief. Help me parent them. I have to say good-bye to one child before I can be a whole parent again.

Someday, but *not* in the early stages, I will need outlets of exercise, hobbies, and new interests to fill the time. I will need to start a new life and find renewed purpose. Don't push me, but be there to encourage me when I'm ready.

Don't wait for me to be "my old self." Losing my child has changed me forever. Fifty years from now, my grief will still be with me.

Love,
The Griever

In Summary:

Listen to me, do but listen, and let that be the comfort you offer me. —Job 21:1–2

1. Grieving is hard work.
2. Understand that the stages of grief are normal: shock, physical symptoms, denial, anger, guilt, depression, acceptance of death, hope to continue. But be aware that there is no textbook formula for the grief process. Everyone moves through the stages in different orders, time frames, and degrees of intensity.

3. Respect the wishes of grievers, and do not assume that you "know what's best for them" based on your experience.
4. Provide an environment of unconditional love, acceptance, and listening.
5. Do not minimize the unique pain and grief of each mourner.
6. Mirror God's love and scriptural truth in Jesus Christ; do not "preach" it.
7. Help the griever to be fully involved in the funeral planning.
8. Support those who grieve as they review their child's life to the last detail. Do not misunderstand dreams, visions, or writing letters to the deceased child. These experiences are normal and comforting.
9. Encourage them to find a creative outlet for their pain. Supply them with needed tools.
10. Do tangible chores such as bringing meals, cleaning, doing yard work, and providing transportation. Arrange financial donations. *You* take care of all the loose ends.
11. Be sensitive to the strain on the marriage and the needs of siblings. Provide a listening ear to the siblings when it is too painful for the parents to fill that role.
12. Be a link to other grievers who have experienced the death of a child. Have information about support groups and hospital or church offerings in the area for those who are interested.
13. Talk about the deceased child. Cry and mourn with the griever.
14. Do not forget the family after the "initial accepted mourning period" passes. Remember holidays and specific anniversary dates in their lives, especially the child's birthdate and date of death. Participate in creating new traditions that honor the child.
15. Be available to support the extended family—

grandparents, aunts, uncles, and others. They must grieve too, and will not want to burden the grieving parents.

16. Be prepared to help but always take your cue from the griever.

When words are most empty, tears are most apt.

—Max Lucado

PLEASE

PLEASE, don't ask me if I'm over it yet.
I'll never be over it.

PLEASE, don't tell me she's in a better place.
She isn't here with me.

PLEASE, don't say at least she isn't suffering.
I haven't come to terms with why she had to suffer at
all.

PLEASE, don't tell me you know how I feel.
Unless you have lost a child.

PLEASE, don't ask me if I feel better.
Bereavement isn't a condition that clears up.

PLEASE, don't tell me at least you had her for so
many years.
What year would you choose for your child to die?

PLEASE, don't tell me God never gives us more
than we can bear.

PLEASE, just say you are sorry.
PLEASE, just say you remember my child, if you do.

PLEASE, just let me talk about my child.

PLEASE, mention my child's name.

PLEASE, just let me cry.

By Rita Moran
Compassionate Friends

*C*hapter 10

Surviving the Unbearable: More Advice from the Experts

Nothing wreaks havoc with our life and our faith like the loss of a child. Families at times feel hopeless, despaired, and abandoned by God. The following account is a very special journey toward regaining God's hope after enduring the dark tunnel. It is also an excellent example of how parents can best help siblings to cope with their loss.

Karen's journey was an ideal life turned upside down. Raised in a loving Christian home, Karen had enjoyed a genuine faith in Jesus Christ since she was a young child. A deep trust in God and desire to obey him marked her life. Her experience of God overflowed with his tender care and goodness. Karen was a talented pianist who gave generously of her gifts to the church and taught music in her home. She had decided against pursuing further opportunities in music to be a dedicated wife and mother of seven-year-old twin girls, Sarah and Michelle, a four-year-old son, and another baby due shortly. Her husband and children were the joy of her life—especially Sarah.

Sarah was extremely bright, active, loving, affectionate—a special little girl. She was good at everything, did well in school and gymnastics, and was also her mother's star piano student. She had a motherly touch, was protective of her sister and brother, and was kind to everyone around her. She brought joy to all.

Sarah had always been very healthy, but one summer's day Karen decided that Sarah should see the doctor about her cold. The doctor informed Karen that Sarah had a cancerous tumor growing in her chest area. A biopsy would need to be done immediately. The good news was that there was an 80 percent chance of recovery from this type of cancer. There was hope.

Karen and Steve were confident that God had always protected them and he would show his power in protecting Sarah now. The doctors said that they could do the biopsy at the local hospital, and Sarah could go right home.

But Sarah never went home. The doctor failed to use the correct pediatric-size tube. Sarah's trachea collapsed, she went into convulsive breathing and cardiac arrest, and then into a coma. Even if she came out of the coma, she would have severe brain damage.

Sarah was rushed to the intensive care unit of the nearest children's hospital. The doctors verified that if the procedure had been done at the children's hospital with specialized pediatric equipment, Sarah would have been fine.

Karen and Steve went home to tell their two children, who adored Sarah, that she would not be coming home. Life had to go on. Karen was about to give birth to a new baby. Steve had a new job and was also in school. How could God have done this to his faithful followers? Life was unraveling, and the questions were deafening.

Sarah's specialists started her on chemotherapy and radiation for the cancer. Though family members were at her bedside around the clock, Sarah was never to come out of her coma.

The first day of school was the hardest moment in the entire ordeal for Karen. She had to take Michelle to school without her twin and protector, Sarah, and face the questions of the staff: "Where is Sarah? Isn't she coming today?" The pain was crushing.

Timothy, Karen and Steve's second son, was born three weeks later. With the demands of a new infant, Karen could not visit Sarah as often as she desired. Michelle and her brother had visited Sarah to talk to her and hold her. Now it was Timothy's turn. Karen placed him in Sarah's arms. He would never know this sister.

To add to the pain, Karen, Steve, and some of their extended family were actively part of a church that believed strongly in healing. Karen and Steve believed in healing. Yes, God *would* heal Sarah. But four months after the onset of the coma, Sarah's doctor called a family conference. Sarah's condition was deteriorating; she was dying. The doctor recommended stopping the cancer treatments. The end had come. Karen and Steve were faced with the toughest decision of their lives. One side of their family said that God would still heal Sarah. She should be kept alive in any fashion. The other side of the family said that perhaps God had already taken Sarah from them and they should accept it.

Karen and Steve painfully came to the realization that their precious Sarah was dying; it was time to let her go. Members of the church opposed their decision and sent prayer teams twenty-four hours a day to her hospital bedside. They were unable to minister to Karen and Steve, but they prayed for healing. Karen had the painful task of asking that they stop, because the nurses' and doctors' care of Sarah was being disrupted. The chaos was not good for Sarah.

Sarah died that week. Not only did Karen and Steve have to face their own intense grief and their children's grief, they also faced a broken relationship with their church. Even members of their own extended family were angry with them and accused them of not being Christians.

Where was God? Had he abandoned them? Where were his loving, protective arms? They had lost their daughter and now they had lost their Christian support system. They had survived pain upon pain upon pain for months. God had been with them through the funeral and first hard month, but now their faith was crumbling and the darkness was engulfing them. If their Bible-based belief in healing and God's protection was untrue, then what *was* true? The questions and doubts flooded in. Karen and Steve entered a dark tunnel of examining every aspect of their faith and relationship with God.

But God never abandons us. He promises to be with his children, even into the "valley of the shadow of death." Though we do not "feel" him, God constantly works for our good. He would lead Karen and Steve through the dark tunnel.

Karen's precious new son was a great source of joy and comfort. Karen desperately missed her role of mothering Sarah, but nurturing and caring for their new baby helped to fill her empty arms and heart.

God gave Karen a determination to rebuild a life for her husband and three children. When severe depression came and she needed to talk, she could reach out to her parents and sister, who were very supportive and always willing to listen. Karen and Steve also realized that physical activity is the best weapon against depression. They immersed themselves in a construction project on their home, and Karen exercised regularly in an aerobics class. Though their marriage was rock-solid, the strains and feelings of guilt common to grieving parents were unavoidable. Karen needed to talk about her pain, but Steve couldn't bear to hear Sarah's name mentioned; the pain was too deep. They finally compromised by talking about Sarah's good times. Karen would talk to friends about the sad times.

Karen stopped teaching piano. Since music touches the deepest parts of our emotions, it is either a great comfort or it is unbearable. Because Karen was a musician and through Sarah she had hoped to continue her music-related dreams, the associations were intensely painful. It was time for Karen to take a break from her music and focus completely on supporting her family. Friends helped with meals and household chores, which freed Karen to spend time with her children. Michelle was the child who suffered most from Sarah's death. Michelle had lost her other half. A twin-sister relationship is the closest of all sibling relationships. Karen understood this and stepped in to be Michelle's partner and spend most of her time with her.

Karen and Steve had done an excellent job of helping their children cope with Sarah's death. They had always been honest and never kept secrets from them. They included their children in every aspect of the loss. They took them to say good-bye to Sarah at her bedside after her death and helped them to attend the funeral. Following the funeral, they left on a weeklong retreat to gain perspective as a new family.

Karen and Steve continued to talk about Sarah, but they were careful not to idolize her or transfer their dreams for Sarah onto Michelle.

Though Karen and Steve had lost their church home, they were still a part of "God's church." God sent a host of Christians from various denominations from the community to support them. Sarah and Michelle's public school was the most consistent, loving source of support. Karen felt most helped by fellow Christians who had suffered similar tragedies and came to put their arms around her, cry with her, and listen to her.

Karen and Steve survived their year's journey through the dark tunnel. Eventually they resolved the broken relationship with their church but never returned there as members. They now attend another church. Today Karen and Steve stand as rocks of true faith and compassionate ministers. When other grieving Christians ask them, "How could God do this to me?" Karen and Steve can say, "We don't understand, either. We miss Sarah desperately, and it will always hurt. But we will travel this road with you. You will survive the darkness and return to a life of faith. We did."

*C*hapter 11

Family Portrait I: Terminal Illness

I met a young woman, Diana, who told me about her sister who died when Diana was eight years old. I asked her if she would write her story to tell helpers what a sibling experiences. She graciously agreed to do so. Her mother and father also willingly contributed their stories. Their gift to us is wisdom and perspective following decades of grief work.

This "family portrait" is a powerful illustration of the principles covered in this book, and a fitting conclusion to this section on terminal illness. Note how the church both helped and did not help them. Note how the medical staff both supported them and did not support them. Observe what brought them comfort and what caused pain. View their different perspectives of the same experience. Think about how you would have helped them.

A Mother's Grief

by Doral Matlock

I lost my firstborn daughter almost thirty years ago and my heart still aches for her. I cry every year on her birthday. This pain lasts a lifetime.

Our family was stricken with the flu in the fall of 1970. My husband, youngest daughter, and I rapidly recovered but Donna, our eldest, did not. After a series of antibiotics failed to work, our doctor recommended hospitalization. Donna had her first needle biopsy and before I realized what was happening, the doctor coldly said, "It's confirmed. She has leukemia," and left the room. I was numb but I followed him out the door to ask questions about treatment. I wanted to know how much time she had left. He answered, "Two to four weeks, two to four months, who knows?" I was shocked at his callous attitude. Finally I asked him if he had children of his own and, his voice softening, he said, "Three." "Then maybe you can understand what we're going through," I replied. Then our doctor walked away.

Donna's seventh birthday was the following day and I cried all the way to the bakery to pick up her "last" birthday cake. Our friends and family joined us in Donna's hospital room, putting on brave masks, to celebrate her birthday.

We called the American Cancer Society for information about treatment options. They recommended Donna be taken to M. D. Anderson Hospital in Houston. We traveled to Texas from our home in California, leaving our youngest daughter, Diana, with relatives. Donna's illness affected everyone in our extended family.

We were relieved to be in a hospital with a very supportive and compassionate staff, specialized in caring for dying children and their families. Parents could spent nights in their children's rooms instead of needing to follow visiting hours policies. Yet I felt so isolated, 2,000 miles away from Diana and loved ones. The phone calls, letters, and packages from California were constant reminders that we were remembered. My husband, Don, traveled between states, trying to keep his job. The school district required that I resign my teaching position. Our savings were dwindling and we learned to graciously accept financial donations. My mother arrived to stay with me and was a tremendous support. She developed intestinal problems due to the stress of Donna's illness.

Donna had improved and was discharged for us to spend Christmas as a family at home. Yet our elation was short-lived. Donna's condition worsened and new chemotherapy treatments began at a nearby children's hospital. I wasn't able to be with my youngest, Diana, on her sixth birthday because I was in the hospital with Donna. This is the pain that tears at a mother's heart. We endured a rollercoaster of endless doctor's appointments, treatments, and hospitalizations. We clung to bits of hope. We learned to live one day at a time and to seize the moment.

I was being trained to mix Donna's medications and inject them through the heparin-lock needle implanted in her vein. We tried to keep her life as normal as possible. It is difficult to discipline a terminally ill child but it is important. We knew that we couldn't change our expectations of her. Donna loved school and was an avid reader. When we took her to our opthalmologist to correct a vision problem, he actually said, "Why waste your money on glasses? She will die soon anyway." How could a doctor—a "healer"—be so cruel?

Soon the disease showed up in Donna's central nervous system and we knew she wouldn't survive much longer. She lost her hair due to the radiation treatments, and we purchased two wigs for her, one brunette and one curly, blond wig just for laughs and fun. An angel, a wonderful housekeeper who took care of everything, came to our house weekly, even if we couldn't give her a check that week. She was critical to my day-to-day survival.

Donna's relapses and high fevers increased and she was moved to Stanford Medical Center. We lived there for most of that last year. Diana had been shuttled between friends and neighbors for too long and we sadly made the heartbreaking decision for her to live with my sister.

Donna was now confined to a wheelchair because of leukemic arthritis. She missed being able to fish and play outside so we bundled her up and took her to a trout farm to fish. It was her last request. Diana was even able to visit that weekend and join the fun. Two weeks later, Donna went into congestive heart failure and died.

We had all fought so gallantly but I knew it was time to let her go. With her dad and me at her side, Donna slipped from this life into the arms of Jesus. I felt that an enormous load had been lifted. No more needles, biopsies, transfusions, treatments, tests . . . . NO MORE SUFFERING. We held a simple graveside service with family and close friends three days later to bury her. The following week we had a memorial service at our church to celebrate Donna's life, rather than mourn her death. She was finally free.

God gave us an unusual gift that month. Through the network at Stanford with other patients and their families, we were invited to travel to Florida to spend a week with a family who had recently lost their son. It was a welcome break before entering real life again.

Donna's illness had consumed me. I was immersed in caring for her and paid little attention to my husband's emotional needs. I couldn't get beyond my own pain to meet him in his grief. Our marriage did not survive. Essentially our relationship was put on hold for three years. We lived in survival mode. We needed counseling but didn't have the time, money, or energy to pursue it. Years later, after further disintegration, we finally divorced. I've often said that divorce is more painful than death, because the corpse is still walking around. I understand that the current divorce rate for couples with terminal children is up to 90 percent.

Our church had encouraged us to stay involved and continue our leadership responsibilities. Looking back, I think they should have encouraged us to take a good break from service. We needed that recovery time.

Our friends and family are the ones who supported us through those dark days. Our community had a blood drive for Donna. Sometimes we would return home to find our yard work done. One good friend was always there to let me talk and cry when I felt lowest. She never tried to "fix" anything or discount my pain. She listened and cared. When I was too paralyzed to reach out for help, she took the initiative and often just showed up on my doorstep.

The first year was the most difficult, reliving our pain with each holiday and Donna's birthday. Don found it too painful to visit her grave, so I often went alone. Sleeping at night was difficult and sometimes I would wake up in sheer panic because I wasn't at the hospital. I was confused. Had I left Donna there alone? After a few months, I moved her, in my dreams, to a rest home. I was disturbed at these bizarre dreams but my pastor assured me that they were a normal part of grieving and letting go.

Six months later, I dreamed that Donna was well and running across a grassy field chasing a kite. I finally felt at peace.

I have felt guilty through the years for not being able to be there for my other daughter, Diana. She knows that we did the best we could in our pain and I have asked for her forgiveness. Today she is married and teaches school also. Two years after Donna died, we had another baby girl, Dayna, who brought much healing and joy to our family. I lived on pins and needles until her tenth birthday, so afraid that we would lose her too.

When people ask me how I survived this ordeal, I tell them that Jesus Christ is my rock and that having faith in God's ultimate plan for our lives is the only way to comprehend this experience. Everyone moves through the recovery process at a different pace. Today I continue teaching, with a special heart for children who are hurting. I help others in recovery groups and am involved in the Make-A-Wish Foundation. We dedicate our efforts to grant wishes to children with life-threatening illnesses and give their families a respite in the storm.

Trimming the tree at Christmas, I am still caught off guard and shed tears of emptiness. We must each pass through the tunnel of grief before we reach the light at the other end. My husband would say, "It never gets easy; it just becomes hard less often."

A Sister's Grief

by Diana Matlock

I lost my sister when I was eight years old. She died from leukemia at nine years of age.

My position in the family is quite unique. I have been the youngest child, an only child, am currently the oldest, and am technically the middle child. Confused? No, I wasn't—just lost.

Donna and I were always social creatures. She, of course, being older, was the leader; I padded dutifully and gullibly behind. Donna was the epitome of the tomboy, I the princess. Consequently, the kids who came over were often the rough-and-tumble kind who climbed our tree house, walked the beam which spanned the distance between the tree and the wisteria-laden trellis covering a walkway, and jumped down. Donna was willowy, I was chunky. Donna was witty, crafty, and saw through people. I trusted everyone, believed everything, and could be conned easily. We loved each other, and she watched out for me, even when I didn't want her to.

When I was in kindergarten I injured my foot and was hospitalized. When I came home, Donna was sick, presumably with the flu. I remember her lying listlessly on the couch watching television. Eventually my parents took her to the hospital but she didn't come home right away. Her stay was not a fix-it ordeal like mine. Eventually I became familiar with such words as *pneumonia, leukemia, IV, chemotherapy* and a myriad of other medical terms—words none of my other kindergarten friends had ever heard.

I was not at the hospital when the doctor told my parents

what was wrong with Donna's body, but I recreated the scene in my mind as Mom shared it over and over again with friends and relatives. The doctor was cold, my parents stunned, and Donna seemingly unknowing. I did not know then the extent to which those events would not just touch but shape my own life.

Over the next three years Donna was in and out of hospitals, my parents filled with the urgency to save their oldest daughter, and I sometimes shuffled off to other households for varying amounts of time. My parents did their best to provide some kind of consistency for me, "the healthy one," but their focus, understandably, for the next thirty-three months was on my older sister.

Donna and I did love each other. I was more willing to show it publicly, much to my sister's embarrassment at times. We joined Blue Birds. Mom became a co-leader. We went camping frequently. Donna and I were in a combination class together at one point. I was delighted to have her there until she started telling me to sit up and pay attention. She let me play with her Hot Wheels track and her electric train but I never could interest her in Barbies. We both enjoyed board games (even though we constantly accused each other of not playing fair) and we loved to draw. Her favorite subjects were horses and hospital things, mine were princesses and mice.

My mom learned how to administer chemotherapy so that Donna could come home. When she was in second grade, I in first, we attended a private school. Donna's hair began falling out as a result of the chemotherapy. Before returning to school, Mom took Donna shopping for wigs. They came home with one which very closely resembled Donna's own hair, dark brown with just the hint of curl at the end; the other was blond and curly, which Donna wore for fun. Most of the time, however, she wore stocking caps. Mom alerted the school staff that Donna would be wearing a wig to school. This wasn't something I had a problem with until my teacher gathered us into our reading circle and told the whole class that my sister would be returning to school wearing a wig. I was embarrassed and just a little angry. The other kids didn't need to know this personal stuff.

She looked just like any other kid. It invoked teasing and mumbled comments which, I am convinced, would not have occurred otherwise.

Unfortunately, Donna was not always able to stay home. Mom says she thanks God that he made me so self-entertaining and easygoing. I suppose it made it easier that I didn't fuss about where I would be staying, although I know she still feels guilty about having had to leave me in the care of others so often and sometimes for so long.

I never lacked love, not just from extended family members but from townspeople as well. I knew I was welcome in whichever household I found myself, be it 5:30 in the morning at the Lecairs when Dad left for work (he and I stayed at home alone for a while when Mom was living at Children's Hospital at Stanford), or bedding down for the night at 8:30 PM at the Rosses. People went out of their way to prepare rooms for me, fix special meals, find things I might like to play with, take me out for ice cream. No, I never lacked love or attention, but I did miss my family. I felt that their lives were continuing without me.

When they went to Texas, I didn't understand why I couldn't go. Grammy went; why not me? When they moved Grandpa's trailer to Stanford, why couldn't I stay there, too? When my aunt went down during the final days of my sister's life, why wasn't I allowed to be there? She was my only sister, my comrade, my idol. Why was I being kept from her? Why didn't my parents want me around?

Each time we were reunited, I had had life experiences in which my parents had had no part, and vice versa. And it wasn't simply a matter of geography; their experiences went beyond anything I could imagine. Donna and I were growing further and further apart during the later stages of her illness. I didn't understand why she didn't seem as excited to see me as I was to see her. I know why now, but I didn't understand it then. She didn't feel well most of the time.

I developed a whole slew of imaginary friends, most based on the characters from the *Speed Racer* or *Kimba* cartoons. I wrote them letters, held conversations with them, took them with me wherever I went. I even had an imaginary pet elephant in the backyard. All were attempts, I suppose, to provide for myself a constantly stable circle of "family" whose focus was solely on me.

After Donna's death, Mom, Dad, and I returned home to a houseful of people. I remember Dad gathering us all in the bedroom. I can't remember what was said, but I remember my dad crying. Later, as we viewed Donna's body in the casket, I remember her looking peaceful in her pink dress, holding a rosary which a nun had given her (even though we are not Catholic, we worship the same God). She seemed only to be asleep. Armed with that memory coupled with the term *passed away*, I quickly fell into a state of denial which lasted a little over four years.

I began having dreams in which I visited Donna in her hole in the wall (crypt in the mausoleum) easily accessible in my subconscious since my parents had not had her body buried in the ground. We would talk, watch TV, share french fries. Everything was fine, unless I asked her about being dead. Then her eyes rolled back into her head and her image started fading. I vowed never to bring up the subject again.

When an acquaintance asked me if I was the one whose sister had died, I replied with a panicked "No!" My friend assured her I was one and the same. The new girl wanted to know why, then, I had denied it. I let her know that my sister wasn't dead.

"Then what is she?" she asked me.

"Donna passed away," I announced triumphantly, knowing secretly in my heart that if she had passed away then she should be coming back. I just had to keep waiting.

And wait I did. Sometimes at night, after particularly rough days, I cried, and in my tears I would admit to missing Donna and wish her back home. When I prayed I often gave God messages for Donna. Whether or not she got them I won't know until I join the throngs in heaven.

The next year was rough, because my parents were grieving, and I, too, felt empty even though I had not yet begun to grieve. My parents were concerned about raising me as an only child, but they couldn't decide whether to adopt or have another child. Just about the time they had decided to adopt, Mom became pregnant. This led to another stressful year. And just as I was not present at Donna's death, I was not present at Dayna's birth (although I did get to pick her name). Passively I added this to my stack of what I thought was evidence that my parents didn't want me around, that I was in the way.

Donna's death occurred just before I entered third grade. In fifth grade two sisters, Sherry and Linda Good, entered the school I attended. Sherry, like me, was chunky and in fifth grade. Linda was slender and in sixth. Both girls had dark brown hair and were thirteen months apart, just like Donna and me. Additionally, their mom was pregnant with a baby girl born months after Dayna. We all became part of a close-knit circle of friends.

The gang of us often got together for slumber(less) parties. Once in seventh grade, however, I asked my mom if just Sherry and Linda could spend the night. Of course they could, so they did. The next morning the two sisters started arguing, which they sometimes did at school. But this time it was in my own home. My heart broke. I was convinced that if one knew she might lose the other, they would never treat each other like that. And I could do nothing to squelch the disagreement.

Watching them glare and spit words at each other, I realized, after four long years, not only was Donna not around for me to argue with, she wasn't around for me to love, nor would she be returning. Her body lay decaying in the casket, her spirit hopefully relieved and rejoicing in heaven. I retreated to my bedroom and burst into tears, crying silently in an attempt to hide my pain.

Eventually, my mom started looking for me and found me sitting on the edge of my bed, my sinuses clogged, my eyes swollen, my cheeks, hands, and forearms slick with tears. Sitting next to me and putting her arm around my shoulders, she asked what was wrong. I couldn't answer. She then asked specifically if it was because Sherry and Linda were fighting. I nodded emphatically and managed to blurt out between two gasps, "I miss Donna!" Mom all but gathered me into her lap and rocked me for what seemed to be an eternity. It must have been painful for her as well. But it was needed, long overdue pain on my part. It was the beginning of the road to reality and acceptance.

I have sometimes found it difficult to get close to people for long periods of time since then. I would rather let them drift away after about five years or so. That way if they don't die, I can get back in touch with them and hopefully we can pick up right where we left off. Or if they do happen to die, I will have the memories and have already started the separation process. A great defense mechanism, but not very socially acceptable, that sometimes makes me downright lonely. But I never want to hurt like that again! I have encountered several deaths since then, many of them extended-family members and close family friends, but none as difficult as the death of my sister. As I grow older, though, I'm beginning to feel braver about taking risks, letting myself be more vulnerable, trusting other people with my emotions.

As Kubler-Ross will tell you, there are many steps to grief. The first, which I mastered, is denial. Somewhere between denial and acceptance is anger. And I experienced anger. I was angry at my parents for making the decision to turn off Donna's life support. I was angry at my aunt for not letting me go with her on that last trip to be with Donna. I was angry with my uncle for telling me my sister had died. I was angry at Dayna for reminding people so much of Donna. And I was angry at the kid in ninth grade, who, after school one day, wished his sister was dead. Unbeknown to that poor, unsuspecting adolescent, he had just provided the break in the levy that contained my anger. The room fell silent as I laid into him loud and long about the pain of losing a sibling.

I am no longer angry. I have, indeed, accepted my sister's death. This same sentiment can be applied to my parents' divorce, as well. I have wondered, however, to what purpose God allowed all of this to transpire, especially since he promises in Romans 8:28 that for those who seek him all things will work together for good. I think I may have found at least part of the answer these last two years in my opportunity to teach children in my classroom, some of whom have lost family members to divorce, drugs, and violence of many kinds. I think I may also have found the purpose in understanding a young, hurting, angry fifth grader who lost his older brother a few years ago to a terminal disease. I truly know how he feels.

A Father's Grief

by Don Matlock

(Read at Donna's funeral)

I once was talking with a young priest who commented, "Parents question the death of a child, when actually the 'why' should be asked at birth." I dismissed his remark as lofty, ambiguous theology. However, his words returned to me, and as I considered them, I came to understand the harsh reality they contained.

Homo sapiens is Latin for "wise man." Granted, this assertion is open to debate, but there are characteristics that distinguish man from other forms of life: a mind that allows qualitative judgment based on intangibles; a soul that demands the worship of God in some manner; and a sex drive that is keyed to emotional involvement rather than triggered by a desire to continue the species.

We love and we have children, but the child is the result rather than the purpose of our love. If procreation were the main purpose of love, I doubt that many people would go through the trials of courtship and marriage. But we do, and we enter into relationships that we expect to last a lifetime. We expect, as does society, that children will result from this relationship. (I am generalizing, knowing that there is always the exception.) We accept the birth of our children as a matter of course. We love our children. We are proud. We carry their pictures in our pockets. Our friends are kept posted on their intellectual, physical, and social development. The children exist, become a part of our lifestyle, and our life continues.

The Bible tells us that "for everything there is a season, a time to live and a time to die," and then reminds us that "it is appointed unto man once to die." If our child dies, we question God's judgment, berate his mercy, and deny his love. When we stop to think, we realize that we bring our child into existence through love with full knowledge that the eventual termination of that life is inevitable. Yet when God decrees that the life is to end, we tend to react with bitterness and rebellion. We create life without a second thought when we should be thinking: Why did God allow us to have this child? What are we to learn from this child? What is the child to learn from us? What paths are to be followed to fulfill God's expectations?

We have our child. We try to raise her to be an individual possessing all of our good qualities and none of the bad. We want her to grow up smarter, richer, handsomer, and better adjusted than we are. We struggle, worry, persevere, and love this child without acknowledging that she is "our" child only because of God's permission.

Since we know full well that every birth will ultimately result in death, it is futile to curse the inevitable. Death is preordained, and nothing has ever prevented it. If we must curse, let us not curse God for the death but ourselves for the birth. If we cannot accept God's decision, then we should studiously avoid any situation where his decision can affect us. We know, whether we admit it or not, that when we have a child, at some time in some way we will lose that child.

Since I knowingly and willingly helped to create a life, I should not complain when that life ends. It will hurt terribly, my heart will ache, my eyes will be filled with tears. The loneliness of separation from my child will seem overwhelming, but I cannot curse God for fulfilling his appointed scheme. In spite of the pain, I will thank God for the joy that my child has brought me, and I am grateful to him for allowing me to share in the brief life of his miracle—my child.

A Father's Epilogue

It has been many years since I wrote these words—years to come to terms with the statements "time heals" or "it gets easier with time." Both are wrong. Time does not heal. I heal. By honestly feeling and acknowledging the grief, the pain, the loneliness, I am healing. It does not get easier with time. At times the anguish and grief of my child's dying is as fresh and as deep as it was eighteen years ago. What has happened with the passage of the years is that it gets hard less often. As time passed, I discovered that it had been an hour, a day, a week, since I had last thought of my child. I also discovered that this was all right. The memory of my child didn't die, nor disappear, nor even diminish for want of my constant attention.

There have been many changes during these intervening years, changes that have been, in their own way, as painful or significant and life-altering as the death of my child. However, in rereading my words, I find one constant. I still thank God for allowing me to share in the brief life of this miracle—my child, my daughter Donna.

This poem was printed in the bulletin for Donna's memorial service.

To All Parents
By Edgar A. Guest

"I'll lend you for a little time a child of mine," He said.
"For you to love him while he lives
and mourn for when he's dead.
It may be six or seven years, or twenty-two or three,
But will you, till I call him back,
take care of him for Me?
He'll bring his charms to gladden you,
and should his stay be brief,
You'll have his lovely memories as solace for your grief.
I cannot promise he will stay, since all from earth return.
But there are lessons taught down there
I want this child to learn,
I've looked the wide world over
in my search for teachers true,
And from the throngs that crowd life's lanes
I have selected you.
Now will you give him all your love,
nor think the labor vain,
Nor hate Me when I come to call to take him back again?"

. . . I fancied that I heard them say,
"Dear Lord, thy will be done!
For all the joy Thy child shall bring,
the risk of grief we'll run.
We'll shelter him with tenderness,
we'll love him while we may.
And for the happiness we've known,
forever grateful stay;
But should the angels call for him
much sooner than we've planned
We'll brave the bitter grief that comes
and try to understand . . ."

Part 3

Helping Grieving Families: Sudden Loss and Complicated Grief

Save me, O God:
for the waters have risen up to my neck.
I sink in muddy depths and have no foothold;
I am swept into deep water, and the flood carries me away.
I am wearied with crying out, my throat is sore,
my eyes grow dim as I wait for God to help me.

—Psalm 69:1–3

*C*hapter 12

When Age Is No Factor

When a parent loses a child, the age of the child is irrelevant. Miscarriage is devastating for couples. Aging parents are equally traumatized when their adult children die. Whether the child was a fifty-year-old son supporting his parents or was lost after three months in the womb, the child is dead, and the pain and grief are the same for the parents. Even the mother who aborts her baby, who chooses to lose her child, endures post-abortion syndrome, a very real grieving process intensified by severe guilt. You must treat each family's grief with the same empathy and tenderness, never judging the severity of the grief in relation to its circumstances.

Miscarriage

> *I had two miscarriages before my daughter was born and I suffered three more miscarriages after her birth. My husband and I desperately wanted to give her a brother or sister. My last miscarriage required a hysterectomy and our dream ended. My most difficult miscarriage occurred when I heard the baby's heartbeat at three months and then*

> *was told in my doctor's office two days later that our baby was dead. This baby did not naturally abort and I carried my dead infant inside me for weeks, lashing out in anger at everyone. I felt guilty for my outbursts but I was on an emotional rollercoaster. My husband hurt for me and was very supportive. He felt helpless and torn up inside.*
>
> *My husband died with cancer this past year. So much loss . . .*
>
> —*A Grieving Mother*

Couples who have no children and desperately want them are totally crushed when the wife miscarries. They lose their unborn child and their dream of parenthood. A mother with other children who miscarries is just as pained. She knows what she has lost, because she has held other babies in her arms. She grieves the loss of a sibling for her children and must deal with their sorrow. *A miscarriage is a death.* The helper must never minimize the situation by saying, "At least you have other children"; "You will have other children"; "It must have been best for the baby, or God wouldn't have taken it."

PeggySue Wells shares the loss of her unborn baby with us. Her family teaches us how to honor the gift of life, no matter how short. The Wells family understood that their unborn child was still *their child*. PeggySue and Keith kept interactive journals with their children to help them express their grief.

Losing Violet

> *My mommy was pregnant with our baby. She did not feel movement because the baby wasn't ready. Then when the baby was ready, she died. Our family made lots of presents for her. My brother, Josiah, and*

Daddy made a box out of wood. We put Violet in the box with the presents. We buried her with violets and my sister made a cross with Violet's name. My dad planted a tree and we planted flowers where we buried Violet so we will never forget her. It was hard to have part of our family die.

—Explained by Estee Wells, six years old

Dear Mom,

Why does God not listen? The Bible tells us, "Ask and you will receive." Why did God take Violet? I JUST DON'T UNDER-STAND! I'm so frustrated! Sometimes I just want to curl up in a ball and SCREAM! I don't want to say this but I am very angry with God. I get upset when people say, "God knows best. He'll help you through this hard time." Well, God could have stopped it. Why didn't He?

From 14-year-old Leilani's journal

A Mother's Grief

by PeggySue Wells

Talking about Violet is not painful. Don't you enjoy talking about your children? I love to say her name. Though Violet was with us only for a short time, she enriched our lives and was a very real part of our family.

I had miscarried another baby the year before Violet was conceived. We named her Hope and losing her was devastating for our six children. I was thrilled to have new life growing inside me to ease our pain. But during my fifth month, I realized there was no movement. The doctor confirmed my suspicions that we had lost another baby. We were drowning in grief again as our excitement turned to sorrow in a single day. We named this baby Violet Trust because we were learning to trust God when we didn't understand His ways.

Medical intervention to remove Violet would have posed greater health risks for me so we decided to wait. The first few weeks were unsettling but then I realized that time was a gift. Instead of waiting for a miscarriage, we planned for an early birth. My son and husband built a small redwood casket. Our daughters each prepared their own gifts, one making a blanket from a piece of my wedding dress. Everyone reacted differently. My husband was attentive but emotionally distant. This was a tough time for him. Our children cried often and sometimes were angry with God for taking the baby. Our son was especially grief-stricken and I assured him that he would meet his sibling in eternity.

The weeks turned into months. Many people worried about me but I wanted to birth this child. Finally Violet Trust was peacefully born in our home. We learned that she was a girl. She was the size of my hand. My husband sobbed, "I didn't expect her to be so beautiful." The only part missing was life. We took pictures of her next to our wedding rings. We buried her on May 1. We wrapped Violet in the satin blanket and placed her in a casket filled with love gifts from her family.

We wept as my husband nailed the casket shut. Then we read poems and Scripture verses that friends had sent for Violet's memorial. We prayed and sang songs. Everything within me protested as she was lowered into the ground. I didn't want Violet to be cold, wet, or alone. Our children placed a homemade white cross on her grave, lettered with her name. We planted a Rose of Sharon Tree there with a multitude of purple and white woods violets. Our child is blooming on the other side of eternity. We have an investment in heaven and I never regret that we had her in our lives for a few months, no matter how difficult. On Violet's one-year birthday, I was able to walk to her grave with her brand new baby sister in my arms. I tell my new infant that she has a big sister named Violet Trust.

In Memory of Violet Trust Wells

*written by her father, Keith Wells,
for Violet's burial*

*We didn't get to run with you, but you beat us to heaven.
We didn't get to teach you, but you taught us to trust.
We didn't get to hear you, but you taught us to listen.
We didn't get to bathe you, but you washed us with tears.
We didn't get to comb your hair,
     but your beauty is beyond all expectations.
We didn't get to change your diaper,
     but you helped us change our hearts forever.
We didn't get to sit on our porch together,
     but we'll always be able to see your place of rest
     from our chairs.
We didn't get to show you our animals or ride the horse,
     but you are now with the Creator of all.
We didn't get to play music with you,
     but today you hear the heavenly choir.
We didn't get to raise you, but you raised our heads
     toward Him whom we can and must trust.
We love you, Violet Trust.*

Parents and siblings need to grieve the loss of an unborn infant. While the death of a child usually strains the marriage relationship, a miscarriage often unites a couple. Wives feel that their husbands are their greatest source of support and understanding.

Helpers should never underestimate the severity of the grief following the loss of a baby in the womb. It is critical that we help grievers say good-bye to their child. Memorial services provide memories that will comfort the family in later years.

Holding a dead infant or planning a funeral for an unborn baby may seem odd or even unhealthy to onlookers who have never experienced a similar loss but it is healing for the grieving family.

Losing Adult Children

Ninety-nine-year-old Mary was often visited in the senior facility where she lived by her favorite son, Tom. Though her body was failing, her mind was as sharp as ever. Tom was her lifeline. He and his sons were a constant source of joy for her. The hardest thing that Mary's grandson had to do was tell Mary that her sixty-nine-year-old child, Tom, was dead. He had died in a tragic suicide. Mary never asked how he died, and the family respected this as her way of indicating that she did not need to know.

Mary attended the funeral in a state of shock. How difficult it must have been for her to endure the next week, which held both Mother's Day and Tom's birthday. He had been a most wonderful Mother's Day present almost seventy years before. A few weeks later Mary required surgery on an ulcer and suffered a stroke. She died soon after. The family realized that Mary had given up any will to live. Without Tom there was no reason to keep fighting for life.

When an adult dies, helpers tend to focus their support on the immediate family—the deceased's spouse and children. People often forget that the deceased has parents who must deal with the loss of their child. Probably the parents are aging, and the child was not only their son or daughter but had changed roles and become their primary support.

I made regular visits to an aging woman in our church a few years ago. Though she was ill and dying, had a dedicated husband who was mourning her coming death, and had other caring children, she was completely focused on the death of her adult son, which had occurred decades earlier. He had been killed in a shooting accident, and the pain of losing him still far exceeded any present pain that she endured.

Helpers must remember that many aging parents lose

children. Their grief is as intense as that of parents of young children, but their options for coping with the pain are more limited. When any human being dies, whether a child in the womb or a sixty-year-old adult, remember to ask, "Who are the grieving parents?"

Fred and Carol Patterson have graciously allowed the accounts they wrote of their adult daughter's death to be printed here. Some years ago Fred and Carol were planning their twenty-fifth wedding anniversary party. They had much to celebrate—their marriage, their friends, the two beautiful grown daughters they had raised, their treasured grandchildren, and countless rich blessings of God. They attended not an anniversary party that week but a funeral.

Human beings deceive themselves into believing that they can control parts of their lives. Fred and Carol teach us that what is most important in life hangs by a fragile thread, held only by God.

A Father's Grief

When the phone rang, I groggily answered, and someone was saying, "Fred—this is Yvonne (my son-in-law's sister). Now, don't panic, but there was a wreck. Sarah and Ryan are fine. Lori and Brian were injured and are being treated at Marshall Hospital. But Lori is being transferred to the U.C. hospital in Sacramento." My heart sank as my mind raced through all the possible results.

Then a calm clutched my mind, and God gave me his word: "There are no ifs"—if they hadn't left so tired, if they hadn't left so early, etc. "If" is hindsight of how we think God should have handled things.

I related everything to Carol, and I could see her mind trying to comprehend the little information we had. I told her there were no ifs. We wrapped our arms around each other and prayed. While Carol was getting dressed, I called all the godly men I knew: our pastor, former pastors, deacons, leaders in the church, and other friends. I simply said, "Lori and Brian have been in a wreck and are in the hospital. Please pray." I didn't reach everyone, but I knew that as soon as they heard about what happened, they would be praying.

When we arrived at the hospital, we were escorted to a waiting room. After a while, an intern liaison came in and told us, "Lori has a torn liver, which was operated on at Marshall Hospital. She received a hard blow to the head, which has caused her brain to swell, but they drilled a hole in her skull to relieve the pressure. She is having a CAT scan now to see how much swelling there is and then will be taken to her room where you can see her."

Our hopes soared at the supposed "good" news. I hung onto God's "no ifs." But Lori never regained consciousness. I have never seen so many tubes, bags, and machines hooked up to anyone. We talked to her, even though she couldn't respond. I kept telling her that Brian and the kids were okay.

We were all worn out by the fourth day. Lori was all puffy and looked like a balloon. I held her hand and told her that Brian and the kids were okay. She squeezed my hand, and I heard (and felt) her in my heart say, "It's all right, Dad. I love you, and I know they are okay, and everything will be fine. God is in charge."

I told the doctor who was present that Lori had squeezed my hand. He looked at me in a condescending way and said, "I don't think so—it was probably just a muscle spasm." It wasn't until then that I knew she was dead, and they were just following the routine of waiting for her brain to die. With all his education, this doctor thought he had the scientific answers, but he overlooked the power of God. God can do all things, including raising the dead to say good-bye.

We were asked to leave the room, and a short time later the doctors came out to tell us that Lori had died. We all gathered in a huddle and cried and sobbed. The quarterback, Jesus, was still in charge, calling all the plays in our lives.

Carol and I almost felt guilty for not falling apart. But we knew that God, in his wonderful mercy, gave us "a peace beyond human understanding."

The church was packed for the memorial service. Everyone at the service came to express their condolences to us at our front-row pew. Our Christian family was so kind and had many wonderful things to say. Some were so shaken that we were ministering to them. I think the greatest compliment, and glory to our Jesus, came from people who said it was more like a marriage ceremony than a memorial service.

We praise God for our wonderful daughters; Lori and Susan were gifts from him. We dedicated them to God when they were babies. I am not an Abraham who has such faith to place Isaac on the altar and sacrifice him (my daughters) by my own hand, but I'll tell you what—God is sufficient in *all* things.

We thank God that he spared Brian, Sarah, and Ryan. The car rolled three or four times and came to rest on its side, with Brian halfway out the door. One more roll probably would have killed Brian. He was sore and needed twenty stitches to the back of his head. The babies (seven months and nineteen months old) didn't have a scratch. To the unsaved this seemed to be quite a coincidence. But for those of us who love Jesus and have experienced his intervention, we know he is the truth and the light. Our lives are in his hands.

A Mother's Grief

Our daughter Lori, her husband Brian, and children Sarah and Ryan left our home about 4:30 AM following a weekend visit with us on June 28, 1982. Baby Ryan had been fussy most of the night. Since our daughter was already awake with the baby, she decided it would be best to begin their trip home. Brian had to be home in time to clean up to be at work by 8:00 AM.

We hugged and kissed everyone good-bye as Brian drove off with his little family. We wished them a safe trip home, as we always did, and went back in the house to try to get a couple more hours of sleep before beginning our own demanding jobs.

The phone rang around 6:30 AM I was a little concerned when

the phone rang in our quiet bedroom so early in the morning. My husband, Fred, answered the call. This was very unusual, because he usually left the phone calls for me to answer. I'm sure the Lord planned it this way.

As soon as Fred started talking, I knew something was very wrong. My heart began to pound, my mouth became dry, and a huge lump came into my throat.

"The kids have been in an auto accident," Brian's sister was saying. "The children appear to be okay. Brian has a bad cut to his head and they are sewing it up. His shoulder and arm are also injured but don't appear to be broken. Lori is in emergency surgery, and due to a head injury, has to be transferred from the Marshall Hospital to the University of Davis Medical Center in Sacramento." This sounded serious. I began a silent prayer.

We learned later that our daughter had offered to drive the last half of the trip home so Brian could get a little extra sleep before he had to go to work. This precious little family got within nine miles of home when our daughter apparently fell asleep at the wheel. The car hit a guardrail on the freeway, causing the car to flip over several times. Lori was the only one thrown partially out of the car. She wasn't wearing a seatbelt! She had the most severe injuries. The children surely had a guardian angel looking over them as Sarah, nineteen months old, was only in an infant seat, and Ryan, seven months, was lying on a pillow asleep on the back seat. Both children were only sore and slightly bruised. There was no human reason the children should have survived. Thank you, Jesus.

As soon as Fred hung up the phone, we hugged each other and prayed. Then Fred started making phone calls to all the "prayer warriors" we knew. After that, we headed for the hospital.

Only a parent who has seen a child (a grown woman of twenty-four but *still our child*) lying in a bed in a coma with obvious severe injuries can know how we felt at that moment. The tears began to flow. Over the next four days there were a lot of tears and fervent prayers.

We learned from a staff social worker that Lori had a severe injury to her head and spine. She was paralyzed from the waist down and remained in a coma. It didn't look good. We kept praying.

On the fourth day following the accident, severe swelling of the brain occurred and couldn't be controlled. Our dear, sweet daughter was gone.

I just couldn't believe it. How could this be? She was only twenty-four years old. She had two small babies to raise. She was a beautiful Christian woman.

Fred and I turned to the Lord for help and comfort. Our ever-present loving Lord was there for us as always. Praise God. At that moment God lifted us above the present situation and held us there through the next several trying days.

We began making phone calls, thanking our friends in Christ for their prayers and support, letting them know that God had allowed Lori to "go home."

Lori was a loving and giving person and was loved in return by young and old alike. She was "in love with love" and had been since she was a little girl. She had spent hours writing poetry and singing. Lori married her high school sweetheart and had two children. All her dreams had come true. She was a loving Christian woman and knew the Lord in a personal way.

On July 6, 1982, the day after our twenty-fifth wedding anniversary, we had a memorial service for our daughter.

What a blessing that service was! Over two hundred friends and family attended. The service was filled with music, beautiful flowers, and a lot of Christian love. The Lord gave us the strength, comfort, and peace to greet each dear family and friend present. The service was full of joy and made everything begin to make some sense.

We know God has a plan and purpose for *everything* that comes into our lives. So we did accept Lori's death, knowing one day we will see the whole picture clearly.

Many hearts were touched during that memorial service.

Over the weeks following the service we learned of several who had rededicated their lives to Christ, marriages that were strengthened, parents who felt a deeper love and appreciation for their children, and an overall awareness of how suddenly our lives here on earth can be changed.

We continually thank God for giving us two beautiful Christian daughters. Our daughter Susan was a great blessing to us during those difficult days and the months that followed. We were able to be a comfort to each other.

Following our daughter's memorial service, and after much prayer and discussion with our son-in-law, we decided it would be best for our grandchildren to be brought home to live with us until better arrangements could be made. We all agreed that these precious little ones would be much better off saying with Gramma and Grandpa all day while Daddy worked than in a daycare center. The babies spent the weeks with us and most weekends with their daddy. The days and weeks went by.

We had the privilege of raising our grandchildren for one-and-a-half years. Then Brian remarried. He and his new wife, Janeene, were able to bring the children home to once again be a family unit. Brian and Janeene have added a daughter, Janell, to their family, and we love them all.

Because of our love for our grandchildren and our full-time devotion to them over that year and a half, we truly did not have time to grieve. We put it on hold for several years. We definitely do not recommend doing this. No matter what the circumstances, there is always a period of grieving. Without living it we cannot have a normal time of healing. Not until nine years later were we able to release the deep sorrow and emptiness we felt for our daughter and carried in our hearts. We will miss her until we meet again in heaven.

*C*hapter 13

*Caterpillar to Butterfly—
Grief Transformed*

Bethany Homeyer's Story

*There is a green sun-drenched valley,
Light with the scent of clover and lilacs,
Where the butterflies dance.
Leaping and swooping, they reflect colors
of every hue and dimension.
There are monarchs and skippers,
Swallowtails and delicate spring azures.
Each dances its unique pattern
of flits, circles, and dives.
Stretching its fragile wings toward the clouds
or brushing its feet on the succulent grass.
There are no roads, paths, or gates
to broach the valley's entrance.
Yet it is visited often in thoughts and dreams.*

Every parent who has sent forth a child
and vainly waited for its return
Comes seeking in the valley of butterflies
And there finds a beautiful spirit.
Stretching its wings to the clouds
And brushing its feet on the grass.
Dancing in swoops, flits, and dives,
Drying its dewy wings in the warm sunshine of
forever.

—*Author Unknown*

I had always told my children, "Do not drink and drive." Nothing could have prepared me for the night that my eighteen-year-old son, Michael, died in an alcohol-related auto accident. I honestly did not think that I was going to make it during those months after his death.

Michael was the youngest of our eight children and the last one at home. He had just started community college. He was very popular in our small Texas town, with a smile that could melt you like butter. He had always been an active young man, playing football, soccer, and baseball. Michael was also a gymnast and very confident about his physical abilities. A hard worker, he was always willing to help with the chores on our four-acre property. We decided that the best way to keep this very energetic boy out of trouble was to keep him busy. He was often in and out of emergency rooms for stitches and minor injuries. Michael was always teasing me and a few weeks before he died, he said, "Mom, did you ever think that you could keep me alive this long?"

The day he died Michael met a new friend, twenty-year-old "Steve." With their girlfriends they were going to a party out in the country. They met at Steve's house where Steve's parents fixed them alcoholic drinks. Then they went to the party and drank more. Steve was drunk when he drove Michael and the girls home. Speeding along at 65 mph on a dark country road in the middle of nowhere, Michael climbed out of the window and stood on the car roof to "windsurf." He fell to his death, breaking his neck. I couldn't believe that my son had done this. My grief was compounded. Michael was a normal, adventurous eighteen-year-old boy but he was a sweet, good kid who always displayed common sense. Alcohol makes people do crazy things.

We received a call from the hospital two hours after the accident. Why so long? The nurse said that Michael was in ICU but that he wasn't going to make it. We had to drive an hour to the hospital, one of the most excruciating hours of my life. When we arrived, the staff explained that they had kept Michael on life support so that we could donate his organs. He had only two scrapes from the fall. All the way to the hospital, I had prayed, "Please, Lord, do not let my son be mangled. I've tried so hard all these years to keep this boy stitched together. Please let him be whole." I couldn't bear the thought of Michael being cut up and hurt anymore. Maybe it wasn't rational, but I couldn't give my permission.

Michael's death three weeks before Christmas affected our entire community. People came from everywhere to be by our side constantly. There was nothing that anyone could say or do that could comfort me. Friends were worried about me and didn't want me to be alone, especially drive anywhere alone. Being a solitary person by nature, I've always enjoyed and needed my solitude. Well-meaning friends robbed me of this. Then a few days after the funeral, everyone left. They went home and returned to their lives. They were done grieving . . . and I was just beginning. I was so angry that they had lives to return to and I didn't. My life would never be normal. I needed to find a "new normal," and that would take several years.

I directed my anger at Steve, the drunk driver, and his parents who encouraged the boys to drink. I needed to blame somebody. Because of family connections with law enforcement, Steve received only a fine and probation and I had to fight for that. The fatality was never put on his record. Steve had offenses prior to and after the accident. He showed no remorse for his actions and his parents were angry with us for holding their son responsible.

My bitterness was eating me alive and I knew that I needed to let go of my anger to be able to move on. I finally had to accept that nothing would bring Michael back. My son was responsible too. He took those drinks willingly and no one forced him onto the car roof. Then I became immersed in guilt. What had I done wrong as a parent? What could I have done differently? Was Michael safe with God?

My husband and I had experienced challenges like any couple in our many years together but nothing like this. Naturally like any teenage son and his father, Michael and he had butted heads. But now Michael would never grow into an adult who could realize how much his father loved him and tried to guide him, and resolve those issues of adolescence. My husband tormented himself, "Did Michael die thinking that I was mad at him?"

"Please, God, keep our children safe," my husband had prayed every night throughout our marriage. That is what he prayed the night of the accident. It would be many months before my husband could offer that prayer to our heavenly father again. Thrown into the empty nest syndrome in the most tragic way, we had to work very hard to sustain our marriage and get to know each other again. Sometimes we weren't sure that our marriage would make it but he is truly my best friend now.

I simply went through the motions of life for the first two years. I was in shock for many months and I don't remember much. Parts of my life are blank from that first year. The second year was even worse. I moved from shock into intense grief, reliving my pain through all the anniversaries. I could feel the grief in my body. I hurt so much.

Being a nature lover, I became interested in butterfly breeding and immersed myself in this hobby, in addition to my full-time job. I was looking for an escape. I didn't want to have one free minute to think. Looking back, I realize that I sometimes put my grief on the shelf until I was able to handle it again.

Then God gave me a glimmer of hope that I would survive. I learned that my walk with God was not daily, but hourly—minute to minute. I cried out to him one day, " God, I can't stand this intense pain anymore. It hurts too much. Why am I left behind? What purpose could you possibly have for me? You know my pain and I am giving it back to you." Miraculously, God enveloped me in peace and the physical pain was gone.

I was learning everything I could from experts about breeding butterflies. The symbolism of the metamorphosis of the butterfly as eternal resurrection fascinated me. We too grew from an egg, lived as a caterpillar, died as a chrysalis, and then will emerge as a beautiful butterfly in a symbol of the resurrection. Soon I left my job to focus completely on my new business, delivering butterflies to be released at funerals, weddings, and any events celebrating a "new life beginning." I began giving talks and interviews about this transformation. I couldn't bring myself to look at Michael's funeral program until years later. To my surprise, I was entranced to find a monarch butterfly pictured on the cover.

Instead of being bitter and angry, today I am grateful and feel very blessed that God never abandoned me. He always kept me snuggled in his hand. I feel only pity and compassion now for Steve and his family. Steve has continually been in trouble and his parents have divorced. The accident changed their lives too. Michael's fiance, who was in the car with him, recently married. She invited me to her wedding. I simply couldn't bear to attend but I did send butterflies to celebrate her day. God did show me a beautiful purpose. When grievers call to order butterflies for a funeral, I am able to share my own experience with them. I truly understand what they are going through. Michael was such a giving soul. I believe now he gives through me.

When we put Michael in that cold, hard ground six years ago, I pleaded with the Lord to know that my son was safe in his arms. How could we survive if that burial was truly the end? We clung to our resurrection hope. Michael had been such an affectionate boy, always holding my hand, putting his arm around my shoulder, or rubbing the top of my head. A few weeks after his death when I was finally alone, I went on my first drive and looked up at the clouds. The golden light was too bright to look at but beneath it I saw Michael and Jesus in white robes. Jesus had his arm around Michael and was rubbing the top of his head. God had answered my husband's nightly prayer. Michael was safe. The gift was for an instant but will last me for a lifetime—until I too make the transformation like a butterfly.

A butterfly lights beside us like a sunbeam,
and for a brief moment its glory and
beauty belong to our world.
But then it flies on again
and though we wish it could have stayed,
we feel lucky to have seen it.

The butterfly is our symbol of HOPE.

For more information contact:

Michael's Fluttering Wings Butterfly Ranch,
Route 1,
Box 447A,
Mathis, TX 78368
Phone: 361-547-5568
www.butterflyrelease.com

Chapter 14

Helpers or Judges?

My heart failed me when you said, "What a train of disaster he
has brought on himself! The root of the trouble lies in him."
                                                    —Job 19:28 NEB

Deaths that bring the deepest grief and pain of all are those of
dying persons who feel they are "unacceptable." As one
griever put it, "If my brother was dying from a brain tumor, I
would feel comfortable telling anyone, confident of immediate
sympathy and support. But telling people, especially Christians,
that my brother is dying of AIDS and that he lived a homosexual
lifestyle . . . that brings a very different initial response, one of
shock and questions."

In this chapter are two such stories. One woman graciously
allowed me to print an anonymous letter about her son's
murder. Another griever has written the story of her family
helping her brother die from AIDS and grieving his death.

Both young men lived lifestyles opposed to biblical principles.
Yet, would any compassionate Christian *really* believe that these
children "deserved what they got"? While reading the previous
chapter, were you more concerned with why Michael was

drinking and partying than feeling the pain of his parents? No one can help hurting people as they die or comfort grieving families who does not grasp the fact that no one sin is more significant than any other. Imagine that we could contract a fatal disease from gossiping, backbiting, bitterness, lying, arrogance, pride, impatience—or judging others. Each one of us falls short of the glory of God. We each make mistakes and desperately need to be enveloped in God's blanket of unconditional love and forgiveness. Christ did not come to heal perfect people. He came to rescue the broken.

My Son Was Murdered

Dear Helper:

Because I am a writer by nature, if I were the only one to be considered, I would tell you about my son's murder in detail. Yet I am unable to do that for several reasons. Murder brings complicated and unresolved grief. Our other children still have not dealt fully with the loss of their brother and my husband is not comfortable with sharing our story. My son's death is still an unsolved homicide and could become an active file if something new came up and this would cause numerous problems for our family.

But I can share with you that there is an extra kind of pain involved when the death is sudden, and another element is added when it is public and "notorious" in its own way. Tom was not living the lifestyle we would have desired at the time of his death. Murders generate newspaper articles that aren't always positive or correct, and both seem to attract people who want to know details rather than share pain—which only adds to the pain. But the other side of that is the wonderful, incredible, and tremendously healing realization that God himself knew the very same pain we did. His own Son was murdered, too. That thought was awesome, in the true sense of that word, to me.

If we are Christians, death should not be looked at as the awful end, but rather as a temporary separation. Tom received Christ as a teenager, and I trust in God's promises. The fact that I know I'll see him again has been a big part of the healing process for me. I really am not concerned about who killed him or why, except that it would bring closure to the situation and ease some of the pain of others in the family. Knowing the "who" or "why" of the crime can't bring him back, and there is always the realization that the "who" is someone else's child.

Although I can talk and write easily about Tom, I often do so with tears that remain very close to the surface. There is strong emotion wrapped up in his life and his death. I refuse to call it untimely, because I believe God determines what is timely and what isn't. We said that in a written statement read by our pastor at his funeral, and I still believe it. God took Tom for a reason; God left us behind for a reason. The "why" of all of that I leave to him who made plans "for our own good" long before we were born.

God also gave us six other wonderful children to console and comfort us, as we do the same, I hope, for them. I hope these brief words will shed some light on the grief of parents who lose a child through murder.

In His Name,
A Grieving Mother

The Killer AIDS

Dear Helper,

My brother died six months ago. Our family, and even a number of doctors, cannot say exactly what caused Kyle's death. Was it the mysterious spot on his lung? Was it severe internal bleeding? His death certificate listed a number of external ailments. The overwhelming fact remains that Kyle died of AIDS.

I am still working through my grief. Sometimes I cry because I miss him so much, and other times I find myself thinking of something to send him or to do during his next visit. I feel foolish when I accidentally speak of him in the present tense. I loved Kyle deeply.

I remember joking about AIDS with friends at work several years earlier. Our boss interrupted our laughter. "You wouldn't joke about AIDS if you knew someone who had it." I was shocked when she didn't laugh at our wordplay on AIDS since she was usually the ringleader of tasteless jokes. I dismissed her comments as liberal sympathy for homosexuals who deserved the disease.

A few months later, I heard a talk show on a Christian radio station. The panel consisted mostly of people with HIV or in varying stages of the disease. I was overwhelmed as I heard accounts of their physical pain as well as emotional pain from rejection. The minister who moderated the group concluded the interview by stating that as a church, and more specifically as individual Christians, we needed to be ready to respond to the AIDS crisis before an individual situation forces us into action. He cautioned against waiting for a situation to arise. Spontaneous decisions are difficult because a response to AIDS becomes clouded with a focus on homosexual sin, discomfort, and fear for one's own health. After the program finished, I remember praying that if God could use me, I wanted to be an example of God's forgiveness and acceptance. I wanted to be the practical extension of God's love. I started reading information about the disease, unaware of what my personal commitment might involve.

After moving to the San Francisco Bay area, we were expecting a visit from my oldest brother. Since he was sixteen years older than me, I was looking forward to his visit. I felt I really hadn't even started to know him until my college days, when I was surprised to find how many things we had in common. He appreciated the arts and music, liked traveling, and enjoyed learning. A student leader and valedictorian of his senior class, Kyle had always been smart, popular, and successful.

I was disappointed when he couldn't come. I can still recall his words when he explained why. "I really am sick," he said. "I have AIDS. I wanted to tell you myself, but I don't know when I'll be well enough to travel." I was engulfed with emotion. I had to deal with the double shock that Kyle was going to die and that he had secretly led a gay lifestyle. In church that evening, while tears flooded down my cheeks, I sat shaking my head no when asked for prayer requests. As a pastor's wife, how would I share this with anyone?

Kyle discovered that he had HIV five years earlier while he was living in Hawaii. He moved back to the mainland planning to break the news of his illness as well as of his lifestyle.

At first his health was so good that it was easy to put things off. Then our family had some other crisis situations. Kyle was concerned about our parents and didn't want to add to their burden. He became weaker but tried to "keep up appearances." Before long it was Thanksgiving, then Christmas, then our parents' anniversary. Kyle didn't want to ruin special family times. There was never a good time to tell us. Finally, after he was hospitalized with pneumonia, Kyle knew he had to tell each of us before we figured it out on our own.

My brother had lived in his own secret prison for several years. A banker with an MBA who had served in Vietnam, Kyle had kept his secret well. He did not expect pity. He was very aware of our family's feelings. He encouraged each of us to get support and was open to our questions. He even recommended the excellent book *How Will I Tell My Mother?* by Steve and Jerry Arterburn to prepare us for what might be ahead and to give us insight into his past life.

Kyle spent a great deal of time talking with me. Though he had accepted Christ in grade school, he had made some poor choices. He explained, "Everyone in my family and even other places said that they loved me, but I always felt that they only loved who they thought I was. I had a big dark secret, and I believed if people knew who I really was, I would be rejected." His fear of rejection was so great that he planned to commit suicide if our parents rejected him after he told them the truth. He knew that homosexuality was in direct opposition to our parents' Christian beliefs, and he'd known a number of friends who were isolated as they lay dying with AIDS. He couldn't face the possibility of rejection in addition to his suffering. Our parents' tearful, enveloping embrace shocked him and marked the beginning of reconciliation in his life.

Our entire family went into action to tangibly love Kyle—increasing phone calls and visits, helping with meals, laundry, cleaning, house repairs, car maintenance, grocery shopping, driving him to doctor appointments, and more. We made ourselves completely available to Kyle, wanting to communicate our love and acceptance of him.

We took advantage of his clinic days to escort him, meet his doctors and other caregivers, and to learn more about AIDS. The staff of the Center for Human Caring was warm and creative. One time when I was visiting Kyle, the center received a number of flowers from a grocery floral department. Everyone helped sort out the fading ones. One volunteer made a special bouquet to take to a patient in the hospital who hadn't had visitors.

The center was a source of support for Kyle. Kyle also tried to participate in an AIDS support group, but the constant death of members and addition of new ones made trust relationships difficult. Kyle certainly didn't avoid facing death. That was impossible. During an especially low point while Kyle was hospitalized, a visitor came. Michael was tan, attractive, and carried his tennis racquet over his shoulder. A month later, Kyle was out of the hospital and doing well when he received word of Michael's death. Our family worked at finding ways to support Kyle emotionally as well as physically in ways that the support group could not offer.

We found that communication was most open when Kyle was with just one person. During one stay at our house, Kyle and I started talking, and I completely missed Sunday school. (As a minister's wife, I usually don't do that.) I was grateful for a husband and a church that was encouraging and understanding when I chose to be with Kyle.

People sent notes and constant reminders of God's love. Friends prayed for Kyle regularly and often asked about his health. Telling people about Kyle's illness was still difficult. There were always so many questions. It was almost as if people were trying to find reasons that this wouldn't happen in their family. Though each member of our family found support from different sources, it was probably most difficult for my parents. They were afraid to tell many of their church friends for fear that they would be judged for accepting him or even more so for being "bad parents" who caused him to be gay. Their own minister and a former pastor were very supportive and encouraging. The most important support person for them was Kyle, as he communicated that they truly were good parents.

Last summer Kyle was accepted into a experimental medication program in San Francisco and lived with me for four months. As my husband and I watched him suffer and become weaker, struggling with pain, we hurt for him. One time, as he lay exhausted in bed with his IV tube hanging from his cheek, he said, "I would never wish this disease on my worst enemy, but if I hadn't contracted it, I would never have found reconciliation with God and with my parents." It took that kind of crisis to bring him back into fellowship with God and his family. Kyle had never been openly rebellious. His secret had tortured and isolated him.

I was reminded that God sees the big picture and is able, through his providence, to work things for our greatest good, even though we may not know how. Sometimes I become frustrated with God for choosing to end Kyle's life so early. And if he did have to, why couldn't he have had a brain tumor or cancer of something that wouldn't make me so uncomfortable when I tell others? However, now I realize that God would not have accomplished his plan that way. Even though Kyle was suffering, in hindsight he would not have chosen different circumstances. Kyle even said that he'd never felt so genuinely loved as when people knew everything about him and chose to love him unconditionally anyway.

While Kyle was with us, I was touched by the response of a number of people in our church. Some of the members I might have categorized as the most offended by Kyle's former gay lifestyle were the most gracious in terms of reaching out to him. He kept saying, "I can't believe people are so nice to me."

People often gave of themselves in ways that were uniquely their own. A family offered to stay with Kyle when we had to be out of town for the weekend. A mother of three boys brought homemade chocolate chip cookies for the times of IV infusions and stayed to visit. A teenager from our church brought newspapers to read. Friends spent time talking to Kyle, praying with him, and making music for him. Kyle asked me, "Don't they know what's wrong with me? Do they realize how I got AIDS? Aren't they afraid of me?" He wasn't used to Christians who were so loving. He knew God's forgiveness, but man's forgiveness was not always predictable. Though there wasn't much anyone could do to comfort Kyle physically, he found joy in their companionship and music.

In August of last summer his condition worsened and he needed to make an emergency trip back to his home doctor. We tried desperately to arrange a flight but couldn't because of complications. Without even being asked, a travel agent in our church went to work on the situation. He not only got a flight for Kyle that day but also arranged skycap service and had a cab waiting in Denver. He even drove us to the airport.

People reached out to me too. One evening while Kyle was resting, a friend showed up at my door with a two-for-one yogurt coupon. She promised we'd take only twenty minutes. I didn't realize how much I needed to get out! People found creative ways to offer support.

It was a privilege to spend time with Kyle in our home. He needed a safe place to make funeral plans. He and my husband, Scott, got along well and talked openly. Kyle wanted Scott to do the service. Kyle wanted it to be upbeat and hopeful. They talked about different ideas. Kyle wrote down song choices such as "Great Is Thy Faithfulness," "It Is Well with My Soul," "Joyful, Joyful, We Adore Thee," and "There Is Joy in the Journey." Though he expected only five or six friends in addition to the family, he wanted to communicate the hope and forgiveness he knew.

After he made the emergency trip to his hometown, he spent several weeks in the hospital. Pneumonia and infection because of the IV tube in his cheek weakened him even more. When he was released, he continued to make arrangements for his death. He finalized his will and made sure all of his accounts were in order and papers were organized. He made plans with a funeral home and consulted family members about their personal wishes. He was very thorough. He didn't want to be a burden.

Our family was all together for Thanksgiving. Kyle and Scott discussed more of the arrangements for the service. Kyle made a list of people who should be notified after his death. Each time we left we wondered if it would be our last time to see him. It was hard to say good-bye. One time Kyle scolded me and told me not to cry when he died. I joked back, "I cried when you moved to Hawaii and I'll cry when you move to heaven. I know you'll be in a wonderful place, but I'm not sure when I'll see you again! I'll miss you."

Kyle's condition continued to deteriorate. Because he preferred to stay at home, my parents visited each week to stay with him, take him to the hospital, and do all they could. In January he was admitted to the hospital again. While in the hospital, one doctor asked Kyle why he was continuing to hang on and suffer. He asked if there was anyone he needed to ask permission to die. Later Kyle asked my parents if they were willing to let him go.

As time went on, Kyle's condition seemed to improve. My parents returned to their own home on Thursday, expecting Kyle to be released from the hospital the following Monday.

On Friday, Kyle's abdominal pain became more severe; he asked a visiting friend to call Mom and Dad from the hospital. When they arrived, he asked them to pray that God would take him. Confident in his hope of eternal life, my parents prayed out loud that God would graciously take him from his suffering. Within a few minutes he died in Mom's and Dad's arms. He died knowing he was loved and accepted rather than rejected and isolated as he once feared.

After I received that phone call, a dear couple came at midnight to cry and pray with us. The love of our church family meant so much, especially with our extended family so far away.

The next several days were a blur. Our entire family stayed at Kyle's place. We grieved together, laughed together, and sometimes drove each other crazy. We shared funny memories. We shared regrets. I had planned to visit Kyle the following weekend.

There was a blizzard on the night of Kyle's funeral. Our former pastor came to sing, and Scott celebrated the freedom of forgiveness that Christ offers each of us. Over a hundred people arrived to express their sympathy. It was truly a joyous celebration of Kyle's earthly and eternal life.

Throughout his life Kyle had a compassion and concern for others. He chose to put the needs of others ahead of his own, even when he was ill. He never wanted to put anyone out of their way on his account, even though he had helped many others.

We cried and hugged Kyle's friends we recognized from hospital visits and others we'd never met. One woman came whose son had died of AIDS a few months before. A young man came. The next day we discovered he also had AIDS. He had heard about Kyle's condition and wanted to share his own testimony, if Kyle wasn't a Christian. The son of a Baptist minister, he had become involved in a homosexual lifestyle. Now he sees AIDS as the escape God provided to bring him back into fellowship. My parents continue to keep in touch with him.

Recently, my parents came to California to visit. We are close, and it was a special time to be together. We looked through sympathy cards and talked about Kyle. They seemed especially grateful to visit the hospital where Kyle had been. At our church they met people who had reached out to Kyle while he was with us. They felt love and support from people they barely knew. We also spent time just having fun together. It had been an especially intense couple of years for my parents, and they deserved a real vacation.

While driving by the coast one afternoon, I mentioned that Kyle especially enjoyed that view, as well as Golden Gate Park nearby. My father said, "He always enjoyed beautiful scenery. I guess he's surrounded by the best now."

At my parents' request I have changed some of the names in Kyle's story. Unfortunately, there are still many people whose response to AIDS is far from compassionate. I'm reminded of Ryan White's grave being continually vandalized. I have purposely tried to protect our family's anonymity. However, I often wish I could have named my parents—not to betray them, but to honor them. They are the "heroes" of this story. Though many people touched Kyle's life, their love and acceptance outweighed all the others.'

Recently a Christian friend told me how proud she was that her sister had the courage to kick her homosexual son out of the house and let him know that he was not welcome back as long as he had "that sin" in his life. My heart broke. How sad it is that we, who have been so freely forgiven, often reject others who are hurting.

I have the utmost respect for my parents' response to Kyle.

In His love,
A Grieving Sister

To summarize this chapter:
1. Our calling is to unconditionally accept and love the dying person and the family, regardless of circumstances. We should avoid the trap of analyzing why this happened, or suggesting the blame of family

members. Judgment has no place here. Unending questions can be painful and intrusive.

2. A profound result of AIDS, which often is an outcome of a "deep, dark secret" that has tormented for years, is that it forces a family to have no more secrets. Open, honest sharing, perhaps done for the first time, becomes the family's way of dealing with the illness and death. God's purpose is healing—the perfect example of "Satan meant it for evil but God meant it for good."

3. Kyle's sister told me that God did not heal Kyle, but He did carry him on the road, miraculously working out every detail. God did this through people—people who brought cookies, made travel arrangements, wrote letters, prayed, sang songs, did household tasks, and more. It struck me that each person probably thought that he or she did little, that their task was insignificant. Yet through all these individual servants, God did much. Helpers must realize that God works out his plan through the little things. All are his available hands for the detail work and the helpers' job is to be alert for those opportunities. A loving, supportive church family is God's greatest tool.

4. Note the support chain that Kyle's story shows us. Kyle's sister and parents helped him as he died. Kyle helped them say good-bye and prepare for his death. After Kyle was gone, his sister continued to help her parents grieve, sharing their pain. Helpers are no substitutes for effective families. The helper's role is to encourage family members to share honestly and help each other grieve.

Chapter 15

Pain Upon Pain: Multiple Losses

How much grief can one family bear? You will read four separate accounts, by a brother, father, sister, and mother who have experienced multiple losses in their lives. Beginning with the death of a child, the circles of loss widened beyond repair.

A Brother's Grief

by Keith Wells

Our family was fishing at a lake in Casper, Wyoming, in September. It was cold and we were bundled in warm coats. As we were busy soaking worms, the stillness was broken by my five-year-old brother slipping on the rocks and falling into the deep water. Panicked, my six-year-old sister jumped into the icy waters to push him up on the rocks but was carried out further. My mother jumped into the lake to save my sister, with my father following close behind. Helping my brother onto the rocks, I then slipped into the lake. My parents pushed both of us back onto the rocks and swam to save our sister. It never occurred to me that my hero, my rugged outdoorsman father, would not be able to save them. They were struggling against the strong current with heavy coats soaked with icy water pressing in on them. The last words my father said to me were, "Go get help!"

We ran to the road for help and I still remember looking back for a second. The lake was empty and chillingly calm. I was four years old and my life changed in a instant. My brother and I became orphans that day. We were whisked away from our home in Casper within the week to live in California with our grandparents. A few years later, my grandfather died of a heart attack and all the grief left my grandmother a bitter, angry woman. I lost not only my parents and my sister, I lost my childhood at that lake. My parents died trying to save us but they could not save all of us.

Today my brother and I have an estranged relationship. As an adult I returned to the scene of the accident, went to the cemetery where my family is buried, visited relatives and even a friend who was fishing with us that day, and talked to the diver who pulled my parents and sister from the bottom of the lake. I still want answers. Today I have my own wife and family of seven children. I have learned from my wife, who was abandoned by her father when she was a child, that her loss is even more painful than losing a parent to death.

A Sister's Grief

I enjoyed a relatively intact life growing up as a pastor's daughter. We certainly had our good times and hard times as a family of four children, but we always had each other, our laughter, our music, and a passion to serve God. But one day everything changed. My older sister died weeks before her wedding in a car accident on a rainy Saturday morning. Soon after, my little sister was diagnosed with leukemia. She died twenty-one days later. My dad was a good man, a faithful servant. But he couldn't bear the pain. He was so broken and disillusioned that one day he just walked out the door and never came back. Our church then asked us to leave because of "the circumstances." Loss and grief left our family in ruins. As a teenager, I was so angry. How could God treat his dedicated servants this way? My mother, who had always raised her hands in praise to God in the good times, did not stop praising Him in the tough times. She would pray, "Lord, my daughter is confused, battered, and angry. Please be tender with her." And He was. Amidst the wreckage of my life, the foundation of my youth remained. I began to remember that God loved me. We have a heavenly father who will never abandon us.

Excerpted from tapes by Chonda Pierce,
Christian vocalist and comedienne

A Mother's Grief

Helen and her family always vacationed at their second home in Sun Valley, Idaho. Their two sons loved the outdoors and mountain life, and this area was the ideal retreat from the stressful executive job that Helen's husband, Matt, held in California. Thanksgiving arrived, and Helen, Matt, and their ten-year-old son, Steven, headed for their vacation home. Thirteen-year-old Paul was remaining at home with friends to participate in a band concert.

Duck hunting season in Idaho was in full swing. Matt and his best friend, both expert outdoorsmen, decided to take Steven duck hunting with them. When they did not return by nightfall, Helen became concerned, but she trusted her husband's abilities in the wild. Later that night, the community organized a search party. The next morning Matt, his friend, and Steven were found frozen to death by the lake. The cause would always be a mystery. What had gone wrong? Had Steven fallen into the lake?

Had the men rescued him and then perished in the freezing temperatures? No one would ever know what actually happened.

Helen's pain was overwhelming. Losing her life's partner was devastating; but losing her precious younger son was even less bearable, and she had no husband to turn to for help. How would she tell Paul that the father he adored and the brother he loved were both gone? She was enveloped in numbness and shock for weeks.

Helen and Matt had many dear friends in Idaho as well as California. They never left her side. She and her husband had always been very social people. Their lives had been filled with activity. She did *not* want to be alone now. Friends chartered a plane and went back with her to California. Friends met her at the plane and brought her home where relatives were already staying. Helen needed people to surround her. Years later, she still did not want to be alone.

Helen and Paul survived the funeral with the support of numerous friends. The two caskets side-by-side—one large, one so small in contrast—were the painful focus of the service.

Paul reacted to the deaths in a way typical of teenagers. He wanted to go to school the next day. He immersed himself in constant activities to numb the pain, a pattern that would continue into adulthood. He would not cry in front of his mother and became angry when she cried. Helen would have to hide her pain from Paul. He could not handle one more burden.

Their first Christmas alone, only a few weeks after the deaths, was the saddest holiday they would spend. Helen could not bear to have their traditional Christmas at home. She even refused to have a Christmas tree. Paul was adamant that they must have a tree, and a group of his high school friends came to help him decorate it. Helen and Paul left to spend Christmas Day with Helen's brother's family in another city, something they had never done before. Paul felt totally betrayed. Not only had he lost his family, but now he had lost all his family's traditions.

Over the years, Helen and Paul pieced their lives back together. Paul went on a journey of searching, which eventually brought him to a genuine faith in Jesus Christ. Helen remarried a wonderful man who had been a dear friend of Matt's—the same man who had met Matt's and Steven's bodies at the airport when they arrived for the funeral. Each year her new husband sent Helen a dozen red roses on Steven's birthday. He wanted her to know that Steven and Matt would never be forgotten.

The most comforting fact that helpers can communicate to grieving families is that helpers will not forget their lost loved ones but will help keep their love and traditions alive.

A Father's Grief

Forty years ago, I went on a shopping trip with my wife and three sons. My wife went into the store while I waited in the car with the boys. I had trouble starting the car. My youngest son, Davey, 18 months, was climbing on me. I told him to move over while I rolled the car down the hill to get it started. The car door opened on his side, he fell out, and the car rolled over him, crushing his head. He was dead well before the store manager drove us to the hospital as I held him. I blame myself for his death. My wife, who was coming out of the store and saw the entire accident, blames herself that she didn't scream louder to warn me. Our two other sons blamed themselves that they weren't watching their brother. We each felt responsible for his death in our own way.

Overwhelmed with grief and despair, my wife took to her bed, unable to function. Overwhelmed with grief and guilt, I often contemplated suicide. I couldn't live with the pain. But I knew that I couldn't cause my wife and children any more suffering. My deep faith in God carried me through that unbearable time. It is a miracle that we survived. For twenty years, I couldn't think about my deceased son or see a picture of him without breaking down. I could forgive myself because I knew the truth. It was an accident. God knew the intent of my

heart. Jesus Christ was my Savior. I had the assurance of God's
promises of forgiveness and purpose for my life.

For over 50 years, my wife and I have had each other. We trust
God completely through all the tragedies of life. Our life has
purpose though God doesn't take away the pain. Through the
years, it does lessen. The memories and pain are not quite as
fresh, though they are always with us.

Through that black time, I told my wife that God would give
us back another son. God was faithful to do that. Yet at age 16,
that son died of leukemia. He was a very special, loving boy who
planned to enter the ministry. For thirty years, an annual
memorial award has been given in his honor at his high school.
I also feel responsible for his death, because I made the decision
not to use bone marrow from his brother to try to save his life. In
those days, the operation wasn't always successful and we
would be putting his brother's life at risk as well.

We received very little support from friends or our church
through either tragedy. We attended a fundamental church. As
my son was dying of leukemia, he was asked to leave the church
choir because he wore wire rim glasses that were "too modern."
One woman from our church visited the hospital often, trying to
convince him that his hair was too long and he needed to repent
of his rebellion. It became harassment and I had to ask her to
stop coming to the hospital. I wrote my own son's funeral service
because I did not want to take any chances that he would be
dishonored.

For many years after my son's death, I made sure that I was
traveling on business at Christmas time. I took my family with
me and we spent Christmas in hotels. It was too painful to be
home. My own father died when I was six years old in 1929 and
my mother's example has been my inspiration. Through all the
pain in her life, my mother was a very forgiving woman,
grounded in her faith. I remember her always singing hymns
and praises to the God she trusted.

Loss takes different forms, sometimes more painful than
death. We haven't seen our youngest son in years. He deeply

resents us and rejects all our efforts to reconcile. He feels that he was an ignored child, receiving little attention from us through those painful years. His grief has left him bitter and angry, often directed at us.

As I approach my 80s, I feel about my deceased sons as King David did about his son: "You cannot come to me but I will come to you."

Survivor Guilt

Grieving siblings travel the toughest journey. Overwhelmed by grief, children and teenagers left behind often unconsciously postpone their grief until adulthood. They are not ready to face it. But eventually they will have to deal with the intense pain, often in addition to addictions they have used to cope with their loss. Survivor guilt is a very real phenomenon. Similar to the war experience when one son is killed in battle while a younger son at home lives, siblings ask, "Why me? Why did I survive?" They live with grief, guilt, anger, and confusion. Not only do they lose a sibling, but they lose their "normal" family. Life will never be the same. When a young person loses a sibling as well as a parent, the trauma is devastating.

*C*hapter 16

Final Family Portrait: The Garwoods

Barbara Garwood's two teenagers, Wayne and Eva, were killed in an auto accident on September 22, 1996. Her third son, Marquis, was seriously injured. Barbara began writing in her journal three weeks later. She has graciously allowed excerpts from her journal to be printed here. Max Garwood shares the writing he did on the night of the accident. Marquis Garwood shares his experience, written two years later. As you walk through the long process of grief with them, use this opportunity to synthesize the material in this book. Note how effectively their church family helped them during the darkest days of their lives and unspeakable grief.

A Mother's Grief

10/15/96

I am on a very long, crooked, and narrow path but I know God is carrying me. I can't do this alone. No way. My life has changed forever and I must use this journal to survive. Maybe someday it will help me or somebody else to read these words.

I remember the day of the accident as a "no fuss" family day. We went to evening church and the kids were coming a few minutes later in our other car. At 6 PM the service began and no kids . . . 6:30 . . . no kids . . . 6:45 . . . no kids. Max and I were becoming so anxious and immediately called home when the service ended. NO ANSWER. I had a sick, heavy feeling in my heart and gut.

We drove home the way they would have driven and saw that there had been an accident. We hurried home to call the dispatcher. She said that there had been two accidents but that she didn't have any more information. She told us to start calling hospitals. We called Lutheran Hospital and Marquis was there. We rushed to the hospital, calling friends from the car phone.

We arrived at the emergency room and were told that Marquis was having a CAT scan. We were shown to a waiting room. Where were Eva and Wayne? Finally a doctor came to tell us that Marquis was in ICU but he was going to be OK. Then two chaplains and a sheriff joined us and we were very, very frightened. We were clinging to hope and found none in their eyes. I knew that they were going to tell me that one of my children was dead . . . which one? Both were dead. Our oldest son and our only daughter had been instantly killed in the accident. Oh, Max was so torn and broken. I couldn't bear to see him like that.

A young man had sped through a yield sign, smashing our car into a utility pole. The car had been cut in two, as had the seatbelts. Eva died in the car and Wayne was thrown through the windshield. It was a miracle that Marquis survived.

Our relatives, church family, pastors, and friends descended on the hospital. We had support like I have never seen. The hospital was full of our friends. We had someone by our side every step of the way. People took off time from work to help us through that week.

The staff asked us if we wanted to donate their organs. Max said it was my decision. I said yes. We needed witnesses. My good friend stayed with me through the entire ordeal. I had to answer every imaginable question about my children's medical histories. It was so painful.

I stayed in the hospital with Marquis that night. Max was so overcome with grief that he wanted to go home to be alone. Brother Paul followed him and made sure that he was OK. Max promised us that he wouldn't do anything rash. He sobbed his heart out at home, lying on each child's bed. He couldn't sleep. I didn't sleep either.

The week was so difficult. I wanted to be with Marquis but I had to bury my other children. Friends were constantly with us and with Marquis at the hospital. People everywhere were praying for us.

Being at the funeral home was dreadful. Could we ever imagine that we would have to pick out caskets for our children? I now know what a heavy heart truly is. After planning the funeral, Max wanted to visit the scene of the accident. I couldn't take it so I lay down in the back of the car. Finally I was glad to be home. Our friends had already been at the house, cleaning, cooking, doing yard work, etc. But I was so weary. I didn't want to see Wayne's and Eva's belongings.

10/23/96

The accident happened a month ago and it still seems unreal. The day of the viewing came and Marquis was discharged from the hospital to attend. I was so tired of being there, sitting alone in the hospital chapel and walking the halls at 3:00 AM.

The caskets were open and I thought the children looked awful. We just wanted to hold them but we were told we couldn't. Wayne's jaw had been broken in seven places. We learned that the morticians had worked very hard for two days to make them presentable. We saw all the things that friends had put in the caskets . . . Christmas ornaments, a shirt that said, "I've gone home to be with Jesus," the other half of a friendship necklace from our daughter's best friend. Eva died before her sixteenth birthday and she had always wanted a bouquet of roses. Her aunt sent sixteen red roses for her. We placed framed pictures of our children by their caskets, including one of Wayne's oil paintings.

About 1500 people attended that day. People stood in line for hours to hug us and tell us they loved us, even strangers we had never met who had experienced similar grief in their lives. I was so tired that I needed to sit down in another room. Even there friends came to tell me special things that our children had said or done—so comforting.

We drove to the cemetery with about ninety cars following, the longest procession that cemetery ever had. It was gently raining. Grandpa insisted on being a pallbearer. He said carrying his grandchildren was the last thing that he could do for them.

There were so many plants delivered that we began giving them to friends who were helping us. Our church had the funeral dinner and delivered meals to us for a month. Wal-Mart, Wayne's employer, provided all the desserts. I've always enjoyed cooking but that's all changed now. I can't face cooking for two less.

12/23/96

Two days before Christmas . . . three months since the accident. Today a friend called Max because he just lost his two children. Our grief is still so fresh. Are we ready for God to use us?

1/13/97

I think that I was supposed to be at my grief support meeting tonight. I can't remember. I just found some trash and items related to Wayne and Eva. I can't throw them away. It's been four months and I still have trouble accepting what happened. I want my children back. I want to hold them. Someday I will. Jesus is coming and we will have a big group hug in heaven. What a reunion!

Marquis is working on his Eagle Scout project. Max returned to law school in addition to his job. We knew if he didn't return right away, he would never go back to finish. He was so close. Eva always drove to class with him and helped him with his computer research at the library. He doesn't like to go alone now so Marquis or I go with him.

1/21/97

Four months . . . I am depressed and not functioning well. I broke three glass things this past week. Max and Marquis are at school today. Friends take me out to lunch but then I return to an empty house . . . so lonely. Before the accident, this tired mom used to want to be alone and just have a little peace and quiet. Well, I have the quiet now.

3/8/97

Over five months and it still hurts. I went to a church program tonight. Everyone sang "Amazing Grace" but I could not sing one word, only cry. That was our family song. I can hardly wait for heaven. I want my babies.

3/16/97

Max had a dream last night. He was sleeping and a tall, blonde woman woke him. He saw Wayne and Eva dressed in shimmering clothing. Wayne looked different. He didn't have his glasses on. They seemed happy. Only one word was spoken. Wayne told his dad, "Soon."

Easter week

I am remembering all our Easter traditions—new clothes, egg hunts, Easter baskets, family dinners. Thank you, God, for good memories.

We visit the graves almost every Sunday. Memories flood our minds with pain. One Sunday I couldn't hold back anymore. I fell on my knees and sobbed. I want to hold them, love them, watch them grow into adults and fulfill their goals and dreams. I feel so robbed. I miss their big strong hugs, especially during those sweet times of forgiveness after a disagreement.

4/7/97

Such a mixture of emotions . . . it seems I go along day by day and keep everything in check. Then suddenly a flood of memories, tears, and emotions erupts.

Happy birthday, Eva! You are celebrating your sixteenth birthday in heaven with Jesus. I am glad that you are there. I just want to be with you too. I went to your grave to plant some flowers today. Dad is sick. Many people remembered your birthday, sending cards and calling us. Marquis didn't want to be at home today, too painful. On Sunday, someone put flowers in the church in memory of your birthday.

4/16/97

Wayne, you would be very proud of your brother. He received a special award for his Eagle project. You and Eva will be very missed at the ceremony but I know that you are watching from heaven.

My world seems to be shrinking and I don't want that. Marquis is moving on with his life. Max is making a whole new world for himself. Everyone is gone. God will show me a new purpose. But I'm not sure I'm ready. I still have so much sorrow in my heart. I don't want to spread that to others. God will sustain me.

5/8/97

God knows how deeply we hurt, how we long to touch your faces and look into your eyes. I hope that you will look down on Sunday to see your daddy graduate from law school. We ache to have you share that day. I'm glad to miss church on Sunday. I would surely spoil Mother's Day for everyone.

7/15/97

Happy twentieth birthday, Wayne! We celebrated your birthday by visiting the cemetery to leave flowers. Then we had a barbecue and did your favorite thing, fireworks. I had found some of yours in a drawer.

7/23/97

It's our anniversary. We've been married twenty-two years. We should be celebrating but we are only thinking about you, dear children. Dad took the bar exam. Everything is in God's hands.

My time on earth is short. I will see you in heaven soon . . . forever. Thank you, heavenly Father, for the promise of eternity in heaven.

9/22/97

One year ago today. We've lived a year-long nightmare. I've dreaded this day. I want to run away and not have to face this day. Marquis, Max, and I went to the cemetery today. I went by myself yesterday to work this through my system. Last Sunday was really, really hard for the whole church. The special music was in your honor. I wanted to lean on friends but I can only lean on God. Max provided carnations for everyone. At the end of the service, each person took one carnation to remember you. We formed a big circle and sang. Later we took the remaining carnations to your graves. Someone else had left roses with a poem about you, Eva.

Then we drove down to the accident scene. Marquis still doesn't remember the accident and I pray that he never will. God protects him from those vivid memories. Drivers kept stopping and asking us questions. Someone even asked for directions! All the interruptions were very upsetting. Marquis clung to Dad and cried really hard. I just stood in shock. This was the first time that Marquis cried with us.

9/22/99

Three years ago I lost my children. Marquis is training to become a paramedic. The young man who caused the accident only had his license suspended and still doesn't understand what he did to our family. He has taken no responsibility or even said that he was sorry. It's too painful to drive by his house. He alone has to face God. I can't carry that burden in addition to my grief.

We drive by the accident scene every time we go to church. We put crosses on their graves the first year and it is comforting to still see flowers left by people. They haven't forgotten us. Today we will remember Wayne and Eva by going to the cemetery and visiting the accident scene at the exact time they left us. Then our good friends are having us come for dinner so we can be surrounded by a loving family on this very difficult day.

A Father's Grief
by Max Garwood, written on the night he lost his children

Emptiness and sorrow surround me as I pen these words. Yet I feel I must record my feelings on the day that Wayne and Eva left us. I am using my daughter's uncapped pen to write this. I want to be alone in this house tonight. The last words I said to my children were, "Do you want to ride to church with us or come later with Wayne?" They decided to come later with their brother, Wayne.

Saturday night we were at the church revival meeting. We were surprised that Eva sat with us instead of her teenage friends. She sat next to me, hugging me and laying her head on my shoulder . . . almost as if she missed me. Oh, how my heart aches for those hugs now.

The clock just chimed 3:30 AM. I've often said when winding the clock that we have no idea of the events that will unfold during the week as the clock winds down. Oh, if we could just unwind time . . .

Tonight at the church service, Eva's friends asked, "When will Eva be here?" I said, "When you see one of our kids, you'll see them all." I didn't know that Wayne and Eva were already dead.

The coyotes are yelping but do not sound nearly as bad as I feel as I see and touch my children's things and cry out. Eva found solace in her writing, but I find little as I write these words. Their presence is everywhere, in their rooms, in their places at the table.

I rejoice in knowing them, in holding them, carrying them to bed, reading to them . . . You gave Wayne to us for nineteen years. We wanted him regardless of what the doctor said about Barb's measles during pregnancy.

Lord, please come for us quickly. I miss my children so dearly. Why most love hurt so deeply?

A Brother's Grief
by Marquis Garwood, written two years after the accident

My lungs felt as though they would explode as I desperately tried to draw one final breath. Then the world was suddenly dark and fierce pain enveloped my body. An entire lifetime of love, memories, joy, pain, and regrets flashed through my mind.

We had enjoyed our traditional Sunday lunch, the one time of the week our family spent together. After feasting on our mom's cooking, the finest food in the county, we relaxed around the house. Wayne and Eva played video games and I went out back to shoot my musket. I was cleaning my musket when mom said,

"Finish cleaning your rifle later. It's time to go to church." Wanting to finish the job, I proposed that Mom and Dad go on ahead to church and Eva and I could drive with Wayne. We followed fifteen minutes later.

The next thing I remember was someone holding an oxygen mask over my face, feeding my lungs the air I no longer had the strength to draw for myself. Everything was dark, but I could breathe. With the oxygen bringing me around, I could feel my entire body erupting with pain.

I recognized the voice of my friend, Dave, a medic/fireman. He told me that I had been in a car accident. Then I lost consciousness. When I woke up, I couldn't see and I was in intense pain. I realized that I was strapped to a backboard with wires and tubes all over me. I was scared, really scared. What terrified me the most was that I was alone.

In and out of consciousness, I was confused, not knowing where I was or what time it was. All I knew was that I hurt and the bed was cold and hard. I was comforted when Dad whispered in my ear.

I could hear Dad and Mom crying. They told me about the accident and that my brother and sister had been killed. My world came crashing down around me. Shock caused my body to convulse and I began to vomit violently, like my guts were being torn out. The hospital staff rushed to shove a tube through my nose to my stomach so I would not aspirate. My physical pain couldn't come close to my emotional pain. I didn't cry. I couldn't because it hurt too bad. The ripping of my heart could not be anesthetized by the doctor's drugs.

My first two days in the hospital seemed to drag in slow motion. Every movement and breath was extremely painful, reminding me that I was not in a bad dream. This was devastatingly real. I would wake up occasionally and see someone I knew. Visitors were usually crying.

Someone had taken the lives of not only my siblings, but my best friends. Lying there staring at the ceiling, I was raging inside. Hating the driver who did this to us would have been easy. I wanted to embrace the hate and bitterness eating away at my heart. I had no strength to fight it. But Jesus did. He changed me once more. The same faith that gave me eternal life would now get me through the dark days ahead.

The love of Christ melted away my fears and drove back the darkness. He Who spared my life would give me the strength to live. It was not how much faith I had but rather in Whom I had faith.

Life has not been easy since that tragic day two years ago. I miss my brother and sister very much. I have suffered with severe migraine headaches since the accident. My heart was rent in pieces. I understand why people numb that pain with alcohol and drugs but those temporary opiates never heal a broken heart. Placing my heart in Jesus' nail-scarred hands is the only answer.

Someday I will be eternally free of pain and reunited with Wayne and Eva. Jesus will wipe away all my tears and He will finally make me whole. Until then I will live my life as though my next breath could be my last.

There Are Days

by Marquis Garwood

(Written on the eve of the third anniversary of their death, September 21, 1999)

> *There are many days that feel as though they will never end.*
> *The deep, throbbing pain deep within will not leave.*
> *I long to hear his voice in the night . . ."Marquis, what do you think about . . . ?"*
> *I no longer have those late nights of conversation*
> *filled with talk of hopes, dreams, and worries of our young lives.*
> *There isn't really any point in going shooting anymore . . . there's no one to go with.*

*No one to wander the fields with, to walk in the dark
trusting each other for each step.*
*I long to hear his voice . . . the voice of the one who knew
my greatest hopes and fears.*
It was never spoken between us that we were friends.
We just were—friends like none other.
*That is all gone now. All my heart can do is ache for the
day when I see him again.*

She was 15. She would never see her 16th.
She dreamed bigger, loftier dreams than any of us.
*She was always in Madrid, on a submarine, or riding her
horses across her mountain range.*
The writer, the lawyer, would never be.
*Her endless dialogues among those characters known
only to her, suddenly ceased like a record that stops
turning.*
*A pen in her hand, a pad in her lap. Smooth ink flowing
onto paper.*
*That is where she was happy. She would have those no
more.*
*Her soft voice and curls walking through our blossoming
orchard.*
Gone.

*I knew them so well. I thought I would have them
forever.*
*Their faces are only faded shadows of images in my
mind.*
The sound of their voices has faded in my mind.
I hear their footsteps, their faint voices falling behind me.
"Marquis . . ."
I turn to see no one.

*C*hapter 17

A Final Note to Helpers

Helpers walk a fine line. We want to support dying children and grieving families but we are mourning too. Yet our own grief cannot become so paralyzing that we are unable to help. I don't think keeping a safe, objective distance is the answer either. Helpers must sincerely feel the grief of those they help, but they should also be aware of their limitations.

Old Testament grievers did not hide their pain. They rent their clothes and wore them as a sign of their grief. In time grievers would repair the ripped seams but they continued wearing the tattered clothes inside out to signify the permanent damage done by grief. Scars remained for a lifetime. Professional mourners saved their tears in bottles. Grief work was shared by a community, with elaborate processions and ceremony. Helpers today do not have these concrete clues to guide us.

Helpers never can assume that their job is over and they can move on. They should be willing to stay in touch with grievers indefinitely. Helping and loving hurting people are lifetime missions. Jesus asked his disciple John to care for and support Mary—for a week? for a month? for the first year? No, for her lifetime.

It is possible that some grieving families will cut off their relationships with you because you are a too painful reminder of their sad journeys. But that is their choice. You can lovingly contact them occasionally while respecting their privacy.

This book was written for helpers, but sections of it, especially family stories and Scripture references, are appropriate to share with grievers at the right time. Your other responsibility is to become familiar with information resources beyond the scope of this book. This is the practical side of helping. You may want to contact health care organizations to receive technical information on specific diseases (e.g., cancer, cystic fibrosis). You will want to become familiar with local bereavement support groups and hospital offerings. You may be interested in developing your own library of books about grief, especially children's books. Visiting your local library is an excellent starting point.

God's Encouragement for Grievers and Helpers

Helpers are links in God's chain of comfort. They help the parents help their child die. They hold the parents as they grieve, and in time they will help other suffering parents. God is creating gold in each of us. He deeply loves the children whom he takes home early. He will never abandon us, no matter how hot the fire or how deep the pain.

> *Should you pass through the sea, I will be with you;*
> *or through rivers, they will not swallow you up.*
> *Should you walk through fire, you will not be*
> *scorched and the flames will not burn you.*
> *For I am Yahweh, your God,*
> *The Holy One of Israel, your Savior.*
> —Isaiah 43:2–3 JB

> *If I go eastward, he is not there;*
> *or westward—still I cannot see him.*
> *If I seek him in the north, he is not to be found,*
> *invisible still when I turn to the south.*

And yet he knows of every step I take!
Let him test me in the crucible;
I shall come out pure gold.

—Job 23:8–10 JB

As you walk through the fire of helping, bearing the burden of grief, you, too, will come out pure gold. I leave you with one final synopsis of grief work, a picture of trusting God in the midst of pain and despair. I call Psalm 77 the "Griever's Psalm." May God go with you on your difficult and privileged journey.

I cried aloud to God,
I cried to God, and he heard me.
In the day of my distress I sought the Lord,
and by night I lifted my outspread hands in prayer.
I lay sweating and nothing would cool me;
I refused all comfort.
When I called God to mind, I groaned;
as I lay thinking, darkness came over my spirit.
My eyelids were tightly closed;
I was dazed and I could not speak.
My thoughts went back to times long past,
I remembered forgotten years;
all night long I was in deep distress,
as I lay thinking, my spirit was sunk in despair.

Will the Lord reject us for evermore
and never again show favour?
Has his unfailing love now failed us utterly,
must his promise time and again be unfulfilled?
Has God forgotten to be gracious,
has he in anger withheld his mercies?
"Has his right hand," I said, "lost its grasp?
Does it hang powerless, the arm of the Most High?"

But then, O Lord, I call to mind thy deeds;
I recall thy wonderful acts in times gone by.
I meditate upon thy works
and muse on all that thou hast done.
O God, thy way is holy;
what god is so great as our God?
Thou art the God who workest miracles;
thou hast shown the nations thy power.
With thy strong arm thou didst redeem thy people,
the sons of Jacob and Joseph.

—Psalm 77:1–15 NEB

Organizations

American Cancer Society, 1599 Clifton Rd., NE., Atlanta, GA 30329

Association for the Care of Children's Health (ACCH), 7910 Woodmont Ave., Ste. 300, Bethesda, MD 20814-3015

Cancer Information Service, 9000 Rockville Pike, Ste. 340, Bethesda, MD 20891 (800) 4-CANCER

Cystic Fibrosis Foundation, 6931 Arlington Rd., #200, Bethesda, MD 20814

Leukemia Society of American, Inc., National Headquarters, 733 3rd. Ave., New York, NY 10017

Mothers of AIDS Patients, P.O. Box 3132, San Diego, CA 92103

National AIDS Clearinghouse, P.O. Box 6003, Rockville, MD, 20850 1-800-458-5231

Pediatric AIDS Foundation, 2407 Wilshire Boulevard, Ste. 613, Santa Monica, CA 90403

Bereaved Parents, P.O. Box 3147, Scottsdale, AZ 85271

The Candlelighters Childhood Cancer Foundation, 1312 18th St., N.W., Washington, D.C. 20036

Children's Hospice International, CHI, 501 Slater's Lane, #20, Alexandria, VA 22314

The Compassionate Friends, P.O. Box 3696, Oak Brook, IL 60522-3696

Make-A-Wish Foundation® of America, 2600 N Central Ave., Ste. 936, Phoenix, AZ 85004 (602) 240-6600; (800) 722-WISH

Make Today Count, 101 1/2 S Union St., Alexandria, VA 22314

The National Hospice Organization, 1901 N. Moore St., #901, Arlington, VA 22209

National Sudden Infant Death Syndrome Foundation, 10500 Little Patuxent Pkwy #420, Columbia, MD 21044

Parents of Murdered Children, 200 E. 8th. St., B-14, Cincinnati, OH 45202

Pregnancy and Infant Loss Center, 1421 E. Wayzata Boulevard, #40, Wayzata, MN 55391

Ronald McDonald Houses, Children's Oncology Services, Inc., 500 N. Michigan Avenue, Chicago, IL 60611

Seasons: Suicide Bereavement, P.O. Box 187, Park City, UT 84060

The Ultimate Rejection—newsletter on suicide from: Suicide Prevention Center, Inc., 184 Salem Avenue, Dayton, OH 45406

For a more detailed resource guide, overview of therapy techniques, and bibliography, you may consult *Music Therapy with Hospitalized Children: A Creative Arts Child Life Approach,* (Froehlich, Mary Ann, editor. [Jeffrey Publications]).

Other books by the author

What's a Smart Woman Like You Doing in a Place
   Like This?

Music Education in the Christian Home

Music Therapy with Hospitalized Children:
   A Creative Arts Child Life Approach

Holding Down the Fort: Help and Encouragement
   for Wives Whose Husbands Travel
                                   with PeggySue Wells

What to Do When You Don't Know What to Say
                                   with PeggySue Wells

Note to the Reader

The publisher invites you to share your response to the message of this book by writing Discovery House Publishers, P. O. Box 3566, Grand Rapids, MI 49501, USA or by calling 1-800-653-8333. For information about other Discovery House publications, contact us at the same address and phone number. Find us on the Internet at http://www.dhp.org/ or send email to <books@dhp.org>.

To my wife, Karen, and son, Kyle

And to our clients, four-legged friends,

and veterinarians…everywhere

 Contents

Miracle on Chigger Hill

The spring breeding season hit us full-on. Four-hundred and thirty-six mares were booked. Not as many as last year, I thought, but still a butt-load of female horses to treat and settle-in-foal before summer temperatures became unbearable.

My partner, Rich Vest, and I split up and began working the breeding farms north and south of our Dallas clinic. We planned on meeting to refuel at the middle-of-nowhere juncture of Four Points under its red neon 'flying horse'. No one knew how or why a gas station ended up on each corner. But there they were, each one endowed with a single crank pump, and a talkative proprietor who jawed about "how things use't be." Other than a faded billboard and dilapidated wood building with 'Ten-cent flat repair' still scrawled on its side, these four amiable gents gave the old county-crossing its only life.

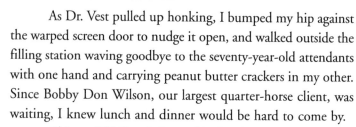
As Dr. Vest pulled up honking, I bumped my hip against the warped screen door to nudge it open, and walked outside the filling station waving goodbye to the seventy-year-old attendants with one hand and carrying peanut butter crackers in my other. Since Bobby Don Wilson, our largest quarter-horse client, was waiting, I knew lunch and dinner would be hard to come by.

Chigger Hill Ranch, located in Single Tree, Population 3, bred more mares than anyone else in these parts. Our work might get done by eight o'clock—or midnight. Bobby Don, his wife, Lady Bug, and their son Donny-Don 'Hutch', mirrored their ranch's legendary reputation for toughness and year-after-year survival. Poor soils had reduced the vegetation on the twelve-thousand-acre spread to just one stunted cottonwood tree that swarmed with bull-bats every evening. Milkweeds and horny toads were abundant.

Dr. Vest's headlights set right on my bumper as we passed pueblo dugouts buried in the flat face of the orange sand-canyon walls. Our path alongside a rock-bed stream narrowed to a hard-worn trail favored by jeeps and wild horses. Bumpy dual-tracks finally opened up through the sagebrush leading us past cedar-post gates to the entrance of Chigger Hill. Tracy, my indispens-able right arm on these spring trips, pointed to the dozens of oil wells strewn about the hillside, while I pointed to the gray stone mansion embedded at the end of the coal-covered bend, com-menting that Bobby Don's been in the horse business longer than those minerals have been in the ground.

Lady Bug and Bobby Don didn't have many visitors. "Don't need none," they would say. "Got our land and our animals." Like trading treaties of the past, Bobby Don and I had agreed to trade goods. He'd provide us with the finest horseflesh in the southwest, with pasture and housing; and we'd artificially inseminate mares and birth foals indefinitely. Our agreement was settled with a handshake.

As a monument to bloodlines and pride in Texas livestock, Chigger Hill held the same sort of historic importance as The Alamo. But it was still a desolate spot. So the high-spirited Lady Bug had no qualms about declaring it *her* town, Single Tree, named after that forlorn cottonwood.

Parts of an antique, two-wheel *carretas* lay in front of sleek, green painted pipe-and-cable paddocks. With their tin roofs reflecting the sky, three one-hundred-stall barns stretched along the far side of the ranch-style house. And Spanish archways marked the corridors leading to the professional air-conditioned and heated breeding rooms. The laboratory separating the sires from dams could hold its own with the best hospital surgical suite of any city. Even the stalls had a clean, fresh smell from the pine shavings that were put down daily. With ready access to computer-enhanced fertility programs, sonograms, incubators, and microscopes, I had difficulty remembering we were there to breed horses, not to perform cloning experiments.

The Wilsons weren't exactly the type to be duplicated, anyway. I'd seen the inside of their home-place…and their barn aisles were much neater. One look at Bobby Don or Hutch put an end to any illusion that Texas cowboys were part of a dying era. None of us harbored a doubt that their horses came first in this family's eyes. These two ol' cowpokes would rather bathe a mule than themselves. Hutch's idea of "soakin' in a tub" meant taking the time to float while skinny-dippin' in the back pasture's stock tank.

And I wasn't sure if this father and son didn't prefer sleeping out-doors under the stars. Bobby Don repeatedly told Lady Bug he wanted his washed shirts hung over the wire fence to dry, "…'cause I like the prairie breeze blowin' through them." Even in bad weather, both men liked the screened-in back porch, with its canvas sleeping cots, more than any other room in the large hacienda.

Myna, my partner's eager trainee, gawked; she had never seen a barbed wire clothesline. From the cab of Dr. Vest's truck, she caught a glimpse of Bobby Don, Hutch, and the sprawling farm she'd heard us talk about. I was fond of telling her that Hutch always reminded me of the four-drawer oak dresser in my bedroom; he had the same solid, short frame, and his massive, square shoulders gave an impression of rare strength. He and his father wore duplicate bronc-creased brims. After a horse trampled on a hat enough times, the shape was set. Neither man was concerned with impressing anyone. Monday was Friday was Sunday on the Chigger Hill spread.

Bobby Don, rounded with age, sat in the cord-bottomed chair kept next to the stud barn entrance. Looking at a magazine and turning the pages with a small stick, I figured he was either projecting the market prices of two-year-old geldings and yearling fillies, or studying to draw brands in the dirt. It didn't really matter. He had enough horses to weather any financial slump. And there was only one brand—eight short sidebars on a circle's rim—the Chigger.

My eyes shifted from father to son. It was hard to tell if Bobby Don was thinking or loafing, until it actually came time to get his brood-mares gathered and bred. Then he was all business. He and Lady Bug would have the mares "teased" before breakfast, even though we weren't scheduled until dusk. Sixty-four mares awaited reproductive examinations on the first day of the season. Many more would follow. Rectal palpations, sono-grams, and uterine cultures would begin our attempts to settle-in-foal all the horses of Single Tree.

"Hey, Doc…" It was always Hutch who did most of the talking. He never moved faster than he had to, and his expression never changed. He pointed a nubbed index finger toward his father and mumbled, "They be a'waitin' on ya." The tip of his digit was lost a few years back when he dallied his lariat around the saddle horn with his finger still inside the loops, and a twelve-hundred-pound mustang jerked on the other end of the rope. It was over in a second.

"Pa's got 'em ready," was our call to work. While we were preparing to tend to business on this first Thursday, seven tail-wrapped rumps greeted us—two sorrels, a bay, three Paints, and a black. From then on, the others blended into a blurred line. Six, sixteen, or forty-two mares would be circling the catch pen, while three, six, or nine mares would be standing in the exam-ination stocks inside the breeding shed. I started from left to right. "Hold 'er tail to the side," I said, aiming a pipette to inseminate yet another of the dozens to be run into the stanchions. "We'll check 'er by sonogram in fourteen days…to see if she stuck. Next!"

Hutch moved three steps to his right, and raised the next sorrel mare's tail. We were moving through another orchestrated pregnancy exam when the worst sound known to a horseman shattered the air. *GONG! GONG!* Bobby Don was ringing the fire alarm bell. *GONG! GONG!* The huge iron bell rang disaster.

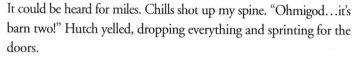

It could be heard for miles. Chills shot up my spine. "Ohmigod…it's barn two!" Hutch yelled, dropping everything and sprinting for the doors.

I didn't know Hutch could move so fast. He dashed past Dr. Vest, who ran from the stallion shed as Myna and Tracy popped their heads through the open window of the laboratory. "What is it?" Tracy asked as I ran by.

"FIRE! FIRE!" I hollered back.

"Cut 'em loose! Turn 'em out!" I heard Hutch and Bobby Don shouting.

Dr. Vest's voice rang out. "That barn's filled with mares and babies!"

His stride was longer than mine. Billowing clouds of dense, black smoke were boiling from the west end of barn aisles as I raced behind Dr. Vest. He followed Bobby Don and Hutch inside. Horses were whinnying in terror. Flames shot high in the sky from the shavings bin on the east end—and I was stopped in my tracks by the intense heat of the inferno. My forearms raised to shield my eyes. I lost sight of my partner and the other men, but I could hear them unlatching gates and shooing horses. Acrid smoke filled my lungs, and my eyes began burning as uncontrollable tears streaked down my cheeks. I choked and coughed, and jumped to the side of the entrance as a filly and colt, followed by string of loose horses, blasted through the wall of shadows in a stampede of panic.

"Doc…Hutch…Bobby…," I cried out over the clatter of hooves. Roaring rumbles silenced any response. I heard another gate unlatch. "Doc…Bobby Don…" There was no reply. I yelled again and again. "Hutch…Doc…"

Trying to enter the barn, I was forced back by the blackness to join Lady Bug. "Where are they?" she asked, her voice quivering. I did not answer. The tin roof buckled from the heat. There wasn't enough water in Dallas County to dampen the timbers as hot ashes swirled into glowing embers and sparks ignited new sites of combustion. Flames leaped and snapped and crackled. It was futile to dowse the fire. More horses and foals raced from the smoldering barn. "Where are they?" Winds whipped the spiraling chimney of fury.

I could see and hear nothing but the fire, and figured those mares and babies couldn't escape the wrath of the blaze on their own. "They're still cuttin' 'em loose," I said. "They must be okay. Lookie yonder." Two figures were moving to safety through the darkness of the smothering air. "It's Bobby Don and Hutch!"

Lady Bug's arms flew open. She didn't mind that both of her kin were covered with smoking smut. Bobby Don's shirt had holes burned through on his shoulders and back, and Hutch's hat brim was covered with flickering-red shavings. Her arms closed around their necks, and her lips made white smudges on Bobby Don's soot-laden face. I swatted at the singeing coals and listened for more thunderous hooves or a whisper of Dr. Vest's well-being.

"Where's Rich?" I asked.

"I saw him last," Hutch puffed, "…in the stall of Port Chevis."

"She was down on the ground," Bobby Don started to explain. "…then, the smoke…" He paused. His eyes looked away. Port Chevis was his wife's favorite mare. "And, then…the flames. Dr. Vest was trying to…" Bobby Don looked back into Lady Bug's eyes.

Dr. Vest was still missing. Another loud roar of flames erupted as the barn timbers teetered. How could anyone be alive in there, I thought. We shielded our eyes in search of life. "Port!" Tracy suddenly hollered, as I turned to see the bay mare galloping free.

Then I gasped as my eyes gazed at a figure coming through the fog of tumbling black smoke. "Rich!"

My partner looked like a ghost emerging from a grave. "Where in tha' hell have you been?" I screeched. Behind him was a falling wall of fire. Dr. Vest was standing with a dazed, still-wet newborn cradled in his arms, against his chest. "Doc," I said, "you had us plum scared sick. What in the world have you been doin'?"

"I've been birthin' babies," he replied with a soot-eatin' grin. He dropped to his knees, wheezing, and laid the baby filly on her side. His hair was charred, and his pant-legs were seared. "Hey, Doc…," he huffed, "these breedin' seasons are gettin' tougher and tougher."

"Yeah, but who is your friend?" I asked, as Port Chevis neighed and the foal began straddling to her feet.

With the help of Hutch and me, Dr. Vest stood erect, coughing, and pointing over his shoulder with his thumb. I protected my face from the scorching heat, trying to imagine what had happened. "Port was in labor," Dr. Vest said, in a strained voice. "I couldn't leave her." Again, he knelt. "Then, the smoke." He paused, in the same silent way that Bobby Don had. "And then…the flames." Gasping and coughing harshly now, his spit was black. "Doc", he said, drawing a circle in the dirt with his finger, "…the fire…somehow…went around us."

"Around her stall?" Bobby Don asked.

Over the roar of the dying fire, he struggled to talk, "Don't

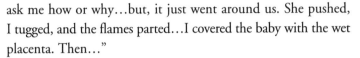
ask me how or why…but, it just went around us. She pushed, I tugged, and the flames parted…I covered the baby with the wet placenta. Then…"

"Don't try to explain," Tracy intervened. "Your throat is raw, and Port Chevis and her baby are fine."

The antique *carretas* lay crumbled in a heap of ashes next to the charred rock foundation of the archway. It was hard to realize that this sixty-year-old barn could be reduced to rubble in a few minutes. Yet behind the black walls was a new beginning. "At least none of the horses were hurt. And weren't nothin' in there that can't be replaced…bigger and better," Bobby Don said. His spirit was dampened, but not snuffed. He's a true Texan, I thought.

Port Chevis neighed while her cute foal nursed for the first time, and nickered.

I caught a hint of a grin on Hutch's mouth as Lady Bug, wagging her finger, reached to hug her son's tree-trunk neck. "You best go wash that dirty smut off your face and behind your ears…both 'em," she whispered. "Bobby Don…go gather them mares. Doc, I reckon I'll be helpin' ya check those last few."

"But, Ma…," Hutch argued.

"Don't be sassin' your mama, boy," Bobby Don said.

"Yes, ma'am," I answered for him. "Myna, Tracy…and Superman, let's get back to what we were doin'." Dr. Vest made a face, objecting to his nickname. "No horses were injured and nobody was killed. Bobby Don and Lady Bug don't see any reason to stop breeding mares. C'mon. It's gettin' dark. Tracy…you hold the tails. Myna, you go help Dr. Vest collect that stallion over there."

Picking up a stick, Bobby Don said, "Doc, I think I'll put the shavings bin…a'way over there." He knelt to draw a 'brown-print' of the new barn in the dirt. "I'll be finished in no time at all." I had no doubt. He drew the Chigger brand where the tin roof would be. "I'll betcha I can find another *carretas*, too…to put by the entrance." I had no doubt. Then he pointed to Port's filly. "Doc, she's a beauty…and some sort of miracle, don'tcha think?" I had not one single doubt.

Three hours later, with the smell from the fire still lingering in the cab of Ol' Blue, I wheeled by our Equi-Tex facility so my tireless technician could find her way home. It was eight o'clock, and dark as pitch. We'd had an eventful day. Tracy's car was parked out back. As the passenger door opened and closed, and the dome light flashed on and off, my tired mind wandered over our years of driving back and forth from the cement towers of the Dallas/Fort Worth metroplex to the vast open ranges. Now feeling equally at home tending a sick cow in a dusty corral or clipping a hamster's toenails in our clinic's polished exam rooms, I couldn't help but reflect on the unusual events that filled my life and work—bringing me to this moment in time.

Spurs and Dominos

ot a summer went by during school when I wasn't working on the family's ranch in Dickens, learning to mend fences and brand steers…only fitting for a wanna-be cowboy, and future animal doctor. Preferring to work part-time for the local vet, rather than doing homework, it was a proud moment when I earned the title of "Head Kennel Boy."

Academics seemed a necessary evil, but after a rollercoaster of ups and downs, I managed to get into Texas A&M. Real luck there meant landing a job at its veterinary school, where I could attend classes during the day—while cleaning cages and sweeping kennel floors at night.

During an unforgettable, undergraduate course in Animal Science, instructor Rodney Putts shared a sobering reality, "I know that most of you are pre-vet majors. This classroom holds three hundred students. I teach six classes. Therefore, only thirty out of eighteen hundred of you will ever submit an application." My feet turned to ice. Dr. Putts continued. "Each year the veterinary school receives 600 or more applications for acceptance into the professional curriculum. Only 128 per year are selected." I didn't have a chance in hell, but listened anyway. "This is the only college in Texas with a veterinary school. And Texans are rarely accepted to out-of-state schools." Then, he paused and grinned, "So, let's cull the herd."

He just said the magic words. Dang, I was a Texan! I was in my rightful place. I determined then and there to study my butt off. My grandpa's simple, but sage, words always haunted me in times like this, "Do what has'ta be done." And my great grandpa, Jon Embry, MD, had practiced medicine with a six-gun strapped to his hip. If he got through his experience…I could get through mine.

My first set of exam grades were dismal. "Shouldn't you consider changing your major?" constantly asked the scholastic advisor. Apparently, an ability with the lariat to rope petals from a sunflower stem at twenty paces meant nothing here at school. Heartbroken, I tightened my belt and plowed ahead. Five years later, my application was submitted to veterinary college. Believing I had beaten the odds, I surely had a whole lot more than the necessary requirements—including practical experience, good grades, excellent reference letters, two bachelor degrees and post-graduate teaching credentials.

But the odds still weren't in my favor; the long-awaited acceptance letter began, "Dear Sir, we regret to inform you that your qualifications at this time do not allow us…" This was devastating news. Now, yet another year would pass.

Completing a master's degree in Parasitology during that next year, I again waited news by working as an associate lab instructor teaching Veterinary Entomology. This time, the letter from the Dean of the College of Veterinary Medicine began, "Congratulations!…" At this point, I figured they admitted me because everyone else either died, quit, changed their majors, or went to medical school. But…that was no matter. Now there were some fun times, too.

* * * * *

I was enthralled when Mac, an ostrich with a broken leg, was shipped to us from the Waco zoo. We had the right specialists at the university. I had never seen this type of huge bird before, and I wanted to play a part. Our surgeons repaired the fracture with some anesthesia and fancy bone-plating techniques. They put screws in the brittle bone matrix, even though the shaft was splintered. But the disproportionate body weight of the patient was a problem, and the results would be questionable. Yet the seven-foot avian awoke from surgery with flying colors, and was moved to a horse stall for his rehabilitation. Eddie Walker, a tall, lanky student known as the "Domino Kid," and I were assigned to shifts, both responsible for the recovery of the remarkable black and white bird.

Eddie and I usually argued about everything, but never when it came to our patients. His occasional gambling in domino parlors paid for his schooling, wild sunglasses, and alligator shoes. With his slick sprayed hair, he looked more the part of a con-artist than an animal doctor.

We called the lame fowl "Spurs," and his six-inch-long, razor-sharp thumb claws quickly gained our respect. Mac had incredible speed and power. Dr. Mitner, the zoo vet, had offered just two warnings: "Boys, them spurs are deadly" and "He'll gitcha." Seein' the still-raw, giant scar down his forearm from one of Mac's glancing pot-shots, left no doubt that the man spoke from experience. We, too, soon learned that extreme accuracy and greased-lightning strikes were Mac's claim to fame. When he struck the wall with his good leg, chunks of the stall's cement cinder-block flew out. Mac was mending nicely though, until one of his blows with the bad leg shattered the surgeon's dreams. Sadly crippled, Mac had to be euthanized.

More of my gramp's words came to mind, "It's whatcha make of it that counts." Normally, necropsy was a dreaded assignment, but Eddie and I decided to keep the ostrich hide for ourselves. Due to public health implications, all tissue samples taken from parts of any carcass had to be properly discarded. Lamely trying to find a loophole in this policy, we took the position that we weren't the "public"—we were "students."

Our classmates circled around us while we worked, so Eddie had to wait for just the right moment to slip the hide under his over-sized lab coat. We met later in the lab to finish processing Mac's "educational endowment." Plucking feathers from such an enormous carcass wasn't easy. My fingers bled with each tug, and I kept looking over my shoulders for any students who might be watching. I finally gave Eddie the all clear signal. "Let's put Mac's hide in the washing machine," he suggested. "It'll soften it."

I balked. "No, he might shrink!" Tanning companies had already given us information on how to scrape the fat from the skin and salt the hide. They'd given us proper storage temperatures, but didn't explain the special technique needed to prepare the paper-thin dermis. Again Eddie and I argued. "No," I repeated, "They told us to handle the skin with care."

"We'll use the gentle cycle," my partner-in-crime replied. The whole saga had become much more complicated than I expected. I couldn't afford gas for my car, yet Eddie was planning to buy Mac a round-trip plane ticket to the chosen tanning company in California. "Relax," he coaxed. "Don't worry, I've got everything under control, and I'll get the money the way I usually do."

But just three days after Eddie assured me we couldn't get caught, Dean Evans summoned us into his office. "We're trapped," I whispered, closing the door behind us. The Dean was fuming! He stood up from behind the fortress of his desk, and his silver hairpiece seemed to stand on end. Folding his stout arms across his chest, as if bracing himself for what was to follow, he began. "The Parks and Wildlife Commissioner in California just called." His voice grew louder and more agitated, "Several Interstate Commerce violations regarding a shipment of endangered species were mentioned—along with *your* names!" I cringed and prepared myself for the worst. His face now turning an alarming red, the Dean shouted, "Well?…Well?…what do you have to say?"

Eddie wasn't rattled at all, and calmly said, "But, Dean, didn't he also thank you for all our care and concern? David and I were simply trying to make a donation to prosperity. We wanted Mac's life to mean something."

I couldn't believe he just said that. Dean Evans sighed deeply. "What?" Nervously combing his fingers through his fake locks, he seemed to have a hard time continuing. "Graduation is only a few months away, ya hear? Now, git...git out of my office!"

We fled as the door latch clicked behind us. This was not the time or place to debate. Both of us groaned, "Damn, that was close." My classmate and I finally agreed on one thing—we swore never to ask how the Commissioner's inquiries were answered. And when Mac's treated hide arrived by Special Delivery six weeks before graduation, we had to come up with a new plan of action—and quickly.

So it was that in August of 1976, Eddie and I proudly claimed our diplomas—wearing brand-new boots, virgin ostrich-skin boots. And after receiving our precious, scrolled parchments from Dean Evans, we handed him a special gift, too—a handsome, ostrich-skin wallet. He simply shook his head while he watched us leave, "Good luck, boys, you're really goin' to need it."

As for Eddie, he parlayed his skills into the opening of sixteen successful domino parlors—managing to specialize in avian medicine on the side—while I hung my degree on the wall and began an internship.

A Ranch Like No Other

igning up to accompany a vet from the U.S. Department of Agriculture, Dr. Zak Farr, I would take off for a special assignment to Kingsville—and the Diamond Ranch. It was under quarantine for Cattle Fever ticks; and I had the honor of being "Head Tick-Picker," responsible for wiping out the disease-vectoring insects. This summer trip would be just the vacation break needed before beginning my pre-arranged practice.

My holiday attitude didn't last long—especially after we were greeted by three armed sombrero-covered guards, *pistoleros* not big on conversation. Our guide would be the ranch's distinguished looking Mexican foreman, Rowdy Mendosa. In fluent English, he said, "You're right on time. Mr. Clay is waiting at the ranch house." Then climbing into our vehicle and pointing his rifle barrel down the asphalt road, he demanded, "Go straight."

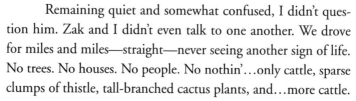
Remaining quiet and somewhat confused, I didn't question him. Zak and I didn't even talk to one another. We drove for miles and miles—straight—never seeing another sign of life. No trees. No houses. No people. No nothin'...only cattle, sparse clumps of thistle, tall-branched cactus plants, and...more cattle.

Approaching an enormous ranchero oasis—a fortress with high brick walls and arching roof tiles—we could make out a few sharp-shooters on the iron-grilled balconies. Sculpted, terra cotta fountains were surrounded by lush, manicured lawns and gardens. It was on the estate's tiled, vaulted verandah that the surprisingly boyish owner, Richard Clay, received us.

Though not a tall man, Clay's erect carriage and no-nonsense manner made him seem larger than life. He confirmed the reason for our visit with a few introductory handshakes, and went on to express his dissatisfaction with the U.S. government. Then uttering something in Portuguese to a young girl, one of several servants who quietly moved about, he asked, "Wine, gentlemen?" A gracious gesture, but it didn't seem like the time or place—and we declined in unison.

"Señor Rowdy is the head of the southern sector of our Texas-based operation. He will be with you at all times. Please follow his instructions *to the letter,* and we will have no problems." His words were precise, well-chosen, definite. We did not interrupt. "He will provide you with a brief history and orientation to the Diamond Ranch." With that, Richard Clay walked, godlike, into the grand house, never to be seen by us again.

Rowdy, who seemed like he could be an amiable sort under different circumstances, led us to the library with its large wall map resembling the kind used for battle maneuvers. Without expression, he began, "Gentlemen, the Diamond Ranch is the largest single family-owned ranch in the world. For five generations the ranch has consisted of seven divisions. You are in the central sector of the Texas branch. Other extensions are located in Brazil, Argentina, Australia, Africa, Wyoming and Mexico. The home division is bordered by Texas, the United States, the Gulf of Mexico and the Rio Grande." There are a hundred and fifty square miles of brush, scorpions, and night-hawkin' wild boars here. And it is estimated that this home division has 15,000 miles of paved roads, plus many unmarked paths. *Federales* have been known to get confused and become lost; some have even disappeared." Now he had my full attention. "We have our own schools, churches, and fire departments. The original *padron* persuaded an entire Mexican village to come here to *Tejas*, defying Santa Ana's orders. So our families are actually third and fourth-generation descendants. Some of the elders have never been off the ranch."

Like a general addressing his troops, Rowdy spoke firmly, seemingly accustomed to the role. "Locations on the map are determined by the numbers on the windmills. A few areas are only accessible by helicopter. Sector entrances are guarded by our workers—and they are armed. Do not question their authority. And remember that your federal identification cards are worthless here." My mind started to play tricks on me as I envisioned the two of us surrounded by 5,000 Mexican soldiers on over a million acres of desert—with no chance of escape. "On occasion, bands of raiding *banditos* from Mexico try to rustle our cattle. But we have our own laws." He cocked his rifle, and a shell casing ejected on the floor. The only other time I'd seen this overly affected gesture was in a western movie. "You will be protected. You will carry only medical supplies, no weapons. Our days will begin and end at dark. And your accommodations will be provided in town. Theo Kirby is the division leader and will meet us and the other sector bosses at Mario's Café in the morning—at 4 A.M. Welcome to the Diamond Ranch."

He then left the room. I had a thousand and one questions, but my lips wouldn't move. A petite Hispanic maid broke the silence. "You have heard of the Governor of Texas, no?" Scents from her overly sweet perfume made me even more light-headed. "He is only the second-most important man. You've just met the *most* powerful...Señor Clay. So, y'all mind your manners, si?"

"Yes, Ma'am," we murmured, "si."

* * * * *

More than a dozen of the wranglers' trucks, emblazoned with the ranch brand, were neatly parked outside of Mario's Café. Inside, at least twenty disgruntled, leathery-looking men wearing sweat-stained cowboy hats sat around the tables. The aroma of tamales this early in the morning did nothing to help my mood. Rifles hung on gun racks, boot-heels displayed spur rowels, and chap-covered legs straddled the heavily-scarred oak chairs. Glaring stares greeted our entrance. I wasn't sure any of these boys spoke English—and didn't want to ask. Clay's cowboys were definitely not thrilled with our presence.

Summoning up a professional air and whatever courage I could muster, I explained our necessary mission and the terms of the quarantine. "Each sector will be diagnosed as 'free from infestation' for the Cattle Fever ticks before any purebreds are allowed to move into different sections of the ranch. No cattle will leave the ranch until they are also confirmed 'free' of

Piroplasmosis infection, *Babesia bigemina* or *B. caballi,* by the federally appointed veterinarian."

Spurs jingled and knuckles popped, but the cowboys' demeanor never changed. With deadpan faces, they then listened to the voice of experience, the respected Zak Farr, and his proposed plan of attack. "We'll begin on the northern border and work our way south. Federal trappers will catch wildlife and collect samples of ticks for identification, while we concentrate on the herds."

Grumbling started to fill the room, and I felt a wave of anxiety. Suddenly, without getting up from his chair, Theo barked, "Now y'all listen up!" All the restless brims seemed to snap to attention at once.

"Each sector will be divided into four pods," Zak continued. "Each pod will be stocked with Shorthorn steers destined for slaughter. Five thousand head of government-issued mixbreds will be here shortly. They will be used as 'vacuum-cleaners' for the ticks, since aerial spray methods can't penetrate the dense brush. Herds will be dipped and examined weekly. After two consecutive 'tick-free and disease-free' examinations, the steers and quarantine lines can move down. Any questions?"

Theo, tall and imposing, finally took the floor. "Dipping vats will be built, corrals disinfected and inspected, cattle assigned and delivered, and other operations delegated in addition to your regular chores. Grumbling started again. "Or, face Mr. Clay." The grumbling stopped. He called out to each man, "Casey, Buck, R.J., Rio..." One by one, they nodded as their individual duties were announced.

The sight burned in my memory—triple-stacked livestock trailers stretching down the road for miles. Every single humid day, thereafter, in the early dawn—for weeks—a hundred or more

Tex-Mex cowboys drove thunderous herds of cattle over a horizon of brambly briars. "WHOOP! YEEHAA! WHOOP!" was all we heard. Day in and day out, it was always the same. Dipping vats splashed, branding irons seared, steers bellowed, and lariats flew. Whiffs of freshly boiled coffee barely covered the smells of burning bovine hair and manure-soaked sands. We worked well into the coolness of the nights—and spent countless hours glued to microscopes, sifting through thousands upon thousands of ticks. Our red-lined eyes were no longer helped by optic drops, but we continued non-stop in our strategic planning for the next five months of quarantine rituals. Slowly, slowly, the restrictions dropped—and I finally caught a glimpse of a smile on the ever-serious Rowdy. At this point, I could identify a species of tick from fifty yards, and Zak could probably draw blood from a yucca plant blindfolded. The last few steers were gathered and released in the dusk of the most beautiful sunset I'd ever seen—the one in our rear-view mirror.

Yelling, "YAHOO!" the businesslike Zak, uncharacteristically and boisterously waved his hat out the window, and the now-grinning Rowdy closed the main gates of the Diamond Ranch behind us. "Where will you go next?" I asked.

"Home, for awhile," Zak said in relief. "And, you?"

"To a pup and kitten practice...in the city. I've seen my last steer and wiped the last chunk of dung from these boots." Sitting up straight, I took to bragging. "Yep, everything I see from now on will be housebroke and on a leash. You'll see, I ain't never gonna have another speck of dirt under these nails."

My summer mentor just laughed and shook his head in disbelief, apparently in-the-know about what was ahead for this fresh kid.

4

Professional Kennel Boy

O n a Monday morning, two hours early—and nervous—I reported to the Squaw Valley Veterinary Hospital just outside the city, in Richardson. Having moved to Dallas with everything I owned crammed into a rented mobile home, I was ready to be a 'doctor'. My uniform was neatly pressed; my shiny new stethoscope freshly unpacked from the box; and my car was loaded with reference books.

The Texas State Board of Examiners had issued my medical license, but I quickly found out that having permission to practice and practicing were two different things.

A knock on the car window startled me. It was followed by a panic-filled voice that shouted, "Are you a doctor?" All I could answer was "Huh?" She screamed again, "Are you a doctor?"

My heart pounded. "Yeah, what's wrong?"

"It's Jamaica!" the lady cried. "He's dyin'! He's havin' a

seizure or somethin'. He's cryin' and floppin' all over the place. I can't stand it!"

Face to face with Dorothy McCabe and her tiny red Pomeranian…my mind went blank. Seizures? What causes seizures? Stress, stroke, encephalomyelitis, hypoglycemia, poisonous plants and insecticides? How do I treat them? Is it epilepsy? An allergic reaction? Dorothy's wide shadow blocked the dimly lit entrance to the clinic, where she cradled her dog in a white blanket. The staff hadn't arrived, so I hastily fumbled with keys sent me earlier, opened the side door, and led her to the nearest exam room. "Now, calm down—and just bring him in here."

As the lights flicked on, Mrs. McCabe stood before me in purple knee socks, and a long green nightgown that had been quickly covered by a black rain coat. I had no idea she was a prominent socialite – or my new boss' favorite client. Small juice-can-like hair curlers dangled about her neck, and facial cream smudges still streaked her eyelids. Jamaica's small head popped out from the blanket. His eyes were alert, and he began barking with glee. "Oh…what's the problem, little fella?" I crooned.

This whole situation caught me by surprise. I was expecting to see a frail canine, traumatized by convulsions—but here were sparkling eyes and playful wiggles. "Ma'am, can I see your dog?"

Reluctant to set him down, Mrs. McCabe's clutch tightened when the pup struggled for more attention. "He looks fine now, but just you wait." Jamaica squirmed and yapped like a normal dog as his owner knelt to the floor and gently unwrapped the fluffy pooch.

Suddenly, Jamaica's combed tail sagged—and the red ball of fluff yelped. He flipped on his right side and thrashed violently. My adrenaline soared and I jumped to his rescue. Then, immediately, he stopped jerking.

"Wait a minute," I said, "…that's not a seizure." Under the owner's watchful eyes, I went through this routine three times. In my arms, Jamaica didn't jerk—but on the floor, he yelped in distress. "Are you sure you're a doctor?" Dorothy whined. "The older vet wouldn't do this. What's wrong with my baby…is he goin' to die?"

"No, no, he's fine," I assured her. But her brightly manicured nails clutched the table. "Fine? How could he be fine?" she choked. "Do you know what you're doin'?"

I reached down deep into Jamaica's thick mane and untangled his right front paw from beneath a thin, blue-sequined collar. After placing him on the floor again, he circled and pranced with excitement—no longer yelping or stumbling. And with a snappy burst, his tail curled over his back.

"There now, that's better," I said. "He just had his arm in a sling. See…he's fine."

Dorothy blushed, was quiet for a moment, then began straightening her curlers. "I must look a mess." Her voice turned to an embarrassed whisper, "Doc, I'm really not crazy."

"No, ma'am. I'm just glad it wasn't anything worse."

Just then, with a slam of the back door, Dr. Morton Stein arrived. I'd heard he was a giant of a man, and it was not an exaggeration. His husky, six-and-a half-foot frame took over the room. He was also known to be gruff—but I thought I'd prepared myself.

Jamaica fit easily in the palm of Doc's large, cupped hand. "Pup, did he fix ya?"

"No, sir, I mean—yes, sir," I answered.

"Still wet behind the ears, ain'tcha son?"

Dorothy winked at both of us, "Oh...Mort, he's fine."

When Dorothy and Jamaica left, Doc introduced me to his five-member staff as the "new doctor," but left no time for small talk. "Hell, people," he shouted, "we've got pets to see." As his crew scattered to their stations, he began complaining about them all. He said he'd been practicing for thirty years...and, to me, that seemed an eternity. On this Monday morning, he continued to rant. "Goddammit! Get to work, folks!" Again, my heart pounded—but Doc put his hand on my shoulder. And with a look of utmost respect, said, "Here, son, come with me."

I imagined he wanted to get my professional opinion on a difficult case. After going over the workings of his organization, and giving me a tour of the large, wood-paneled clinic, he finally stopped at a door marked with a large K. Then, rather offhandedly, he said, "The regular kennel boy will not be returning to work." So here I was again...baths, dips, cage cleanings, and floor moppings seemed to be my only future. Thirty barking, howling dogs and a dozen short-tempered cats were to be part of my first caseload.

Weeks passed. I slipped into my routine. But at the end of every day, after walking the dogs one by one, I went up front to the main clinic just to see what it would feel like. A day came when Doc, running behind schedule, asked if I'd help him with the next ovarian hysterectomy. I jumped at the chance to do my first 'spay' as a full-fledged doctor. He nodded his approval as I tied the last skin suture in record time. "How was that?" I asked.

"Not too bad," he grumbled. "Y'know, I need a day off. Brenda, my wife, has been wantin' to take me to the Orient."

That would take longer than a day, I thought, trying to conceal my enthusiasm for practicing solo.

A new kennel boy was hired. After learning the front desk protocol, and arranging the pharmacy to my liking, Doc left for a month. The staff and I worked well together, operating the clinic as smoothly as ever. On his return, Doc was elated at what was accomplished in his absence…but had one small change. I was back in the kennels again…but not for long.

In spite of a ragged beginning, Doc and I managed to develop a good working partnership. My time with him was probably the best learning experience a young vet could have. But after a year, I decided to leave and start building my own place—Twin Oaks Veterinary Hospital. Little did I know, then, that Twin Oaks would be just the first of five clinics.

Doc offered me a bit of parting advice, which I've never forgotten. "It doesn't take much to be a veterinarian. But it requires a lot of experience to be a 'good doctor'."

It would be years before I really knew what he meant. Only after unexpected lessons seldom given in veterinary school—in my least favorite areas of accounting, architectural design, advertising, funding, environmental laws, business taxes, personnel management, computer science, insurance, inventory control, equipment procurement, and corporate contracts—would I begin to understand.

Doc Stein was right. I'd come full circle—and earned the highest rank of any veterinarian, "Head Kennel Boy of My Own Place." With a certain satisfaction, I look forward to knowing that a walk through the kennel wards will always be the first and last thing I do each day.

Birth of a Clinic

I n the middle of the brick-lined, sleepy little town of
Carrolton, we were in a building frenzy. My new clinic
bustled, not with clients or patients, but construction
workers, broken pipes, and on-again-off-again electric-
ity. Like most folks in small towns, our neighbors at historic
Perry's Hardware and the old cream-soda fountain behind Mr.
Blanton's drugstore liked passing the time of day by watching the
hectic goings-on.

It was a madhouse. Fluorescent bulbs in the surgery room
kept flashing on and off. My feet seemed perpetually tangled in
extension cords. And sawdust hovered over everything in a low-
slung fog. Freshly glued Formica countertops buckled, and hinges
pulled away from exam room doors.

From cardboard crates, I began assembling a career. Boxes
of medical supplies were stacked in every corner, and equipment
remained in plastic wrappers. I wanted everything done perfectly,

down to the stenciled information on the front glass window. But the letterman had misspelled 'hours' and we ended up with 'HORS'.

This solo adventure could not have taken off without Karen Anne, my new bride. While I grumbled, looking for vaccines, she was scrubbing down all the shelves. In sawdust-smudged work clothes, her long brunet hair falling from a clip behind her baseball cap, she still looked as pretty as when we met years earlier. When she stretched up the steps of our work ladder in her Wrangler jeans, I remembered first seeing her shapely legs reaching for the stirrups of a saddle. A fifth-generation Texan raised on cornbread and catfish, this wife of mine was as tough as she was soft. At home anywhere, she could sip tea at a social or cuss a workman in Tex-Mex. That's what I liked.

"Will we ever get this clinic in order?" she asked.

The carpenter hollered, "Hey, Doc, how high do ya want these cabinets in radiology?"

I'd given him a set of blueprints drawn on my kitchen table. "Right there," I said, pointing to the height mark on the wall, "…just like the plans say."

"What plans?"

It didn't matter who the workmen were or what they were doing. They all had the same response, "What plans?"

We'd been at this for months. Window widths, floor drains, dryer vents, colors, ceiling height—every possible question came up, even down to a debate on the length of yellow stripes in the parking lot.

Karen just about lost all patience, "Did you know the bathroom wallpaper is peeling—and the sink is backed up?" She tried flushing the toilet, and screamed as water came gushing from under the floorboards. A roll of new office carpeting in the hall-way quickly diverted the water flow as hundreds of tiny, Styrofoam packing noodles floated into the reception area. "Hank!" Karen yelled to our foreman, as she stood there with water spewing around her ankles. The happy-go-lucky Hank, who thrived on chaos, just hollered back, "I'm acomin', Mrs. Doc."

Even Karen's feisty mom, Juanita, always there to help us out, decided to join the madness. "The air conditioner won't work, darlin', I quit!"

The lights went out again, and it was just 9 A.M. "Lunch time," crowed the painters. "We cain't paint in the dark."

Hank took charge, amiably restoring order. "Nobody can quit. Hell, y'all ain't done nothin', yet."

"Darlin', I can't see your face in front of my hand," Juanita said, as she tripped over a box of medicines—shattering bottles. That was the last straw. We both sat on the floor, laughing. And just as I began wondering if this would ever work out, the front door opened.

"Are y'all open?" asked a small, slender lady.

"Why sure we are, cutie," Hank's scruffy voice echoed from under the porcelain sink.

I sloshed to the front desk, forcing my best smile, "Yes, ma'am, can I help ya?"

The sweet woman grinned, "I'm Mrs. Honeycutt. Are you *sure* you're open?"

Karen and her mother ducked into another room, as the well-dressed woman lugged her huge, black alley cat into the exam room. Bruiser, a well-endowed tom with battle scars on his thick jowls, pinned his ears back and fully extended his claws. "Doc,

I think I should have him neutered and declawed." Bruiser hissed and spit.

"He'll need his shots—for distemper, feline leukemia, and rabies…especially rabies," I said. A sudden paw swipe from the unhappy patient went scraping down the back of my hand, and after another determined swat and growl, blood trickled from my wrist. "A friendly little cuss, ain't he?"

Like a short-order waiter, I repeated, "Let's see, now, that'll be rabies, neuter and a declaw."

"No, no…just the rabies shot for now," said Mrs. Honeycutt, apparently changing her mind about leaving the ill-tempered feline overnight in our clinic's confusion. Unable to help himself, Hank's voice again cut through the noise with a crude remark, then he added, "Doc…and scratch the claws," while his crew laughed with him.

At the moment I gave the muscular tomcat his injection, sirens blasted and lights flashed. Bruiser freaked, and was about to tear through the walls if Mrs. Honeycutt and I didn't use our combined strength—and will—to hold him steady.

"The security systems are working now, Doc," Hank hollered. "Now, missy, y'all come back now, ya hear?" He waved to Bruiser's owner with a grease-covered palm, as I handed her a vaccination tag and asked if there was anything else I could do.

"Why, yes," she said as she turned to walk out the door. "You can send the bill to my ex-husband."

"No problem," Hank said, "We'll be glad to," and the door closed behind my very first client.

As I stood there, dumbfounded, with no payment, Karen said, "Don't worry, honey, someday you'll have a real hospital and a real staff. Until then, my mother can work the front desk and charge clients as they leave."

"Over his dead body," Juanita chimed in. "But I do know two girls who need jobs—and one of 'em is even a registered veterinary technician."

I cringed, trying to ignore her suggestion. These were things I never wanted to mess with; doctoring animals was all I wanted to do. Firing my favorite person, Juanita, wouldn't be a problem, but hiring the right staff would be—and I should do that myself.

When the phone rang, Hank bellowed, "Hey, Doc...the phones work now, too."

"Su-ugar, it's someone from Mr. Hall's stable," cooed my irreplaceable mother-in-law.

6

A.J. and Big Bertha

J. Hall's place was just up the road; a 'ranch' of sixty flimsy plywood stalls seemingly painted over and over again in any and every color. I already knew it and him well, having been there with Doc Stein. Fees for boarding horses were quickly traded for cases of beer or bottles of whiskey, with empties used as reflectors for his fences—the old-timer's personal contribution to recycling.

Border to border, Texas can boast more quarrelsome characters than any other state. And A.J. topped the list. Bragging that his barn was the only stable in town that did everything right, the stubby-bearded horse trader would tell you straight out, "Ain't no place finer." In his crushed straw hat, smiling his snaggle-toothed smile, A.J. never tired of telling folks that he had birthed more, bred more, ridden more, treated more, traded and raced more horses than anyone else.

As I pulled up next to his homemade horse trailer that tilted on two flat tires, a woman introducing herself as Lila greeted me. Worried that her gelding was lame, she led me down the maze of cluttered aisles to Champ's stall—and a look at the chestnut's left foreleg did indeed show a bowed tendon. Strange grunts and snorts interrupted my exam, as Bertha, A.J.'s mammoth pet sow, began loudly rooting under the slats. Never far behind his 300-pound pig, A.J. leaned over the stall listening to our conversation. With these two, it was always hard to tell who was grunting or snorting the loudest.

As usual, A.J. criticized my diagnosis and medications I planned to use. Elaborating to Lila on his vast experience with lame horses, he turned to his own nag, Lucky Lady, "When ol' Lucky here had that tendon problem, I treated 'er different than Doc. I dun' 'er better…not thataway…used that pink stuff myself. But then…we missed runnin' the Derby that day. Ah, hell, the Derby ain't everythin', you know? My mare's still the fastest horse in the county…mite older now, but still the fastest. Yep, runs like the wind. By the way, Doc, I wantcha to look at Bold Warrior's feet when y'all gets done…can you do it today?" I could swear this old fella never took a breath.

Champ jumped sideways as Bertha snorted again. "Whoa, son," I crooned, continuing to wrap the leg with a soothing poultice. "Now. A.J.…would you take the pig away? I'll look at Bold's loose shoe in a minute."

"Leave? Don'tcha wanta see the pictures of Bertha's last litter of piglets? Had 'em on the back porch…all by herself." Then, with Lucky and Bertha snug beside him, A.J. shuffled out through the weeds, mumbling to himself, "Ya know, even ol' Doc Stein don't do 'em thataway, neither. He uses my pink stuff."

I laughed as Lila Jasper whispered, "That pig bothers me, too, Doc. The three of them—it's like watchin' the three stooges. A.J. knows everything about everything – just ask 'im. In fact, he asked me not to call a vet."

I doubted if A.J.'s horse, Bold Warrior, ever lived up to his name. The old dapple-grey must have been bought at a "clarance sale." I'd handled him before, when Doc Stein was out of town. Knotted in burrs, his mane and coat dull and shaggy, Bold stood untied in a small paddock put together with fencing made of rotted tree limbs woven between rusted cable. Any holes were plugged with worn rubber tires.

When I flipped the gate latch to announce my presence, Bold remained anchored, intent on staring at a couple of horses tree-tied about twenty yards away. "Whoa, now…hey, son, turn around here. Bold?" Normally he would turn to face me, gentle-broke that he was. But he seemed defiant. I repeated myself again and again, then softly stroked his coat and eased forward along his shoulder to place the halter around his neck. "C'mon, now." I thought, one gentle tug on the lead rope and he'd move away from the fence. Then, another tug.

Bold planted his hooves. I'd seen that look in a stallion's eyes before. There had to be a mare in heat close by…but, regrettably, this occurred to me a second too late. Rearing and spinning, Bold's body flexed and went one way, while mine went the other. I yelled, seeing nothing but hooves and dirt—then everything blurred.

After being out for a second, I awoke to a throbbing ache in my head, and a searing pain running through my shoulder.

Stumbling to my feet, I scrambled toward the gate but fell over again. A.J. came running. "Doc, what tha hell happened?"

Cussing, "Your damn stud nailed me!" I felt an oozing down my neck...then more shooting pains.

"My horse? Bold Warrior did...that? Naw, couldn't uv."

Angry, but too dizzy to stand, I managed to grab my jacket and put pressure on the lacerations, since my face, hands and clothes were covered with blood. I winced and looked for Bold Warrior, who stood calmly poised by the back fence as if all was well. The type of pain in my shoulder convinced me that this had to be a fracture. Helping me to my feet, A.J. reached for a blood spattered horseshoe on top of the fence rail. "Look, Doc," he smiled, "Thanks...at least ya got his shoe off."

Telling him that Bold must have hooked it off the fence himself when he turned to trounce me, A.J. grinned his toothless grin. "Does that mean you're not gonna charge me for his shoe removal? C'mon, I'll getcha to the hospital."

As soon as they sewed me up and set my broken arm, I went back to the clinic. The diminutive Juanita stretched on her tiptoes to see my sutures, and couldn't resist jibing, "Honey, the doctor could sew and sew and never fix what's inside your noggin'." I pretended to fire her again, and she happily added, "Thanks, Pum'kin, now let's get to work on finding you some decent help for this place."

The classifieds worked, we thought. Edith was the first to apply and first to be hired, but fainted at the sight of blood —and was gone in a day. Marilyn came next, and seemed perfect in every way; she had worked for a dentist—and didn't faint. Even Karen and Juanita nodded their approval.

The future seemed rosy, and the days began to bounce along in good order, until we noticed Marilyn's 'vision trouble'. Juanita spotted the problem, commenting, "It seems that our new gal can't see workin' on Tuesday, Friday, or Saturday." Marilyn finally quit without notice. After that, receptionists came and went…all pleasant but none with any genuine interest in our problem critters. We couldn't depend on Juanita forever—and the uncertainty was making us all edgy.

A few weeks into our practice—just past midnight—an emergency message came in from A.J.'s place that Champ was ailing again and wouldn't eat. Accustomed to jumping out of bed at any hour, I said I'd be right out. When I got there, the house and barn were dark—and no one seemed to be around. I yelled for A.J., and just heard a faint grunt. Concerned, I began knocking with my fist on the door of the long screened-in back porch, "Mr. Hall? C'mon now, git up!" Then suddenly the most awful snorting and chomping sound echoed through the night. "Oh, hell…Bertha's awake!" Her cloven hooves rumbling down the planks of the porch sounded like a runaway train. "Geeze!" I didn't look back. I'd forgotten that Big Bertha took her 'guard-pig' role very seriously. I could feel her hot breath as her teeth kept gnashing and grinding in hot pursuit. Becoming a super-charged sprinter with a mad sow nipping at my heels, I hurtled myself on the hood of Ol' Blue. "Holy crap!" Then, jumping off, I scrambled up the barn loft. Bertha circled beneath my perch, billowing dust and pawing the ground like an angry bull. "Dang! …shoo, Bertha…shoo. Go away!" But, like an excited coonhound with her prey treed, the hefty porker held her attack-stand at the base of the ladder.

A faint light brought A.J.'s stooped silhouette into view. Laughing and giggling, he cajoled Bertha to calm down. "Come on down, Doc, she won't bother ya…let's go look at Lila's gelding." Using every bit of restraint I could manage, I held my tongue.

Examining Champ, while still keeping an eye on Bertha, I asked A.J. why he called me when the horse wasn't sick. "That's what I told Lila," he said, "…but she insisted he wasn't eatin'."

After inspecting the feed trough and finding every kernel of grain moldy, I finally lost my temper, "Dern, A.J., no wonder, his rations are spoiled!" Fetching fresh oats, the horse trader watched while Champ hungrily gobbled down a scoop of grain. "See, Doc, I told ya he wasn't sick."

"Then why did you call me at one o'clock in the morning? Y'all rolled me out of bed for nothing."

"Yeah, well…no, Doc…it wern't for nothin', at least Bertha got some exercise."

That was it. Getting home at 2:30—totally exasperated— I called Juanita, half blurting, asking her if she could have the two girls she knew be at the clinic first thing in the morning.

Considering the hour, Juanita was calm and not the least surprised. "You won't need my help anymore, Sweetie. Your new receptionist will be Rachel Styles—and the new technician, Tracy Barnes, can join you in a week." In that moment, she did more for me than anyone ever did—before or since. These two, Rachel and Tracy, were to become the indispensable backbone of my animal practice.

City Meets Country

F our hours of sleep, and I felt revitalized and anxious to meet Rachel. In those first few moments after she walked through the door, none of us could speak. Every red hair of her piled-high curls was sprayed in place, and silver-green eye shadow glowed over false eyelashes. In her early twenties, fastidious and fashion conscious, Rachel had previously been a clerk in one of Dallas' high-end boutiques.

This new receptionist was quick to arrange her desk—and just as quick to retrieve a bottle of nail polish from her bag to '…touch up her tips'. Meanwhile, all our phone lines were buzzing. Picking up one line, as she spread her fingers and blew on her nails, Rachel sweetly said, "Sorry, we don't open for another five minutes." I stood frozen in disbelief, counting to myself—watching her watch the clock. Heaven forbid that our clientele might disturb her morning ritual. At this point, I was sure Juanita must be playing a trick on me.

But Rachel was for real, and after chalking off the first few months of her employment as 'getting started', I decided she was a valuable asset. Dependable, direct, fun to talk with, and a whiz at office skills, the only ability missing—the most vital —was a concept of time and distance. Farm calls were scheduled in such a way as to keep me ricocheting across four Texas counties like a jackrabbit dodging buckshot.

Thinking a diplomatic maneuver could solve this dilemma, I posted an enormous map of the Dallas area behind the reception counter. Marking forty-two prominent barn locations with red thumbtacks, I felt sure the strategy would help her in coordinating appointments. Listening from the next office, it was apparent the map plan didn't work. "Yes, sir...he'll be there at 1 P.M. Yes, ma'am...I'll have him there by 1:30." These two house calls were fifty miles apart. This went on for several minutes, with long treatments scheduled for places twenty and thirty miles from one another. After hearing Rachel tell one caller I could have his 84 calves dehorned in fifteen minutes, I realized that she not only needed a better idea of what I do, but she also should come with me, meet the clients she talked to every day, and actually see their farms and stables.

Our 'field trip' started on a balmy spring day; no clouds in the sky, and no blowing winds that could muss Rachel's beehive hairdo. It was time for her to see the real world, and I handed her a pair of blue-drab coveralls. With confidence, the citified young lady announced that the first appointment in her book was with Los Royale Stables.

I turned Ol' Blue south. Our estimated time of arrival was thirty minutes. Rachel was destined to see some startling contrasts among our clientele. On our list of regulars, Los Royale was the most aristocratic. One hundred Thoroughbred horses were cared for on a plantation northwest of Dallas. Jaguars, Mercedes, and chauffeur-driven limousines lined the front of the architecturally designed 'barn' that reflected the city's skyscrapers on its glossy, cathedral-shaped mahogany doors. Crystal chandeliers hung in the lobby of the management offices. Welcome, I thought, to the equine industry.

Decorations for the upcoming international Grand Prix Horse Show gave the covered arena area a festive look. Grooms and trainers scurried about maintaining precise deadlines. This was a fantasy world of opulence that stunned Rachel.

We'd come to perform the last of seven ultrasound treatments on Sneaky Pete, who had strained his ankle. After twelve years as a Hunter-Jumper, the gelding suffered from a lameness common to an over-extension and tearing of the ligaments. Sneaky's left front ankle was swollen and sore, but radiographs showed no evidence of fracture. Signs of calcification indicated a recurring limp. Coolant bandages, non-steroidal anti-inflammatory medications, stall rest, and hand-walking exercise had worked well with the ultrasound treatments. He'd be back in competition in no time at all.

Sneaky didn't have a mean bone in his body. His kind eye and good character matched his handsome dark-bay haircoat. There was no danger in Rachel being here, and the therapy application was painless. She held his lead rope with disinterest, while checking her makeup under the barn lighting in a pocket mirror. Sneaky immediately sensed the presence of an amateur. Playful since a colt, he'd come by his name honestly.

Prolonged confinement of this athlete made Sneaky restless. With pent-up energy, he nuzzled and jostled my hat, then
shuffled his hooves in the shavings—just to stir the dust—as I
ran the flat probe across his afflicted area. He was getting ready
for his move on Rachel. Remodeling her 'Texas big-hair' with one
lip-smackin' bite was just too much to resist. With a quick nibble and yank, the ruckus began. "Hey, you!" Rachel screamed, as
I jumped for safety and Sneaky trotted to the corner, seemingly
happy with himself. He turned to look at Rachel sitting on her
fanny in the middle of the stall. Physically unharmed, but fash-
ionably bruised, she exploded, "He did that on purpose," and
began cussing Sneaky out with words even I'd never heard.

"Oh, he was just funnin' ya," I said. "But, y'know…you
can't be daydreaming in here." I warned. "He's a thousand pounds
of muscle…with a mind of his own."

We continued our rounds through the stable, as Rachel
picked straw from her hair and slivers of wood chips from her
pant-legs. Reading the brass nameplates on each stall, she rattled
off what she remembered about each, "Fly Boy…his owner owes
us money. Foxy Lady…that owner is very demanding on the
phone. And, Cookie Dough…that owner is a real gent."

"Where to next, Rachel?" Proudly referring to her
appointment book, she said, "Dripping Creek Farm…isn't that
Jake's place?"

I turned my rig to the northeast, crossing the Collin
County line. At the farm entrance, Jake directed us in as we
weaved through parts of old tractors. "This is it?" Rachel asked,
disappointed. Spitting on the ground, Jake motioned for us to
follow. "And that's him?"

Jake, a retired cowboy, had let his former skinny build fatten out. Now sporting a pot belly, he made an easy living running a stable for wanna-be cowpokes, those weekend wranglers—usually lawyers and salesmen—who used the farm to ride their 'hobby horses'. But the farm had gone to pot, too; new pieces of lumber mingled with termite-infested boards. Rusty tin curled from the roof's edge...and holes became skylights.

We were there to see Bourbon Street, a four-year-old Palomino. Jake had mentioned a bad right front foot on the animal. But, with Jake, "one" animal usually meant several.

No southern gentleman, Jake began giving Rachel a bad time. "Fashionable duds, Toots. Hey...Doc, you oughta let this scrawny kid out more often."

I tried to referee. But, with a dirty look that was all Texan, Rachel said, "Aw, Jake...stick it in your ear."

The horse's owner, Larry Parks, was a drugstore cowboy...someone I wouldn't let ride a soda fountain stool. I knew him—and there was no telling what Bourbon's problem might be; but, at least, he was gentle.

Wet mud and hard manure packed Bourbon's soles, and hoof-testers showed sensitivity over each frog. "Geeze, no wonder," I grumbled as I cleaned the bottoms of his feet. Bourbon leaned heavily against my crouched back while I held each hoof between my knees and pared deep into the grooves. A rotten, necrotic stench came from the frog tissues as I peeled away. "Jake, he's got thrush." I gagged. "Has he ever been trimmed?"

"'Bout a year ago, I spec," Jake said. Rachel's nose wrinkled at the pungent smell and her eyes watered. She asked me about thrush, and I told her this type of rotting infection was caused by dirty stalls and owners who don't pick the muck out of their horse's feet.

"That's Parks for ya," said Jake. "He never picks Bourbon's feet…just rides him hard and puts 'im up wet. I've tried my darndest to tell 'im, Doc." Blotting his brow with a ker-chief, Jake stuffed his lip with a fresh dip of snuff. "Hell, I might as well be talkin' to a stump. Damn city folks. That Larry ain't been out here in months." Jake patted Bourbon's rump. "Poor ol' boy. It's a shame, Doc."

Rachel choked, fanning herself with cupped fingers, "Yuck!…that's a horrible smell…and it's preventable?"

"I'm tellin' you gal, it's just plain neglect," said Jake with a nudge. "Yeah, ain't nothin' worse than lettin' a good horse go like this."

"Here, Jake." I handed him a bottle of topical astringent medicine. "Put this on his soles daily. Now, who's next?"

Dodging a pinch from Rachel's fake nails, he said, "Just my ol' ropin' pony, Doc. She's right over yonder." His mare, stretching her legs, looked to have the same energy level as Jake. Kicked-back and calm, with a chest as broad as a barn door and a powerful butt, the Paint horse shook dust from her mane. Jake spoke proudly, "She's tough as nails and a ropin' fool. But, Doc, she's off on her onside rear."

It took awhile to examine Whiskey—and the extra time threw us way behind schedule. I could see no swelling or abnor-mality when flexing or extending the left limb. When I asked Jake how long this has been going on, he just sighed that it had been on and off. Since this explained nothing, we needed to spend some time here. Now distracted and bored, Rachel stood idly by as I had Jake trot Whiskey up and down the barn aisle. Finally I caught a glint of a characteristic 'hitch' in the mare's gait. At a walk, the affliction caused her to slap her sole on the ground. The hoof pulled back just before contacting the dirt during the normal forward stride. "Did you see that?" I asked. Self-absorbed again, Rachel didn't hear me.

Whiskey River had ossifying myopathy, a chronic injury to the muscles in her rear leg, probably associated with the sudden sliding stops during roping events. When Jake brought the horse closer, I felt a hard mass of scar tissue, like a rock, buried between the muscles on the back of her thigh. Figuring this loss in elasticity was causing the abrupt shortening of stride, I told him that Whiskey was going to need it surgically removed.

Rachel chimed in, "As soon as you can pay for it…since you still owe us money."

Turning to me, Jake said, "Ah, Doc will give me credit …or, better yet…take it out of Rachel's pay. Lord knows…she spends a fortune on all that face putty." Again, I played referee, and arranged for him to bring Whiskey by the clinic the next morning.

Starting the truck, I then asked Rachel where we were going next. Adjusting the rearview mirror, and dabbing her lips with gloss, she said, "Now, it's lunch." Reminding her that a time to eat was not scheduled in the book, she said, "Okay, okay, then we'll just go on to Bent Oak Farm."

★ ★ ★ ★ ★

Turning southwest and crisscrossing two counties in bumper-to-bumper traffic, we were now in a bind. We still needed to draw eight blood samples from Emma Weston's horses…before doubling back again to northwest Denton County and the Herman Hawks' Double Tree Ranch. Arriving shortly after 4 P.M., it was evident that the time wasted and distance traveled was staggering—but I remained silent—hoping this inefficient retracing had impact on Rachel.

Herman had a mule with a runny nose, and, since we were there already, his neighbor asked me to vaccinate three of his horses. At this point, Rachel just wanted to wait in the truck. Her patience had worn thin. As she saw the sun beginning to drop, she moaned, "I'm thirsty and hungry…and I need to go to the restroom." We weren't but two miles from our clinic, but she didn't notice.

Rolling into a gas station for a rest stop and cold drink, we were four hours late for our 1:45 appointment. "Now, it's Luke's place…and just where is Luke's?" Rachel wearily asked. Trying to keep a straight face, I said it was an hour due east of here…less than five hundred yards from Jake's place. "Didn't you check the map?"

She didn't answer. And I continued to pray that this back and forth routine was sinking in. Again, we crossed another county line. Ol' Blue had been gassed up twice since we began.

When Luke's gate came into view, Rachel gasped. Seeing was believing—and this was a sight to behold. Seldom sober and always in a crisis, Luke managed the 'rent-line capital of the world'. His hovel was converted into a local tavern and menagerie. Fighting cocks, stray dogs, wild pigs, and broken fences surrounded the abandoned trailer that once had 18 wheels —and that he, now, called home.

Stumbling as he walked, Luke waved to us with the ever-present bottle of rum in one hand. "Who's the purdy gal, Doc?"

In a formal fashion, I said, "Why that's Rachel. She's the one who answers the phone when you call."

"Well I'll be damned. Howdy, little lady…y'all get out and stay awhile."

Luke had called us about scouring calves. He often went to auctions and bought three-day-old dairy bulls with diarrhea for five bucks each. If any died, he took care of the carcass in the woods behind his trailer. That was only one reason for permeating smells that took over his farm. Owning twenty horses rescued from the killing floors of the slaughterhouse, raising roosters and sheep for companions, and feeding garbage to the pigs —all helped contribute to other odors. Everybody had a job. Two goats mowed the grass down to the roots…and Mildred, his Holstein cow, provided milk.

"What's today's problem, Luke?" I asked. Holding a brightly colored rooster up by his heels, he said, "It's this cock…he cain't eat nothin' right."

I pointed to the beak and said, "No wonder, the bottom of his mouth is ripped open. See Rachel?" Weakly murmuring, "I've seen quite enough, thanks," she appeared to turn green.

From the bottom-side of his jaw, we could see the roof of the rooster's oral cavity as his tongue jerked in and out of the hole and food fell to the ground. He flapped and feathers flew, as I held him on his side and sewed the laceration shut. The bird was then able to immediately swallow what he pecked.

Luke next led the way to a dung-filled, dilapidated lean-to that even I didn't want to enter. Through a cloud of flies, he brought out a bay Thoroughbred stallion in pretty bad shape. Once a beauty, Command Performance still had good markings…one white sock on his right fore, and a thin, white stripe running down between his dejected eyes to the tip of his nose. But the stallion's hip was punctured. Having purchased him at an auction a few weeks earlier for fifty dollars, Luke assumed he'd been shot.

Wondering why she turned away, I asked Rachel what was wrong. Her answer was clear, "What's not?" She tried not to watch as I cleaned the opening of Command's wound. "Luke," I said, "he wasn't shot…he's got hip pointer…probably from a race starting gate. Those bone pieces finally abscessed, and his body is trying to spit them out."

"Can you help 'im, Doc?" Luke asked. With the aid of a local anesthetic, I laid the point of Command's hip open with a scalpel, and, one by one, was able to remove four golf-ball-sized bone chips. Drainage was maintained with a penrose tube, and antibiotic solutions were used to flush the vacated cavity. After searching for possible smaller chips, I closed the skin.

Luke celebrated the stud's good fortune with a swig from a new jug. "Mighty fine job, Doc." Turning pale, Rachel anticipated that the worst was still to come. Sure enough, Luke announced, "Now, the calves."

Twenty emaciated black and white calves gathered around us. Luke provided them with brimming buckets of grain, but watery diarrhea pulled them down. In truth, he was their only hope. Moses, his pet brown and white steer, was saved from the last bunch, and now helped him plow the garden. The fat bovine nudged Rachel for attention with his cold muzzle, while she knelt to let an orphan calf lick her hand.

Wormer and sulfa medicine were fetched while Luke gathered the calves in a circle. They each had to be treated for the scours with a drenching combination which would slow the bowels and remedy their problem, a protozoan parasite of feedlot calves. Suddenly, Rachel caught me by surprise by rolling up her sleeves and grabbing the first calf. "I can hold 'im while Luke catches another."

The calves were as cute as could be, weighing between 80 and 120 pounds. Rachel didn't weigh much more, and I admired her grit. When one of the calves squalled and she fought to restrain him, he kicked her in the shin—and they both slipped into the diarrhea-soaked dirt. This made my day—and was better than watching mud wrestling on TV. Rachel remained determined, and hung on as the calf sprayed her coveralls and slung foamy drool in her hair. Tears of laughter ran down my face. "Way to go," I cheered, as she won the battle.

She continued like a trooper, holding down each writhing calf while I drenched them.

Her rubber boots kept sticking in the slush, and she slipped and fell repeatedly. But, quit...she did not. With mascara running down her face, Rachel was covered with manure from head to toe. But grinning with fatigue, she caught the last one and hollered. "Whew! That's it...we're outta here."

It was evening when I wrote up Luke's bill. My trusty helper chipped dung from her arms, and I congratulated her, "Ya'done good." Returning from his trailer, clutching a wad of bills wrapped in rubber bands, Luke said, "Damn good," as he counted out the money for his payment.

Heading on home toward the clinic, Rachel said, "Y'know, Luke's never owed us a dime."

"That's why his thumbtack on our clinic map is gold."

Deciding to tell her about Luke Gifford, I whispered, "Don't tell anyone, but that man has more money than God. Money simply has no meaning to him. Luke's is a home for the down and out. The compassion I've seen him show simply has no pricetag. Ya see…even though everything out there looks like it's dyin'… at least it's breathin' today with a second chance. Who knows what tomorrow might bring. Hell, he's their savior."

Rachel nodded, then dozed off. If nothing else, I hoped our expedition had bridged our communication gap. I pulled Ol' Blue up to the clinic. It was 'dark-thirty'. We both knew we missed the dehorning appointment, and would need to reschedule it for the next day.

Walking inside the clinic and yawning after her well-deserved nap, Rachel just stood in front of the huge wall map. The gold thumbtack stood out. And I began tracing the course of our day with long strips of colored ribbon that formed a criss-cross pattern.

"I get it," Rachel said, "I get it…I best be checkin' the map from now on."

All in all, our field trip had some good results: Sneaky Pete won the Grand Prix, Fly Boy's owner paid her bill, Whiskey River charged from another roping box, Command Performance healed without complication, thirteen of Luke's calves grew into fat little steers, and…my gasoline expenses dropped in half. And, Rachel, becoming a super-whiz at Texas geography, never offered to ride with me again.

8

Night Call

The agitated caller almost yelled, "Wake up, Doc. This is Della Broadstreet...and my cat's goin' crazy!" I squinted at the digital clock flashing 3:00 A.M.

Our clinic hadn't been set up yet for emergency night referrals, so I groggily asked her how she got my home number.

Della went on non-stop, "Cindy's pawin' at her face, slobbering like she's rabid and smacking her gums constantly...and it was your sister who referred me."

Still not fully awake, I asked her to repeat the cat's situation and to let me know if she felt this was an emergency. Adding to the confusion was the fact that my sister's name is also Cindy—and I figured she was sleeping soundly by now. But she owed me.

Calming questions didn't alter Della's frantic state of mind. She said the cat's behavior had just started, and that Cindy kept rubbing her face on the carpet in great discomfort. "Ohmigod, there she goes again."

Trying to stifle a yawn, though not unconcerned, I asked her to meet me at the clinic in ten minutes. After hearing my futile attempts to console Della over the phone, Karen decided she'd quickly dress, too, and come along to help me out.

Clutching her yellow tabby, Della got to the clinic just a few minutes after we did. As I flipped on the exam room lights, I was surprised to see that she was a lovely girl of about twenty-one. But she nervously flitted about the room in a rather scatter-brained manner.

Her kitten had no facial swelling that would indicate a bee sting or spider bite. However, excessive saliva drooled from the corner of her mouth. The little three-month-old's pupils were dilated in fright, and she huddled herself tightly in a ball. Looking for any other abnormal signs, I asked Della if she could have gotten into anything toxic.

"What?" She seemed confused, and Karen simplified it for her, "Anything poisonous?"

Della quickly answered all my questions with a no, she hadn't gotten into anything poisonous, she hadn't been outside, and she hadn't suffered from any traumatic fall or blow.

"Any emesis?"

"Vomiting," Karen translated again.

"No."

"Has she been playing with string or anything?" I asked, prodding Cindy's small mouth open.

"No," Della continued, "I was sitting on the living room floor wrapping my son's birthday present when she started goin' nuts."

Attempting to comfort the jabbering girl, Karen tried talking with her about her son and the party being planned for him.

After examining the cat's palate, I interrupted their conversation, "There it is." And I peeled away a tiny strip of Scotch tape from the roof of Cindy's mouth. "Hey, girl…that should feel better." The sweet tabby licked her whiskers and gently pawed at the sticky foreign material on the tip of my finger, as if to identify her brief misfortune. Then, with a contented purr, she began grooming her chin.

Holding up the strip of tape in disbelief, Della stammered, "Well, Doc…I'll be damned."

"Me, too," I laughed with relief, wishing all emergencies had such simple solutions. As Karen led the young blond woman and her Scotch tape-eating kitty to the door, I looked at my watch. "Shoot, maybe there's just enough time for a quick nap before coming in to work."

The Indispensable

ove it! Move it!" The pony-tailed, blond dynamo barked orders like a staff sergeant. A consummate perfectionist, Tracy Barnes, my new five-and-a-half-foot technician, thrived on giving me a hard time, and I snapped to attention like any other soldier.

Karen loved Tracy from the moment she first shot through our door. And from that time on, she continued to move at jet speed. She had to; the clinic hours had extended from dark to dark, or whenever the phones stopped ringing. And, for me, it made sense to start leaving a change of clothes in the back of the truck and in the office closet, since half my day was spent at the clinic and the other half in the field. Our nights were the same. The small community was booming—horse investments and land values escalated—and our Twin Oaks Veterinary Hospital followed suit.

Tracy was always cool under pressure. With a degree in nursing, she'd been a medic's aide in Vietnam. And, while working in a veteran's hospital, she managed a return to school to become a veterinary tech…all while surviving a divorce. A combination of Apache Indian, Southern Baptist, and East Texas cowgirl—I called her "a hell-cat with a purr." Karen described her as "gracefully frank." Both were true.

This technician of ours could hold off a vein, administer medications, befriend a mean dog, restrain a bronc, flank a calf, run blood chemistry tests, monitor anesthesia—or even take out the trash…all in a day's work. I've only seen her make one mistake, twice…and, years apart. Twice she misjudged an animal's sex, with no harm except my continual teasing.

Following one particularly long day, I glanced up at the clock. It was 10:00 P.M. Pitch black outside, but every light in our building burned brightly. "Tracy, the day's over."

"Maybe for you." She breezed by me, and disappeared down the hall. I started to move a medicine bottle to the first shelf in the pharmacy. And from the other room came her voice, "Not there. That bottle goes two spaces over and up on the next shelf." Wondering what kind of sixth sense she had, I reached for the top shelf when her small frame suddenly darted beneath my arm. Grabbing the bottle I'd just misplaced, she moved it to its proper position as I protested. But she scolded, "You'll be lookin' for this in the morning and complainin' 'cause you cain't find it."

"I'da found it."

"Yeah, sure. After I tracked it down for ya." She was right. Without her, the clinic doors might as well have stayed closed. The pace was too hectic for either of us to stop and search for a misplaced bottle.

The clock struck 10:30. I tiptoed to Tracy's favorite domain, the small animal surgery suite—just to be sure everything was in shutdown mode. Over the intercom, from god-knows-where in the building, her voice rang out again, "Doc, get out of my room."

I answered, "I'm not in your room."

"Then, how'd you answer my call?"

Efficiency was Tracy's middle name, especially in the design and organization of our small animal surgery room. Always ready, the stainless steel hydraulic table could be illuminated by large surgical lamps in a moment's notice for the performance of serious procedures. Instrument trays and sterile equipment packs laid next to the anesthesia machine. Respirators, heart monitors, IV bottles, bone drills and surgical gowns surrounded us—and the emergency 'crash cart' sat in the corner. That room was either a place of elation or sadness, as minutes became hours when an operation hinged on a tiny heartbeat or single breath. Tracy and I concentrated on thoroughness. I did the surgeries, while Tracy assisted. From tumor removals to spinal disc surgery, we developed as a team, instinctive to one another's needs. Each of us had our job, and mistakes were rarely allowed.

11:00 P.M. We left the clinic. At 5:00 A.M. an emergency call came in from Caitlin Kent telling us that her black cat, Boots, was having trouble delivering her kittens. "She's been straining for hours…but, no babies."

Tracy answered my call on the first ring, and without waiting to hear a voice, simply said, "Hello, Doc…I'll meetcha there."

When we arrived, Tracy already had the room prepared.

Caitlin asked, "Maybe I waited too long…do you think the babies are still alive?"

Boots' big blue eyes enlarged with each uterine contraction as she tried to force the hopeless delivery. Her tummy tightened and tail curled as her rear legs went limp from the pelvic pressure. Explaining her situation to Caitlin, I scrubbed down, "There's one in the birth canal plugging up the works. Boots needs a C-section right away."

Caitlin nodded consent and Boots was anesthetized. After opening her abdomen and exposing the uterus, kittens were extracted one by one. Within minutes, seven hungry mouths cried for food and mobbed the exhausted mom, all finding a nipple. The multi-colored kittens were healthy with bright pink noses. And Caitlin was thrilled that one even looked liked Boots, with white paws and a teensy white tuft on the tip of one ear.

"I can't believe they all made it, Doc. Seven of 'em?" I told her we got lucky, considering how long Boots had been in labor.

As usual, Tracy was blunt, "Ah, Doc's just bein' modest. He gave Boots her ninth life…or rather eighth, seven kittens and a mama."

7:00 A.M. After a brief moment of elation, I went looking for the coffee pot, as Tracy looked around at the aftermath of our morning delivery. Instruments lay scattered on trays, gauze sponges were all about, and surgical drapes were crumpled on the table. "Geeze, Doc, look at my room." Snapping a roll of paper towels under her arm, she zoomed in and out, organizing and scrubbing. After a few minutes, she ordered, "Okay, Doc, let's get ready for all the surgeries we've scheduled today."

10

Partner for Life

ith so many four-legged patients coming through the door, Tracy and I were kept racing against the clock. When I brought Dr. Richard Vest on board, relief was thought to be in sight. Soon enough, he, too, was working non-stop, and none of us seemed to know what day it was anymore.

Rich—though I liked calling him Dr. Vest since he'd earned the title—was our new associate. And from the back, it was difficult to tell us apart. We appeared to be mirror images of one another—right down to the same age, similar upbringing, favorite clothes and boots—to the same crease in our hats. He just had two years less experience in clinical practice.

On his first day, I decided to take him with me on farm calls—figuring he'd worked too long and hard to be kept in kennel work. Besides, I needed the help. We were called to work the

Muddy Creek Quarter Horse Ranch, near Prosper, the site of an exclusive auction.

Young colts and fillies were bucking and pawing as a herd of fifty or more was brought into the holding pens. Unbroken two-year-olds and other fine breeding stock of the highest pedigree were scheduled to go before the auctioneer. But no bid could be cast until Dr. Vest and I verified the total health of each horse. Every one had to be examined for soundness of wind and limb, radiographed, wormed, and vaccinated. Their owner and the foreman of Muddy Creek, Buck Tennyson, was under great pressure to have this all done before the start of the auction.

Dr. Vest didn't hesitate, "Welp, let's get 'em done." My kinda man, I thought, as we entered the mayhem of the back corrals, and worked each horse one by one.

Like a seasoned pro, Dr. Vest tube-wormed one after the other in record time. Buck, usually quiet and reserved, leaned over to me and whispered, "Doc, this new fellow might be a keeper." It was somewhat of a courtesy to say very little at times like this. But when I told him he might be right, I also wondered if I could be that lucky. If our new doctor survives the day of this sale…then, I'd know for sure.

Red and white checkered tablecloths dressed the gourmet feast, and open bars surrounded the invitation-only audience of 'high-troughed' bankers and oil men.

The who's who of ranchers milled around, while champagne fountains flowed and whole sides of roasting beef revolved on giant spits over hickory smoked coals. Five-star chefs, in starched white butcher's coats and black Stetson hats, smiled and carved meat for the fortunate here decked out in their silk suits, with sterling silver hatbands, eel skin boots, and diamond studded cuff links. Western-attired valets ushered motorcades; and bid-attendants escorted mink-wrapped ladies to their tables. All very magnificent…

Dr. Vest was standing by my side when the sale began. A hush muffled the crowd as the lights dimmed, and a tuxedo-clad auctioneer began his 'twist-a-jaw' calculated to excite the audience and whet everyone's appetite for the presentation of the ranch's stallion—Hippocrates. The horse and his portfolio should have been on the cover of the *Wall Street Journal*; his estimated value was thirteen-and-a-half million dollars, single stud fees for limited booking exceeded $48,000, and prodigy sales averaged more than $150,000 each. Not to be overlooked, of course, were his three million dollars in winnings.

Normally not one to show off, Buck couldn't help but proudly stand when his beautiful sorrel stud was introduced in a show-stopping number equal to any Las Vegas production. I, of course, only looked for anything on that stage that could be of possible harm to the horse. Buck was anxious; I was nervous. But Dr. Vest seemed unfazed. Strobe lights flicked on and off, and the audience quieted as a foggy mist enveloped the grandiose stage. A large movie screen descended from the rafters showing film clips displaying the stallion's attributes. Then, against the musical crescendo of the orchestra, Hippocrates pranced on stage, his grandeur highlighted by a shower of pulsating spotlights. And, in the glory of the moment, the muscular stallion bowed before the applause, as croons of oohs and aahs drifted from table to table.

A circular beam of light slowly widened to next reveal the first-born Hippocrates-sired filly of the season, Karina. She wasn't quite yet a yearling, but knew how to bat her eyes and milk a crowd, swishing her flaxen mane and sashaying from side to side. The auctioneer opened, "I've got 100!" Hands raised all around the room. Each time the filly struck a pose on the runway, bidders felt their hearts flutter and purse strings snap.

"Now one and three! Who'll make it six?"

"Yo!" a voice from the back yelled as the auctioneer took off again…and again.

"Now more! I've got seven open, three closed, and four. Lookin' for nine. Who'll gimme eight?"

"Yo!"

"All right, there's eight!" Another gent raised a hand. "Nine! Where's TWO?" he exclaimed. "Any more? Goin' once. Takin' two and a double, or two and an ace!"

A voice roared up from the front, "Yeah!"

"Two and one! Now, two and two. Lookin' for three. Goin' once, twice, and sold for $210,000," the auctioneer shouted, "…to the gentleman in the front row."

That was just the warm-up, I told Dr. Vest. "Hippocrates' first-born son is number four in the program." Rich just nodded, saying he knew…then nonchalantly folded his arms as if the glittering excitement was no big deal. Tipping his hat to the bidders who bought the next two fillies for $110,000 and $130,000, Rich said, "The serious buyers will wait for their chance to bask in the sun."

The auctioneer took a deep breath, and Buck crossed his fingers. The $80,000 he spent on the party wasn't much when compared to a possible five million in sales. But Buck was superstitious. And a lot depended on the next few moments.

From an elevated platform, Hippocrates' son, the three-year-old champion, Earthstar, was dramatically lowered through a silver cloud of swirling smoke. Bold and fit...a noble presence. "Okay, five! Now, six, eight, nine ...and ONE!" The auction boss stuttered; he had difficulty keeping track of all the bidders. Markers waved from every corner of the room. "Okay, ONE comin' TWO!" For a second, the audience was silent. Dr. Vest looked away, losing the continuity of the auctioneer's drive. "Gimme one and one. Shootin' doubles! Won't settle for three! Askin' six. How 'bout five? Who'll gimme five?"

A banker near the front snapped, "YO!"

"Ain't a bad shindig," Dr. Vest finally said, "What's the count?"

"One-and-a-half million dollars," I answered, "...so it's best you keep your hands in your pockets."

Instead, Dr. Vest held six fingers in the air. "There's six." The auctioneer acknowledged. "Who'll make it eight?"

My jaw hit the floor. I looked at Rich as if he were crazy and gasped, "Have you lost your mind?"

An oilman hollered, "Yeah!"

"Seven!" the auctioneer shouted.

With one finger bent, Dr. Vest bid again. The auctioneer choked. "Keep it comin', ladies and gents. Add five! Who'll gimme eight? Can't be late. Or, make it nine!" Bids of almost two million had been reached—and Dr. Vest had the floor. A shallow rumble spread among the guests as the markers slowed. All eyes were on the banker and oilman to see if either would answer Rich's bid. "Gimme TWO!" The silver-haired banker shook his head, undecided. Everyone waited. "Goin' once!"

That broke the ice. "Goin' twice!" Dr. Vest still didn't blink an eye.

Then a female yelled out her first bid, "Yes!" The wife of the oilman had spoken up, and he nodded in agreement as she shouted, "DOUBLE TEN!"

Two million dollars. My throat tightened. "Rich, do you have that much money? Do ya?"

"Two and five? Anyone for two and five?" the auctioneer asked to a cheer that was swelling. Once, twice and SOLD! To the lady for TWO MILLION DOLLARS!"

Shrugging his shoulders, Dr. Vest started to walk away. "Just wait a damn minute here," I said. "Could you have covered that bet?"

"We'll never know," said Rich, as he tipped the brim of his hat up, so I could see his eyes. With all the confidence of a Yankee politician, he said, "No, but that's not how it turned out …so let's get back to work." Then, stopping in his tracks, he leaned toward my ear and mumbled, "By the way, Doc…when's payday?"

Yeah, I reckoned, he's a keeper all right.

I had no way of knowing then that this fellow—this daredevil—would become such a good friend and business partner during the next fourteen 'never-a-dull-moment' years of our Dallas practice.

Snapper's Sabbath

HOA, DAD!" my four-year-old son screamed, just as we were peacefully driving along on our way to church. Jumping up and down in the front seat, with his arms waving wildly, he yelled, "WHOA UP, DAD!" I slammed on the brakes, thinking he'd somehow hurt himself. The tires screeched, and I heard bottles of medicines in my vet pack smashing together as Ol' Blue slid to a stop.

K.C. couldn't contain himself, hollering, "C'mon, quick!" Jerking his little Stetson hat from his head and bolting from the cab, he hit the ground running. "Didn'tcha see 'im?" He ran down the shoulder of the road, with hat in hand, then stopped and turned to me. Motioning for me to come quickly, he cried, "Over here, look!"

Not knowing what to expect, I pulled the rifle from the gun rack and ran to him as fast as I could. "See what, K.C.?"

I cocked my Winchester, imagining the worst.

Excitedly pointing to the ground, he said, "The turtle! Over here, dad!" Sure enough, a large hard-shelled turtle lay at the edge of the pavement. He was as big around as my belt buckle. And he'd obviously been hit by a car or truck. K.C. sighed, "Aaah, just look at that…would ya?"

The turtle didn't move. And the sight was upsetting for my young son, so I tried to calm him down. "Ain't much we can do for him now, K.C." Standing there, quietly, I patted my boy on the shoulder, "He's…"

"Are ya sure?" His eyes were riveted on the turtle. "Look! SEE?" I set my rifle down and knelt to examine the helpless creature more closely. Tears began to well up in K.C.'s eyes. "I saw his leg move. SEE?…he's still alive." The turtle pulled his head inside his shell, and appeared to quiver.

"Welp, let's have a look at 'im," I murmured. Then, noticing the pulverized shell, I hesitated. "Son…he sure looks pretty banged up."

Rubbing his eyes, K.C. sniffled, "Yeah…but can'tcha save 'im?"

My heart sank. I wanted to spare my son's feelings and save the turtle's life, but knew my limitations.

"Oh, please…can't we try? Dad, please…" K.C. pleaded.

Through the hole in the back of his shell, I could see the turtle struggling to breathe. His chest moved in and out, ever so slightly. "I wonder what kind of turtle it is?"

"It's a snapper," my boy proudly exclaimed.

"How do you know that?"

"I saw his sharp beak, dad."

Scooping the injured victim into my hands, I chuckled, "But turtles don't have beaks."

"Well, *he* does!" K.C. insisted. And, of course, he was right.

When I told him we might not be able to save the turtle…he looked up at me with total trust, and said, "But, dad, you're a vet."

He had me there. His big brown eyes searched mine, and I couldn't resist, "Okay, I suppose we could try, son…let's take 'im to the clinic."

K.C. scrambled around on his rescue mission…and reminded me of myself at that age. I watched him hurriedly collect insects for Snapper's meals, and put them in the crown of his hat —in the same way I'd once gathered handfuls of grain for an injured prairie dog.

"We need somethin' to put him in," I said. And this lad of mine knew just what to do. Running to the truck, he rummaged through the vet box and fetched a feed bucket, his short legs almost stumbling over it as he dragged it back to me. We carefully placed Snapper, three grasshoppers, and a dozen pieces of fragmented shell into the rubber container. The top of the turtle's protective covering was so badly shattered that a gaping hole left his delicate flesh exposed.

Exhilarated at being able to take care of this 'emergency', K.C. mimicked the words he always heard me say, and shouted, "Okay, dad, we're ready…let's roll…"

At the clinic, Snapper was centered on the illuminated surgery table. Under my boy's watchful eye, I meticulously raised crushed portions of the shell with medical instruments, trying to decipher the correct position of the splintered pieces as though they were parts to a puzzle. Chips of shell were soaked in antibiotic solution, then arranged into a form that resembled the original helmet. Snapper flinched when I moistened his tender skin with antiseptic. Even after all the patching, it was obvious that parts of the shell were missing. A jagged and cracked three-inch hole was still open in Snapper's roof. Exposure to the elements would prove lethal, I thought, yet I had to do something. "K.C., I've got to find a way to anchor more of these pieces."

Never at a loss, my small assistant said, " If we had some shingles...then you could patch 'im like ya did the barn."

Going into our storage room, I began searching the shelves for something to serve as meshing support...and spotted a roll of screen door wire. If the metal netting was sterilized and acrylic hoof-binding glue used as an adhesive...this might work.

As I returned to the surgery room, K.C. was busy talking to Snapper, assuring him that we were doing everything possible to put him back together again. I went about the business of adhering the shell fragments to the mesh with the gummy resin compound. When I sealed the remainder of the hole with a small bit of green vinyl cloth, K.C. said, "Wow! Pretty neat, dad!"

Stepping back to admire my work, I had to agree. I'd done what I could—even though Snapper's back resembled a miniature, open-domed Texas Stadium. And I still remained skeptical about the reptile's prognosis.

We were both elated over our good deed. But after looking down at our soiled Sunday clothes, I said, "Son, I guess you know we're both in trouble...'cause we missed church. So you better show your mom this turtle as soon as we walk through the door. Or, we'll both be in the doghouse. And...son...you darn well better take care of Snapper."

"Oh, I will...I will," he crowed.

As we pulled into the drive, K.C. yelled with excitement, "Mom...mommy...Dad made me a 'convertible turtle'! And he can stay in *my* room!"

Since we already had more than the usual number of cats, dogs, and birds, Karen just gave me one of her 'looks', to which I responded, "Now, honey...remember, it's the Sabbath."

One more pet really made no difference, and Karen blessed our new turtle patient. After praising our morning's work, she then showed K.C. how to turn one of our old aquariums into Snapper's new home.

Over the years, she and I watched them both grow. And we simply kept adding more items to our shopping list...such as those special insects and greens needed for a lucky turtle's diet.

Advertising Honky-Tonks

Odors coming from one of the exam rooms were unrecognizable, so I took a deep breath before entering. Lone Star and Texas Scream, two armadillos, were running loose on the floor tiles. Their entrepreneurial owner, Gerald MacSweeney, had created a small advertising business with the competitive team. Every Friday and Saturday night, for the past year, these handsome roadside-captured creatures entertained in clubs around town, by racing each other around Gerald's homemade track.

Their featured attraction had replaced darts and frog-jumping as the contest of choice. Honky-tonks, such as Bad Boy Lil's and Stagecoach Ambush, sold ads of painted logos and slogans on the armadillos' shells...making them mini-billboards.

Lone Star had a Texas flag scripted on his right side, and a beer ad on his left. Texas Scream, on the other hand, bore the emblem of a steak house restaurant, and a symbol for an auto parts store. Running in circles, they looked like small, decorated race cars. I was just glad they were not subjected to wearing neon lights. Gerald herded them with a long shepherd's staff, since they were a mite too heavy to carry everywhere.

I figured their only natural enemies were trucks and shot-guns—for they could live many years in the wild. The only ones brought to us before had been shot for uprooting plants and veg-etables. But we never treated such a backwoods' animal for a reg-ular ailment.

The individual snorts coming from these two were amus-ing. But, I needed to cover my nose with the palm of my hand, for the stench from the musk and nervous excretions was over-whelming. The attempt was futile, though. After a forced exhale, I saw that Lone Star was suffering from an infection…and Texas Scream showed a yellowish discoloration of the skin.

The fair-haired owner stood across from me at the end of the exam table. He was skinny as a twig, and almost seven feet tall. An interesting looking fellow, I thought, in his striped shirt and dark green, shiny suit. The ponytail hanging between his shoulder blades showed him to be a young man, in his twenties, maybe. His long arms stretched to thick, leather gloves on his hands…and his knees popped as he knelt to pick up Texas Scream. When he asked, "Doc, do you know anything 'bout treatin' these critters?" his tenor voice was octaves higher than I expected it to be.

"Not really," I said, as Texas Scream was plopped on the table. Her paws paddled, and her claws tried to find traction on the slick Formica surface. Pointing to the creature's cute little ears, and nasty tail, I joked, "Aren't these supposed to be the Texas State Bird?"

Gerald smiled weakly, and with his long fingers gripping the back of the armadillo's covering, he turned Texas Scream so that I might better see the severe hue of her leathery hide. She hissed in a throaty growl, as he said, "She's got a beer-belly, Doc...and, she ain't got no energy."

"Does she drink?" I asked.

"Like a fish," he replied, with a sheepish grin.

That was her problem, all right...jaundice, bloodshot eyes, and bad performance on the job. "Well, she's got chronic alcoholism and cirrhosis of the liver. Her diet is wrong. She doesn't get enough sleep. And, she drinks too much."

Interrupting, Gerald said, "That's what I thought...in fact, I'd been thinkin' 'bout turning her loose in the woods, so she'd get her natural ways back—and her health." I agreed that this was the best course of action for the animal.

Dipping down to the floor again, Gerald brought up his other pet and money maker, "What about Lone Star? He stinks to high heaven."

With gloved hands, I examined the accordion segments of the carapace. Hard bands of dense shell were separated by fleshy, soft connective tissue strips...allowing the armadillo to curl his protective shield. Lone Star ducked his head, yet didn't move. Multiple, draining tracks of pus came from under the plates of armor. The canals contained a foul smelling bacterial liquid, which I figured was a staphylococcus infection. I flinched when Gerald said, "...been drainin' like that for days."

Oral antibiotics would be no problem to administer, but the bacteria wasn't really in his body. The pockets were trapped in the space between Lone Star's dermis and his outer shell. I needed

Gerald to bend Lone Star, so I might inject medicines through the soft tissues, directly into the blind pouch. I had no idea if the armadillo would let me do this. Asking Tracy for a two-inch stylet, I told Gerald to lay Lone Star on his side and curl him, so I could tap the needle into the site of the infectious material.

I chose my site, as Gerald stared at the needle. I paused a moment, and he continued to stare. Wiping the spot with alcohol, and spreading the elastic bands, I aimed the injection. Still staring at the needle, Gerald's Goliath shadow swayed, then his hand slipped. He lost his grip, and his face turned pale. I glanced up, but not in time. Gerald was rocking back on his heels. WHAM! His back slammed against the wall, before he went slumping to the floor in a dead-away faint.

I yelled for Tracy, looking to be sure the lad was okay and catching Lone Star as he tried to jump from the table. "Fetch us a wet towel, please."

"I'ma comin', she said, as she stepped over the man's lanky frame. While she held Lone Star, I checked on Gerald, and laid the damp cloth on his forehead. Coming to, he got himself into the exam room chair, and we told him to put his head between his knees and rest a spell.

Tracy and I went about the business of treating Lone Star. "Bend him in a circle, and hold 'im tight…while I infiltrate along these segmented lines." THUD! Again, Gerald was out like a light, coiled in the chair with his chin on his chest.

Tracy hollered for either Dr. Vest or Rachel to help him to the reception area. "He's fainted twice." Half awake, Gerald's knees were still buckling, and Rachel asked him to put his arm over her shoulder. She was strong, but it was still a struggle for her to guide someone three times her size to the cushioned bench out front.

I slipped the stylet in place, and Lone Star didn't blink. In fact, he appeared downright relieved and comfortable when I used a large animal IV set to flush a liter of mixed antibiotic/saline solution under his shell, chugging in 100 cc's here and there. The medicine acted as an 'under-the-shell' lavage. Catching a glimpse of Gerald now sitting up, I called out, "We're almost done, just let this drain in and out."

"I'm okay," said Gerald. He raised his head, blinked, saw us working…started to say something. "I'm…" THUD! All Rachel could do was break his fall. But she was able to find Dr. Vest to help her roll Gerald's limp torso over. This time, he lay flat on the floor, and my partner suggested we let him lie there a while.

Completing the work on Lone Star, I set him down on the floor…and he scampered around Texas Scream, snorting and sniffing. He feels better already, I thought, closing the exam room door and stepping over Gerald. Talking to Dr. Vest about another topic, we finally knelt to tap Gerald on the cheeks. He began mumbling in a confused state, asking, "When is it?" We let him rest with his head on a towel, while Dr. Vest kept an eye on him.

We needed to examine the bacteria aspirated from under Lone Star's carapace, knowing that armadillos can serve as carriers for other organisms. So I swirled the test tube with care.

Gerald started to rise up to a sitting position, when Dr. Vest looked over at me to say, "Did y'all know armadillos can carry the bacteria for leprosy?" THUD! Gerald's head fell back against the towel. Looking down at his peaceful expression, something told me this young man would be getting out of the ad business. "Boy, wait 'til I tell him we're going to need to treat Lone Star again." Dr. Vest tapped his cheeks, "Gerald, it's time to wake up."

When the boy was able to stand and move, our wonderful Rachel made him feel better, saying, "Wow, Mr. MacSweeney, that was a record!" Then she turned Lone Star and Texas Scream loose in the lobby to keep him company, while he got his bearings.

Before he left, I cautioned, "Now, I wantcha to bring Lone Star back tomorrow...but, I'd rather you waited in the car during his treatment. We also think it'd be a good idea for you to see a doctor about those fainting spells."

Turning out to be quite a responsible fellow, Gerald not only brought Lone Star in for subsequent treatments—but released both armadillos back to nature. They didn't go far, though, showing a preference for his folks' farm, and its bounty of vegetables. They were pets, after all, and the family didn't seem to mind.

We see Gerald in town, from time to time. And, as it turns out, he still writes slogans and jingles—but for the greeting card business.

Peaches Goes Ballistic

Dr. Vest called out in exasperation, "Hey, Doc…can you help me in here?" Wondering what could be giving him trouble, I quickly opened the door to the small animal exam room. Rich had the ablest of hands, but he was no match for the creature now sitting on the table. Peaches, the apricot poodle—weighing in at three pounds—had a reputation, and Rich's dilemma was understandable. Greeting Peaches' glum owners with some trepidation myself, I tried to be pleasant. "So…I guess we're all here to trim his toenails again."

Jill, a sweet curly-headed brunet, covered her cheeks to hide a blush. She and her new husband, Brandon, knew I was making light of Peaches' terrorist tactics during this common, but, in his case, most dangerous service performed in our hospital. The young couple nodded. Brandon was reluctant to get his large, linebacker frame any closer to the table and its occupant. But

Jill cuddled and smooched on Peaches' topknot while the pooch bathed her with playful kisses.

Dr. Vest stood ready, with a 'no-bite' muzzle cupped in his hand. Defending their 'baby', Brandon emphasized that Peaches is always sweet at home, and, as we know, never minds getting his shots or any other type of treatment. "But," he added, "…if a bear was to touch his feet, he'd rip off his leg and beat 'im to death with the bloody stump." A little blunt, maybe, but not far from the truth.

Peaches was a powder puff all right, until it came down to this painless task. The last time we attempted a trim, he was slightly anesthetized for dental work. Even then, he jerked his paws away from my grasp when I began to clip the white pointed tips. At one time or another—despite kindness, treats or bribes—he managed to take a chunk out of each one of us.

I hollered for Tracy to bring in a bunch of double-thick leather gloves, and asked her to assist us. Peaches sat quietly and innocently in the middle of the table, partially wrapped in a baby blanket covered with hearts. Tracy thought we were pulling her leg. "It's going to take three of us to hold this bitty piece of fluff?"

"No," I answered, "…it's going to take five—three men and two women. I looked at Jill. "Do you remember how we did this before?" As in previous rehearsals, we each donned our 'battle-gear'—sliding catch-gloves up to our elbows for protection—and hoped we were ready.

Distracting Peaches with 'baby talk' as she scratched his neck, Jill let my hands and hers exchange without causing suspicion. Peaches' eyes shot back and forth. In our split-second maneuver, I interlocked my fingers in a 'whiplash' collar behind his ears, and Brandon immediately scooped the poodle's body up into his muscular arms, pinning him firmly against his chest. I thought, at that moment, that I'd seen calves 'thrown and tied' with less effort. Oddly, Peaches remained calm until Dr. Vest touched his right front paw. Then snapping, jerking, and squirming...Peaches let us know the 'fight was on'. "Grab his back legs," pleaded Dr. Vest. "And, Tracy, trim the left front nails."

Overly shrill in his determination to stop us, Peaches yelped, screamed and twisted, tangling a leg in one of Brandon's pockets. Despite the frenzy, Tracy did her best to snip away at any nails she could get hold of during the blur of movement.

The tiny ball of rage tried every trick in the book to escape. He'd relax, then explode—screeching like he was being killed. I didn't want to imagine what the folks waiting in our reception room might be thinking. Trying out a whole new strategy, Peaches now kicked like a kangaroo, choking and frothing at the same time. Sweat-laden hair was all over the place, and I couldn't be sure who it came from. Brandon's face was red...he wasn't about to lose his grip, and neither was I.

On Peaches' previous visit, after piercing the leather glove, his canine teeth went deep into the first joint of my index finger; I could still feel the stiffness. During that same episode, the 'baby' lacerated the back of Brandon's hand and chomped on his forearm in three different places, before bending his head around to nail Dr. Vest with a blood-letting snap across the heel of his palm.

Tracy continued snipping nails as fast as she could. Dr. Vest gasped as he looked down at the front of his smock and smelled the pungent odor of Peaches' spraying mark. "Doc, this is the hardest thing we've done. Where does this tenacious little thing get all his incredible strength?"

I agreed that a toenail trim is the most chancy procedure a vet will ever perform. "You're liable to receive the worst kind of lacerations." We knew some major, primal instinct was at work, since no critters tolerated this well. Cats came undone at just the sight of clippers. And we'd see birds prepare for attack if anyone tried to mess with their claws. Since time began—whether needed as weapons for protection or tools for hunting—claws or nails meant survival.

"I'm done!" Tracy said as she patted away at the slight perspiration on her forehead. "Set him back on the table."

Jill's hands took over, as mine relaxed their grasp, and she resumed her petting strokes and 'baby talk'. "Go-ood boy," praised Brandon. "That's the best you've ever been," they crooned together.

Clearly the winner in all rounds, the pint-sized apricot looked straight up at each of us with a low growl, as if to say, "Sure…just try this again, and none of you will leave here in one piece."

Ol' Blue Trucks Along

Driving into the midday sun on the way to a call, trusty Ol' Blue backfired and the baling wire keeping the hood down nearly snapped. It's damn near time to trade her in for another blue truck, I thought. Any other color but blue was out of the question.

The moniker for all my pickups was affectionately dubbed by my cowboy hero, Pete Channel. "Hell, son, your horse has a name…so, why not give one to your truck? Who do ya spend more time with, your wife or your pickup?" Then, in a ceremonial christening of sorts, Pete spit tobacco juice on the tires of the first Ol' Blue. The name stuck—and, from then on, everyone knew Ol' Blue was part of me.

Pete's word meant a lot in these parts. Even now, when telling friends about our clinic, some folks will say, "I can't rightly remember his name, but I use the vet that drives the blue truck, Ol' Blue they call it."

Pete was foreman of the small Samuel Ranch, a 6,000-acre cattle spread stretching across the improved pastures of Frisco. It was hard to tell just how old he was—other than knowing he was probably thirty years older than me, and a hundred years wiser.

This man, short in stature, stood tall in reputation—a living legend. Always in starched shirts and denim jeans, Pete's high-topped calf skin boots, legging chaps, and jangling rowel spurs tagged his character. But the real hallmark was the constant, and overwhelming, sight of his engraved belt buckle about the size of a dinner plate. It read 'Cowboy Rodeo Champion 1954'.

Not outwardly rich, just good ol' folks, Pete and his quiet, raven-haired wife, Rosy, lived in a modest, wood-framed house next to the grand historical mansion built by Cody Samuel. She would either be watching soap operas or driving around town in her battered '63 Chevy, while he was bouncing over the ranch in his rattletrap farm truck checking on the herds.

We all first met shortly after the big canine parvovirus epidemic began. Finding his favorite ranch horse, Hand Shaker, suffering from the severe lameness called 'founder', Pete gave the gelding some old-fashioned remedies of the day. He finally called Twin Oaks. "Doc, I poured coke down his throat this mornin', but he ain't changed. I giv'd him a whole pouch of my good chewin' tobacco, too—and even stood 'im in the mud. I couldn't find no Glauber's salt or castor oil…so, I decided to call you. Do ya think he needs one of them enemas?"

I listened in awe, agreeing to come out to the farm—admitting to myself that I was a mite nervous about meeting this legendary figure. Going around to the clinic's backyard, I quickly did some squirming and rolling around in the dirt until my coveralls looked dusty and worn. After all, for the famous Pete Channel, at least, I needed to look experienced.

Hand Shaker was in bad shape, and there was no time for a regular exam. Sweating and trembling from the onset of crippling pain in the last stages of the disease, he was ready to look for a place to lay down and die. I needed to jolt his senses to get him to walk out from the mud. So, as Pete would have done, I gave him a strong, swift pat on the hindquarters. It took a while, but, with great effort, he slowly made the few steps. The sorrel's hooves were hot to the touch and his pulse was thready. Hand Shaker rocked back and forth to relieve the painful pressure in his forefeet, but his legs buckled. I frantically tried to stabilize his awkward position. His heart was racing—and so was mine. The good-tempered workhorse repeatedly stumbled and collapsed. He'd stand, try to walk, then crumble.

"Pete, this ain't good," wishing with all my heart that I didn't have to say this.

"Give 'im something, Doc." Mustering all the strength I had to balance the gelding, I administered anti-inflammatory pain relievers in the jugular vein. As Pete held the horse's muzzle, I pumped a gallon of mineral oil into Hand Shaker, using a gastro-intestinal stomach tube. But, again, the blaze-faced horse collapsed with eyes half-shut in pain. Obviously shaken, Peter begged, "Git up ther', sweetheart!" I reached for more injections and thumped the vessel hiding in the neck furrow. "Doc, it's his feet, not his neck, that's ahurtin'. Why stick 'im again?" I palpated the jugular and set another needle, as blood aspirated into the syringe hub before I pushed the plunger.

The medications kicked into effect. Thank God, I thought. Hand Shaker wobbled when I released his halter, then stood on his own appearing to be more comfortable.

Seeing this, Pete quieted down, too. I asked him to walk the horse back into the mud and, "…take 'im slow 'cause he's still a mite woozy." Waiting for the gelding's heart rate to drop and sweating to subside, I told Pete I'd be back the next day to check on him and x-ray the hooves for possible rotation of the bone away from the hoof wall.

"What do ya thank?" the foreman asked in his long Texas drawl.

"I think Hand Shaker's going to be just fine—and hopefully, there's no permanent damage." With a huge sigh of relief, I added, "Right about now, I think I could use a chaw of your good tobacco." Pete's grin changed to a toothed-smile. Offering a pinch from his leafy plug, he patted me on the shoulder…and I knew then I'd been accepted as his 'animal doctor'. After a spell of "fence sittin', horse watchin', and spittin'," we moseyed over to my worn-out truck.

"Well, I'll be damn, will you look at that? Hell, Doc, it's too bad you ain't got no decent wheels to go with all that doctorin' knowledge. Guess we'll hav'ta fix that…I ain't gonna have my vet lookin' mangy."

Two days later, three vehicles pulled up in front of the clinic. Rosy, in her white sunbonnet, sat behind the wheel of the old Chevy; three well-dressed gentlemen in dark suits emerged from a Lincoln; and with his silver-belly hat resting on the dashboard—Pete stood next to a beautiful new three-quarter-ton pickup.

"How are ya, Doc? It's a fine mornin'...ain't it? Yep, fine mornin' indeed." Pete proudly went on to make introductions, "This here is Mr. Howard...he owns the Ford dealership in town. This slick-haired farm boy is Tom...chairman of the board of that big bank over yonder. And, this yankee is Bob Hansen...he'll be writin' your insurance."

"What? Insurance for what?" I stammered.

Tipping his hat back, and kicking against the front tire of the new truck, Pete said, "Yep, this is goin' to be yours, Doc. These gents want to improve your professional image. So, let's get to work." He spoke as if he were herding cattle, "Now, y'all git-a-long, now, ya hear? Just let 'em handle it, Doc, they'll do ya right."

My hands held the keys, but I stood there stunned. Now the unbelievably proud owner of a blue Ford pickup, I had full insurance and small payments even I could afford.

To this day, I don't quite know how much of this transaction Pete either paid for—or negotiated—and he'd never tell me.

But the first Ol' Blue was birthed just this way—Pete's way...no fuss, no gloat, no brag. "Yep, that truck'll spruce up your image mighty fine, Doc, mighty fine indeed."

★ ★ ★ ★ ★

Another month of Sundays passed before I heard from Pete again. He left an emergency message that one of his prize Longhorn cows went 'down' in the pasture trying to give birth. On her back in a small gully, unable to right herself, the 1500-pound, tan and white heifer had a calf stuck halfway out of her uterus. She was fighting her frozen position, and at the same time straining with labor pains hard enough to tear up her reproductive tract.

I groaned at the sight, "Damn, she's pelvic locked, and the baby's hung tighter than a monkey's paw in a cookie jaw. But, the little son-of-a-gun is still alive."

Pete was furious because the calf was the spitting image of Chuck Vaden's black Angus bull in the next pasture. "Damn fool, I oughta castrate 'im!"

When I said it wasn't the bull's fault, Pete chuckled. "Not the bull...I mean Chuck Vaden, I oughta castrate 'im. I know, I know, Chuck ain't the worry now, that calf is."

The two of us went plunging into the pasture's creek bottom to rescue the cow and her black baby...me in my new truck, and Pete on foot. Tying a rope around the heifer's horns and securing it to Ol' Blue's bumper, we tried to pull the mother across the wet grass and out of the ditch. Peter pushed on her rear, and I slowly drove. Mud, grass and twigs spun out from beneath the tires. Pete's face and hat were splattered. "Whoa, Doc...aw, shit. This ain't workin'!" The cow hadn't budged.

I decided to birth the calf right there—and reached for the cow's head to check the rope. She wasn't as exhausted as I figured. As the heifer suddenly sprang to her feet, Pete yelled, "Look out!" and hit the deck face first. The roped pulled tight and cut the air. "Git 'er!" he yelled. Then the lariat snapped like a string—and the cow sprinted away. We both went chasing after the scampering cow, who still had her baby 'hip-locked' and flopping. Galloping along, the calf's head and front legs bobbed helplessly up and down—but the baby was alive and bawling.

The heifer proved to be faster than us. Pete, winded, managed between breaths to ask me to keep going after the cow. But after another hundred yards or so, I, too, gasped for air. Both panting, we slowly returned to the truck to think up a new plan. Laughing now, Pete was convinced we should drive to the back of the pasture where he knew the cow would stop to rest. "She'll be next to the pond." I disagreed with him, but he argued, "She's my damn cow...trust me."

Sure enough, ten minutes later, there she was standing in the very spot Pete described. He jumped out and into the back bed of the truck. "Just use Ol' Blue to head 'er off. I'll rope the hussy...if you'll block her path." He swung a perfect loop over the cow's horns while I maneuvered Ol' Blue like a huge horse. Leaping from the truck, Pete hollered, "I got 'er, Doc." At the same time, I bailed from the cab, screaming, "Keep her head tight."

With grass churning everywhere, Pete held the rope as tight as he could, and I slung a restraint rope. Then he dallied the lariat's slack several times around Ol' Blue's bumper. "Bigod, I got 'er. She won't be breakin' this one loose." The cow's cloven claws were planted deep in the wet sod, and she slid down on her side. Fatigued, her rib cage contracted up and down in great huffs and puffs, and, for a moment, she stopped fighting. It was all the time I needed. Luckily, the cow's running movement had changed the position of the unborn just enough to make the delivery fairly easy. With a little extra lubrication, some manual rotation of the torso and forequarters, and a strong tug, the newborn escaped its bondage. Dazed, but strong, the calf immediately tried to stand. Elated, I shouted, "All right, one of our plans worked."

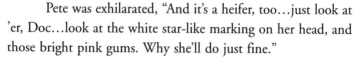
Pete was exhilarated, "And it's a heifer, too…just look at 'er, Doc…look at the white star-like marking on her head, and those bright pink gums. Why she'll do just fine."

Unexpectedly, in a powerful display of frenzy, the mother erupted again, jumping up and pulling the slack from the lariat, jerking my bumper loose. I went sprawling flat into the mud, as the shaft of one horn passed over my body and angry hooves pawed the ground. Her bad temper left no doubt as to the object of her attack. She charged again—and I dodged her again. But still bent on letting off steam, the old cow took out her aggression on Ol' Blue.

I cringed as she marched into my truck, burying her horns deep into the side panels. The banging and crunching sounds seemed to go on forever, as she went about the business of pulverizing Ol' Blue. That angry mass of muscle, horns, and hooves plowed up and down the sides of my Detroit beauty, ripping her apart—until the rope snapped and she finished mangling the grill. Helplessly hollering "NO! NO!" I watched as the old hussy finished off her work by smashing her left hoof through one of the headlights.

Ol' Blue was destroyed. I was crushed. Pete just grinned and shrugged his shoulders. There was nothing else either of us could do. Now thoroughly satisfied, the cow, with newborn in tow, calmly trotted off toward the main herd to graze.

Seeing me sitting there on the ground in anguish, Pete tried to cheer me up. "Welp, I guess that's just part of it. Now ya got dents and experience, Doc." We began debating just what the insurance could possibly replace.

As soon as I got back to the clinic, Bob Hansen called. "I heard you had a little problem." He stopped laughing long enough to tell me I should take the truck in to Howard's dealership for an estimate of damages." At this point, an estimate wouldn't help, I explained. "The only things not gored were me, Pete—and the left door panel."

"Then," Bob said, "...we'll be filing this first claim as 'Acute Cow-Annihilation of Ford Pickup'.

Talkin' Texan

ob would end up filing a string of unusual claims on my behalf. After running into the corner of Lazy C Stables, 'Barn Alert' became the second. Then on a visit to Indian Head Farm, a yearling colt named Bonsai decided to escape from the round-pen, clearing the wall and landing on Ol' Blue's hood—making 'Flying Pony' the third claim.

Enough was enough. Ten months later, after my 98,000-mile abuse test, I traded in for a blue super-cab that I thought capable of getting through just about any job-related incident. The original nickname stuck, but, unfortunately, more claims followed. When I ran over some old tractor parts in Mr. Walton's field, Bob entered 'Tractor Attack'. And just two weeks later, Ol' Blue was pummeled by hail. The resulting damage led Bob to get even more creative with 'Sky Rocks'.

It was inevitable that Bob would finally call in a serious mood, "Doc, we need to talk. How about lunch?"

On the day of our appointment, Rachel stepped into the surgery room as I was completing a fracture repair on a young Doberman. She worriedly asked if I was going to be much longer because Bob had just arrived in a black limousine accompanied by a "strange lookin' man." Tracy whispered, "Probably the insurance company's 'hit man.'"

Still wearing my scrub suit, I stepped out to the front desk where Bob introduced me to a Mr. Jay Slavocheknesky, a tall, handsomely-groomed gentleman who spoke with a slight foreign accent. Quickly removing my surgical gloves, I vigorously shook his hand, saying, "Howdy."

Bob was nervous, and motioned me closer. "He's my boss...the president. He's from the Chicago main office."

Bob winced when I, trying to be courteous, stumbled over his name, "Well, Mr. Slavo-neesi. Welcome to Texas."

Uninterested in small talk, the president got right to the point, "Thank you...but are you the owner of the truck called Old Blue?" I was proud to tell him that I was, indeed.

"Please come with us," he responded, "...and we'll talk further at lunch."

Bob quickly opened the doors of the limo as Tracy handed me my hat. We must have been a sight when we arrived at The Spur, a plush dining club in downtown Dallas. The tuxedoed doorman balked as he stepped forward and opened the car's doors. I got out, saying, "Thank ya, sonny," while Bob covered his discomfort with a twenty dollar bill.

The maitre d' firmly offered me a dinner jacket. There we were, seated at a view window, two executives dressed to the hilt, and me, wearing a dinner jacket, sneakers, a cowboy hat, and surgical scrub bottoms. But Mr. S. kindly felt the need to apologize for the restaurant's dress code. "Sorry, but my secretary in New York made the arrangements."

Anxious to please, Bob fawned, "Oh, it's perfect," while I was still trying to figure out why a man from Chicago had a secretary in New York.

My Texas slang must have been confusing to Mr. S., because Bob felt the need to conduct a translation of everything I said. He also went on to say that his boss was here for the annual board meeting, and, while in town, wanted to meet the owner of Old Blue.

With great diplomacy, Mr. S. intervened, "I've been intrigued by some of the claims submitted on your behalf." When I invited him to ask me about any of them, he pulled a long sheet of paper from his briefcase. "I have a list of just a few: 'Ostrich Egg', 'Buffalo Girl', 'Locust Raid', and 'Armadillo Windshield.'"

Bob chimed in, "Oh, Doc can explain each one."

I told him that the egg claim was really very simple—that I had run over an ostrich nest when leaving the Yellow Rose Exotic Farm near Denton. "The big bird laid her $3,000 egg in a clump of hay next to the road leading from the camel pens...and I inadvertently drove through it." Mr. S. smiled slightly as I went on. "Of course, the crunch of a several-thousand-dollar egg caused quite a stir at the farm. The owner tried to be understanding, but I had the feeling he'da been less upset if I'da run over his wife."

Mr. S. looked over at Bob and grinned, "We replaced the value of the egg after the owner of the farm argued that there was no difference between hitting a car or an egg. We agreed."

"That was mighty nice of y'all, too," I said, in all sincerity. Mr. S. read the next item, "And 'Buffalo Girl'?"

I suggested that we finish our lunch first, saying I'd prefer to have the foreman of Samuel Ranch tell him that story.

Pete Channel was sitting on his front porch drinking coffee and chewing tobacco when he greeted us. And Mr. S. appeared fascinated by him. Over the jingle of his spurs, Pete started talking, "Here now, Sonny, park your riggin' on that ther' bench."

Mama's voice rang out from behind the screen door, "Y'all want some calf-fries?"

Bob quickly answered, "No," to avoid any more translations.

"Y'all pull up a chair," Pete said, "and sit a spell." Mr. S. remained standing, and it was hard to know what he was thinking. Pete wouldn't let it go, "What's the matter, yankee? Sit, son, sit. And what brings the likes of y'all to these parts?"

Turning a little pale, Bob looked at the dusty log bench and his boss' black suit. Trying to oblige, Mr. S. knelt on the step instead, seemingly entranced by Pete's way.

When Bob told him we were there to talk about 'Buffalo Girl', Pete spit and looked Mr. S. square in the eye. "That was the roughest bronc ride I've ever had," he began. "Best I recollect, Doc and me went to Yellow Rose Farm to find Sam...'cause in tha good ol' days, me and him punched cattle together in the Fort Worth stockyards. Anyway, them buffalo out there was plum loco, y'know? Now, mind ya...they wasn't big. But they was buffalo...snot-nosed, muzzle-blind, woolly-smellin'...and, they was easily spooked. Now Sam, ya see, was a weldin' by one of the sheds. I was mindin' my own business, when next thing I know sparks started flyin' and the weldin' torch hissed like a snake."

Pete paused and spit again, shaking his head back and forth, and snubbing his hat. Gripping the arms of his rocking chair tighter, like a true Texas storyteller, he said, "Now, sonny...them round-headed, slobber-faced calves bellar'd and spooked, and them buffalo cows took offense to Ol' Blue. I grabbed all the leather I could find. But...yep...they charged. It was the damn-dus thing I'd ever saw. I tossed like a minnow on dry land when the first cow hit the off-side door like a rhino, over and over. I bounced clean over to the other seat, and back again."

Pete stood and walked to the edge of the porch. Mr. S.'s eyes followed him. The permanent scent of cattle drifted through the air. For a moment, the only sound came from Pete's spurs. Mr. S. didn't move. While peering at the horizon, Pete went on. "Got a thousand good cattle out there. Nope, you couldn't give me one of them buffalo heifers. Nope, they ain't good for nothin'."

Mr. S. slowly stood up and shook Pete's hand. We drove back to the clinic without another word being spoken. Pulling into the drive, and pointing to a hole in the fiberglass wheel-well of the newest Ol' Blue, I couldn't resist breaking the silence with another fact, "Mozzie, the owner of the Double D Ranch, threw a bucket filled with oats at her rottweiler for chasin' the barn cats. The dog got away, but Ol' Blue didn't."

Trying to talk Texan, Mr. S. slurred, "'Slingin' Oatmeal' ...okay, I'll handle this one personally."

I never did see the insurance company's president again. And neither Bob nor Mr. S. ever again asked me about other claims. It might have been hard for them to understand how a cloud of swarming grasshoppers chewed Ol' Blue's paint right down to the metal. But, this was Texas—and they just had to ask.

My pickup backfired again. "Ah, c'mon, gal," I pleaded, "you've got another 100,000 miles left in ya."

Boarding Scruffy

n a Friday morning, in the middle of a spray of flying gravel and dust, Dr. Vest and I simultaneously pulled up at our clinic. I was returning from an early morning calf delivery at ol' man Frederick's place, and Dr. Vest had already removed a retained placenta from Audrey Lynn Brisco's mare. It wasn't quite dawn.

Tracy called out, "Doc, it's Mrs. Kendall on line 1." The common noises of the clinic erupted louder than usual, and I motioned our kennel boy, Billy, to close the kennel door. "Hey, Nelly, how's it goin'? I'm sorry I'm havin' trouble hearing you." Rachel was filling the exam rooms with dogs and cats, Billy was cleaning the small animal cages, and, back in the barn, horses were whinnying to be fed. Nelly Sue Kendall was speaking so very softly. "Ma'am, can you speak up a bit?"

"Good morning," she said, in her gentle manner. "Doc, I forgot how much y'all charge to board a dog." Since fifty dogs were now barking in the back kennels, I joked that we didn't charge enough.

"Do you think you might have room for my little dog, Scruffy?" When I told her we'll always have room for Scruffy, she said she'd be right over.

Scruffy was a fuzzy geriatric schnauzer, whose bushy eyebrows shaded his glazed eyes. Arthritis had stiffened his walk, but he still shuffled along with short determined strides like a little old man. Scruffy already had grey whiskers when we first met, and was on heart medicines and diuretics. I remembered that he hated baths, but loved having his ears rubbed. Since he'd been at the clinic on numerous occasions, I assumed that the eighty-three-year-old former school teacher would simply drop him off as usual. "Hey, Scruffy's comin' in," I shouted to Rachel, who was too busy to give me any comment.

Instead, she yelled, "Doc, you need to go out to Mr. Skinner's. He has a cut horse." She couldn't send Dr. Vest because he was involved with a C-section on Mrs. Lord's spaniel, so I yelled back, "Tell Mr. Skinner to apply a dry pressure bandage, and I'll be there as soon as I can." I swore to myself, "Damn, everything seems to happen at once around here."

Rachel nagged again, "Hurry, Doc—he says she's bleeding badly."

"I'm goin', I'm goin'," I said, and jumped into Ol' Blue, not giving another thought to Nelly and Scruffy.

Norman Skinner's horse must have been frolicking near the work shed. A sheet of tin had sliced deeply into the left rear heel and blood was squirting through the wraps. The hemorrhage was easily stopped, however, with proper pressure on the posterior digital artery and vein. The chestnut mare would mend just fine with antibiotic dressings, support bandages—and time.

I rushed back to the clinic, bolting out of the cab. As I came through the door, Tracy informed me that a Siamese with an abscess from a cat fight was in room #2, and Mrs. Kendall was up front waiting. Dr. Vest jumped in to say he'd treat the cat, and I could see Nelly again.

I trotted to the front counter to greet her. "How are ya this fine afternoon?"

"Doc," she scolded, always priding herself on punctuality, "Afternoon? It's ten in the morning."

"It's good to see ya, anyway," I said, giving her a kiss on the cheek. In looking over Scruffy's medical chart, I saw that he hadn't been in to the clinic for almost a year, and was surprised it could have been so long. "Where's Scruffy?"

"In the car," said Nelly Sue, as she placed her glasses on the counter and raised her trembling hand as if to explain something. Then she paused, apparently forgetting what she was about to say. Her voice quivered, "Oh, I'm goin' to visit my sister in St. Louis, so I wantcha to take good care of my little Scruffy."

"You know we will, he's never a problem," I assured her.

Nelly Sue stood serenely poised with a baby blanket under one arm. She adjusted her white gloves and handed me Scruffy's bedcloth. On the floor was a small dog bed. With her cane, she pointed to it and said, "This goes in his cage, too."

I asked her to get Scruffy while I took his toys and belongings back into the kennel. "I'll get him all fixed up, with a big bowl of food."

"Food bowl," said Nelly to herself as she slowly walked out the door. And she kept repeating, "He needs fresh water…fresh…fresh water. And food…fresh food. I'll get his food bowl, too."

She must not have heard me, I thought. Placing a large container of cool water in Scruffy's cage, I carefully arranged the blanket and bed next to a bowl of our special dog food. Then, I waited…and, waited.

Getting distracted when the spaniel began awakening from surgery, I left for a moment to check on her progress. Mrs. Kendall called out from the reception area, "Doc, oh, Doc…can I put him in his quarters now?"

"Sure," I answered, "I'll be right there." But when I went back to settle her pooch in for his stay, I stood there dumbfounded—unable to speak.

"Here," Nelly instructed, "just set 'im on the bed." She handed me a small cedar box—Scruffy's ashes! "Doc, he died about a month ago in his sleep. I had him cremated. But, I sure wouldn't want anything to happen to 'im while I'm away." Her voice cracked. "He always liked stayin' here."

I quietly said, "He'll be fine, Nelly Sue," and I placed the velvet-lined box in the center of the pet bed. "Don't worry…he'll be fine." And I closed the cage door.

"Now, I'll pick you up in a month," Nelly murmured to Scruffy's remains, "…be good now, ya hear?"

Teeth of Fury

A rare treat…Dr. Vest and I managed to finish our coffee before heading out on morning rounds. Rachel had us on a tight schedule until the afternoon. Maybe then, I'd have the chance to get Bud Winston's horses ready for the flight of a lifetime—to South America. I promised the renowned horse trainer and breeder that I'd be there sometime today.

After finishing our rounds, Rich and I returned to the clinic within a minute of one another. I could see his rig approaching in my rearview mirror. Our timing was always perfect—late.

Suddenly a stream of livestock trailers began turning into the parking area of the clinic. The sight puzzled me. Pipe-fence corrals separated our small animal facilities from the large animal barn. And as the last pickup slid to a stop in front of our barn stalls, I recognized the logo of the high school's agricultural program painted on the slats above a blood-spattered wheelwell. Students began jumping out of the vehicles, as Tracy exited the kennels on a dead run. Rachel pointed and yelled to us from the back door. "A pack of stray dogs attacked the lamb barn at the school!"

I leaped from Ol' Blue and rushed forward, as Dr. Vest followed. Maimed and torn sheep, all bawling and in a panic state, lined the sides of each van. A short, blond boy anxiously explained, "They didn't have a chance. The dogs had already killed two before we found 'em this morning." In his arms, he somberly held a ram. "And mine...he just died a few minutes ago...on the way here."

Everywhere we looked, there were hemorrhage-saturated white wool coats. A dozen teens, boys and girls, gently pulled one lamb after another from the trailers. Blood stains smeared the concrete. Different voices called out from every direction, "Doc, over here. Look at this one!...Come over here...Please, Doc...take a look here!"

Dr. Vest knelt to help the first injured animal he came to. And I went straight for a small 'kid' that Tracy was helping. When she removed her hands from the lamb's throat, it bled profusely. "I can't stop the bleeding. Her jugular veins, on both sides, have been lacerated." Reaching down to apply firm pressure with my palms, blood oozed from between my fingers. Tracy ran into the clinic to get what we needed. Bandage materials were packed around the lamb's neck, but then we saw that the femoral artery, on the inside of the baby's thigh, had also erupted. Through the softly matted wool, I grasped what I could. I kept one hand on her throat, and the other on the relentless seepage from beneath the curls on her hind leg. Tracy began wrapping rolled gauze over her neck wounds, and I tied a tourniquet above the stifle. The lamb groaned, a guttural sound, and panted rapidly. Her tongue and gums blanched from anemia as her eyes helplessly stared at us. Her value, we knew, could only be measured in sentiment, but we didn't hesitate to try and save her. "Hand me an IV bottle," I said.

"There's no need," Tracy sadly replied.

Jennifer Meeks cried. Fourteen, and hopelessly in love with her newborn lamb, the frail young girl dropped to her knees beside the fatally injured pet. Tracy held Jen until the child's choking sobs subsided.

Our barn aisle resembled a hospital tent on a battlefield. Sheep were pawing against the stall walls in a rhythmic pattern—like fallen soldiers unable to arise. Jennifer seemed to be the leader of the group—and we had to keep her busy. To distract her and the other children away from their grief, we assigned each a task and an injured victim.

As in a triage, Dr. Vest designated numbers in accordance with the severity of each patient's wounds. Twenty-six sheep lay scattered at our feet as we methodically passed through the ravaged flock. IV bottles were passed down the line. "Jennifer, hold his head still," I said, threading a venous catheter, then handing Jen the life-supporting fluids for a young ram. "You, over there, son...spray the superficial wounds on this one."

Jennifer rose to the occasion. "Clint, pay attention to Doc," she commanded.

"That's number five," Dr. Vest yelled.

The deep gashes were sewn first. Stitching as fast as possible, Rich and I administered shock-therapy medications when necessary, monitored IV drips, and stroked through the lambs' locks as cut after cut was discovered. Wool, blood-soaked sponges, and empty cans of antiseptic spray littered the path behind us. "Are we up to sixteen, now?" I asked. My hands cramped and my knees ached. Rachel continued opening more packages of suture material, while Tracy threaded more needles. Across the aisle, I noticed Dr. Vest examining the foreleg of a lame ewe. Asking if it was broken, he replied, "Nope, but she's got a gash on her side as long as my arm."

I paused for a breath, when Jennifer pointed to a stumbling lamb trying to gasp for air. From ten feet away, we could see her gums were blue from oxygen loss. I jumped over three other sheep to see her. Her windpipe had collapsed, and I hollered for a trach-tube, asking Tracy to grab her head. There was no time for any anesthetic. While Jen held the lamb's legs, I performed an emergency tracheotomy with a pocket knife. And as I held the airway open with my fingers, Dr. Vest inserted the tube and taped it in place. "She can breathe on her own, now," he said.

"I think that's twenty-two," my partner commented.

We finished mending the last four, and slowly stood up. So much for a quiet afternoon, I thought. Dr. Vest stretched out his arched back, and said, "Ya know, there had to be at least six to eight dogs to do this amount of damage. And I'm kinda surprised they continued their attack through the entire flock…they had to have been in some sort of wild frenzy. We'll need to do some investigating…there are a lot of questions. Where did the pack come from? Has anyone seen them before, or since? Did they belong to anyone, or were they really all strays? We could use some town support for this…in fact, I'm going to call the sheriff's office right now."

We'd been on our hands and knees for hours. Since the attack, five lambs had died, but twenty-one would slowly recover. Rich muttered. "I almost forgot, I still have to do that endometritis surgery on Dixie, Mrs. Synder's chow."

"Yeah, and I've got to get Bud Winston's horses ready to fly—and pack myself."

When Jennifer asked who was flying where and when, Tracy answered, "Doc's goin' to Brazil tomorrow with a bunch of million-dollar horses. You can be sure there's never a dull moment around here."

Putting an arm around Jennifer, Dr. Vest said, "Jen, you've been a real trooper. Y'all can bed down the rest of these lambs, and I'll check on 'em again in a little while. Clint, while the lambs are here at the clinic for several days, please take the boys and mend those fences around the school's lamb barn. We don't want this to happen again."

It was impressive, I thought, the way these children responded. They all did what had to be done, despite the circumstances. And most of them still lingered on in the barn, spending a little extra time with their own pets.

I jumped into Ol' Blue, "Tracy, do I have what I need for the trip?" She nodded affirmatively, while Rachel waved goodbye from the back door. Dr. Vest turned to scan the flock of sheep —now resting and quiet—saying he hoped to have some clues about the dog pack by the time I got back.

Gravel spun from beneath my tires. "I'll be back before ya can blink…if not sooner."

"Tell Bud…" Rich yelled out, "…congratulations on his fantastic horse deal."

In the Air

monumental transaction had taken place at the Hollow Bend Quarter Horse Ranch in Collin County. Bud Winston sold $4.5 million worth of horseflesh to a syndicated Brazilian conglomerate. Having paid $950,000 for a single two-year-old colt, the group was anxious to have it and their new herd personally delivered.

Passing the fruit stand in Lolaville, I turned right on the chalk road leading to the small bridge crossing at Round Rock Creek. Red reflectors next to an oversized, blue wooden mailbox marked the entrance to Bud's ranch. His Spanish-style home rested beneath a knoll next to a stand of willow trees. But, here, Bud's barn and corrals took prominence, stretching over the hilltops surrounding his property.

Bud was waiting for me. A hefty, jovial sort of fellow with a boisterous laugh, he took everything with a grain of salt. He loved telling tall stories, and his gift of gab was notorious. His sharply creased straw hat was banded in braided horse hair, as was the belt on his worn, faded blue jeans. Blessed with years of experience, this well-liked rancher had seen just about everything in the horse business.

I never knew Bud to worry about anything. But, today, he seemed a mite nervous. Usually, my presence started a half-hour discussion about everything except the reason for my visit. Not today—he said very little. Obviously concerned, he took to pacing. Thinking I could razz him out of this mood, I said, "Welp, pardner, I sure hope none of 'em croak during the trip."

Grinning, Bud finally spoke up, "Bite your tongue, Doc. Hell, you're as ornery as they come. Don't even think such a thing. The truth is I've got a gut full of bad feelings 'bout this trip."

I assured him we'd all be fine, and actually bet him that we wouldn't have one problem. "I'll take that bet," he quickly added. Shoot, a Texan will damn near bet on anything, I thought. "Six-bits or a dollar?" I confirmed our wager with a counter of a dollar that we don't have the slightest problem.

We set about the important business at hand—protective leg wrappings and prophylactic 'oiling' for each horse. After I finished 'tubing' each mount, the plan called for equine transport vans to haul the horses to Houston during the night, to avoid the extreme heat and humidity of the Gulf-port town. At first light, I would meet the caravan of expensive breeding stock at the Export Customs Station. Then, a 747 cargo-jet would fly us non-stop to Palma, Brazil.

This was a well-organized maneuver—all pre-flight blood tests, government forms, and arrival arrangements were in place. Each horse was consigned to a holding stock and individually walked up the vans' ramps. Older mares, more accustomed to travel, were loaded first, while young fillies and colts came on last.

Everything progressed according to plan—almost too smoothly. Although one colt balked on the ramp and danced in the stocks, a quickly administered injection of a mild tranquilizer calmed his antics. All sixteen horses were secure and ready to roll. Even grooms rode in the rear of each van to ensure their travelers' safety. At the slightest problem, they were to pull a special 'panic cord' alerting the driver to stop.

As the transport started to roll, I waived to Yank, the lead driver and Bud's longtime foreman, "We're right on time. I'll see y'all in Houston." Holding up his fingers, crossed for luck, Bud's parting words to me were, "Doc, my check won't clear the bank until they're landed on Brazilian soil. So, please...take care of my babies. And, for godsakes...don't let anything happen to that good colt."

* * * * *

In the early morning darkness of the next day, my dad and I tromped across an open field to a wood-rotten barn where he kept his yellow, vintage bi-wing plane covered with a canvas tarp. Pa let me borrow "Lizzie" whenever I needed her. And he never stopped harping on me to be careful and not scratch her paint. I never asked him why he worried so much about her paint, when she had been through the heavy action of World War II. He helped me push Lizzie's creaking frame out into the dewy air. Checking the oil and kicking the tires, he wiggled the flaps while I fueled the tanks. "Don't slosh any of that," he ordered, "she's tender." The red prong jumped to 'full', and I shimmied up into the tight front seat. Pa stroked the propeller until Lizzie was ready to crank. "Ready? Clear!" He ran a ways out from the tip of the wings, hollering, "Go, now...go!"

Smoke billowed from Lizzie's exhaust, but she purred smoothly. I'd flown this old single-engine Steerman since I was tall enough to reach the stirrups on a saddle. My dad had used the air-craft to spray crops before I was born. Over time, he modified the wing-lengths, fuel tanks, and storage bay for ranch use. Under the seats were sliding drawers for my medicines. And, inside the hull, he'd attached my 'calf-jack'. Shotguns and shells were added weight, but she wasn't taxed. She even rolled over gopher holes with ease.

Always amazed at my dad's ingenuity and practicality, I benefited greatly from his determination to keep this 'family' transportation going so well for the past fifty years. Two days a week, during calving and foaling seasons, Ol' Blue sat idle while I hopscotched, hundreds of miles, from one cow-paddy to another. Most farms had at least one soft, flat pasture where I could land. The standing joke along my routes was that ranch-ers only had to look out over the horizon to determine if I'd be early or late. They knew whether to look for a blue dust trail on the road, or a yellow dot in the sky.

* * * * *

Taxiing Lizzie down the narrow asphalt runway in Houston, I felt relieved to know I was right on schedule to meet the vans. After checking in at Customs, Dr. Amos Hooper, the Federal Debarkation Veterinarian, blurted out, "The golden ponies haven't arrived yet!"

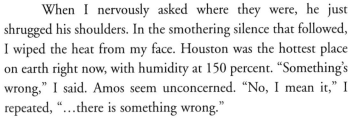

When I nervously asked where they were, he just shrugged his shoulders. In the smothering silence that followed, I wiped the heat from my face. Houston was the hottest place on earth right now, with humidity at 150 percent. "Something's wrong," I said. Amos seem unconcerned. "No, I mean it," I repeated, "...there is something wrong."

At that moment, the Customs Agent picked up the ringing phone on the counter, and quickly handed me the receiver, "It's for you, Doc."

It was Yank reporting that one of the vans broke down and they were stranded just outside Mexia, but he had radioed the ranch for another van. Amos interrupted, "I know where they are, but that's two hours away."

"Not by plane, it isn't. Yank, we're on our way."

Dr. Hooper almost backed out, admitting his fear of flying. But his sense of duty prevailed, and throughout the flight, he gamely clutched the seat cushions like they were life preservers. We cut through the clouds for almost an hour before spotting the van caravan and its broken-down rig. "Hang on!" I yelled, rolling the plane and diving across the highway to alert Yank. Groaning, "Holy Mother of...," Amos closed his eyes when I pointed to a patch of dirt about 500 yards east of the vans, and the plane's nose dropped. He was still repeating, "Ohmigod..." over and over, as grasshoppers splattered the windshield and the landing gear clipped off a few wild sunflower blooms. Our wheels touched down, the brakes locked, and dust swirled around the cockpit. Amos sat like a wooden stump, unable to move.

I patted him on the shoulder, "C'mon, let's look at the horses—they've got to be melting."

With the help of a few 'medical cocktails,' each horse was slowly transferred to the new coach that pulled up shortly after we got there. And, again, we were on our way to Houston. The responsible Yank, uptight at this break in our schedule, now smiled his mustachioed smile. Looking at the sun, we figured we still had time to make our flight. Amos now had the choice to go back with me, or with Yank. He looked at the highway, then the plane…then back to me.

Now into the spirit, Amos yelled, "YeeHaa!" when the engine revved, and Lizzie's nose jerked away from the ground. Vertical takeoffs were always my favorite things. "Houston…we are airborne," Amos announced over the radio transmitter, as we topped the trees.

* * * * *

As he came wheeling into the airport, Yank laid on his air-horn to announce his arrival. At the bar inside the terminal, Amos had just finished sharing his hair-raising adventure with the other agents. Normally, International Customs protocol was a long, drawn-out process. But, today, as the expanded wings of the 747 jetliner taxied down the concourse, Amos just pointed to the silver 'hippodrome', and waved us through.

One by one, the horses were unloaded from the vans and walked up to the cavernous belly of the stadium-like plane. At the rear, a massive ramp was lowered. Inside, plush padded scaffolding had been erected into individual holding stocks with wood slatted floors. And piped-in music played tunes contrived to soothe any mood of man or beast. I'd never seen anything like it before. While a cool breeze of compressed air added to the inviting environment, I paused to appreciate it all. Struck by the architectural design and detail, it looked as though the lobby of a South American luxury hotel had been moved into the body of the jet. Over the intercom, a resonant voice welcomed us aboard.

Yank and I secured the halter chains, and checked the butt-bars behind each mount. Night Squaw, a sorrel mare, pitched a small fit because she didn't get the seat she wanted, and two of the studs begged to get closer to her. But, all in all, every horse stood quiet and calm as the tail-ramp closed behind us.

We figured the lift-off would be the most frightening for the horses. After fastening my seatbelt, I studied the eyes of each horse. Not a single steed appeared uncomfortable, until we leveled at 23,000 feet. Then, Buenos Pecos, a bay gelding, whipped his tail and neighed—which started a flurry of shuffling hooves and nervous clatter.

Hearing the mild disturbance, the co-pilot called to us through the speaker to see if everything was okay. "Ain't nothin' we can't fix," I replied, as we walked among the horses, talking to them and soothing their restless spirits.

Though I didn't meet them prior to takeoff, Captain John Blackwell and his co-pilot, Gary McFearson, were apparently a couple of characters. Enjoying this whole mission, they joked from the cockpit, "Maybe our inflight movie, *Pegasus,* will calm them down."

Turbulence shook the plane. "There's one helluva storm up ahead," the captain added, "Maybe you can save some of the tranquilizers for us, too...Hold on to your hats, we're climbing to 35,000 feet."

A feeling of weightlessness gripped my stomach. Chocolate Dip, one of the older stallions, became strangely aroused by the upward surge and decided he was going to mate with his stall-partner, Night Squaw's full-sister, Morning Dove. Scaling the walkway, Yank and I aborted his intentions.

Again, the plane rattled—and I began to feel like a worm trapped inside the gizzard of a big bird. "Whoa, now, whoa," I crooned to the herd. "How much longer?" I asked the boys in control. "Two more hours," Captain Blackwell's raspy voice answered back.

Then, I saw it…Double Image, Bud's prize colt, starting to show signs of acute colic. His stomach must have felt the same flip-flop as mine. Without warning, the plane began to violently shake and bounce. "Storm's dead ahead," announced the captain.

Grabbing my medicine bag, I yelled, "We've got a belly-ache." Double Image stretched to urinate, but didn't. His eyes dulled, and his tail sagged. "Can I help?"asked the co-pilot. When I hollered, "Get down here, quick," Gary immediately climbed below. In his pressed uniform, the bald-headed city boy with fancy-trimmed black beard said he didn't know one end of a horse from the other. I didn't care, we needed the help.

The colt flexed his flank muscles, curled his lips, and his knees wobbled. "Hold his head…don't let him lay down. Grab his halter!" I yelled to Gary. The plane vibrated and pitched, and lightening strikes flashed outside the windows. Double Image's hocks trembled. He broke with a cold sweat. Thunder clapped. I injected him with pain relievers and smacked him on the side of the neck—to get his attention. "WHOA!" I yelled, trying to stop his collapse in the padded stock. "Stand up ther'."

Fermented gastric fumes came billowing out from the end of our nasogastric tube. "Gary, keep him on his feet." We both grunted and strained. Yank helped me push Double Image against the railing. We fought with all our might to ward off the 900-pound colt's attempts to combat his painful cramps. "We can't let him fall!" Soon, the hold of the plane smelled like a rotten silo. I exhausted every trick I knew. Double Image's black muscular frame swayed with fatigue. Crumbling to his knees, he tried to stand…staggered…and, buckled again. His legs banged against the post—and the butt-bar bent. The colt's hindquarters splayed, and the veins on one side of his face dilated with an adrenaline rush of fear.

"Watch out!" Double Image's hooves went slipping from the deck, pawing the metallic covering of the plane's body. His right rear hoof slammed against the escape-hatch door. His left hoof creased a metal panel, and sent echoes of alarm throughout the hull. "Gary, hand me a rope!"

"What in the hell is going on back there?" came the captain's voice. "Colic!" I answered.

While Yank had his hands full keeping the herd from picking up on the anxiety, Gary and I literally lifted Double Image to a standing position. "We've got to keep that hoof away from the wall." Wrapping a lasso loop around his right rear ankle to divert his crushing kicks away from the plane's shell, I commanded, "Git up ther'!" smacking the colt on the rump. His ears perked up, and his hooves came together. "Now, stand!" But, again and again, as the plane crackled with aftershocks of the storm, the colt's youthful temperament couldn't cope. Rivets rattled, support beams buckled, and metal panels bowed. The chain on Double Image's halter snapped, reeling to the floor like an anchor.

Then, suddenly, the noise stopped. Double Image shook his mane, as if awakening from a bad dream. We used our voices to further distract him. Whispering in his ear, "Good boy…whoa…settle down…whoa," the colt finally stood without help. The pain had subsided. The cold sweat dried, and his hooves locked firmly on the deck.

We looked down at the rope burns on our hands. Then, noticing a crumpled seam in the hull—right where Double Image had pawed last, I asked Gary if it would hold together. "What if he had kicked a hole right there?" Gary matter-of-factly said, "Well, then, I guess you and I would've been the first to reach land."

Captain Blackwell announced our descent, as Gary grinned and reached for something under my seat. Handing me a roll of duct-tape, he said, "Here, if it'll make you feel better, put a strip of this over that spot." Then, he climbed back through the hatch to the cockpit.

Screeching tires sounded good to me. "We're on the ground," proclaimed the captain. Horses pawed the stocks' decking as if it were dirt. "We're finally here, babies!"

Since we ended up with more than one problem on this trip, I would owe Bud Winston a whole bunch of dollars, if I ever again knelt to kiss Texas dust. Thank God, I thought, as I led Double Image, Night Squaw, and the others down the ramp to Brazilian soil.

Two businesslike gents, in seersucker suits, stepped forward. "Any problems?" asked the new owners. I didn't lie, "Not one," I said, turning to shake Captain Blackwell's hand. He was younger than I imagined. I kept on talking, "There were just a few black clouds between here and Dallas…right, boys?" Captain Blackwell backed me up. "Yeah, right, not a single hitch." His confident smile and official ranking gave him credibility.

Juan Montez, Double Image's new trainer, seemed relieved—and he was instantly charmed by the colt. If he only knew what had gone on just ten minutes earlier. Speaking a combination of Portuguese and English, Juan tried to carry on a conversation. Several men in the group now laughed, and pointed off toward the city, apparently inviting us to see the wonders of Rio de Janeiro. I could have been easily persuaded to see the accommodations where Double Image would be bred and housed, and, certainly, the Amazon River, the beaches and marketplace. But time, energy, and a passport were three things missing. All the horses' papers were in order. But I never thought to do anything about mine. Yank, on the other hand, had prepared for this and decided to stay on for a few days. He also wanted to report back to Bud on how the herd was doing.

After this quick and cordial owners' meeting and time for refueling, we decided to get back home. For the next eight hours, I stared at the weakened seam in the belly of the plane and wondered, in my paranoia, if it would hold together. But if Gary and Captain Blackwell felt secure, why shouldn't I? To humor me, Gary kept the tape coming, and I continued to apply layer after layer, until the panel was probably braced stronger than the original hull.

Relieved when the Gulf coast came into view, and the nose dropped…I thought of Amos and I, too, clutched the seat like a life preserver. Then I felt the jar of touchdown, and smelled the scent of oil. We had landed in heaven—Texas.

Time, Spirit...and 'Little Bit'

achel was overheard talking with a client on the phone, "No, ma'am," she said, "...she won't feel a thing. Doc's really good with 'em. Yes, you can bring her in about noon, Mrs. Beck."

After you've been in practice for awhile, euthanasia becomes an increasing part of the territory. But I heard myself saying, "Damn, why can't they just live forever?"

I knew who Rachel was talking to. I'd birthed Telia Beck's older dog, Little Bit. This tiny Maltese, a favorite of ours, had been a longtime patient. Little Bit's kidney functions, urination patterns, and general physical condition had been declining for some time, and we'd been expecting the owner's call for months. Still, it wasn't going to be easy. I'd gotten so attached to the sweet mutt...my whole staff loved the dog.

"She'll be in around noon," Tracy said quietly, as she put Little Bit's file on my desk. "I heard," was all I could say.

I remembered how our relationship began. At 2:00 on a Friday, I told the lovely Telia Beck that her puppy would be ready to go home around 4:30. Taking a minute to stop in the bank across the street, but seeing it jammed with people, I rushed in and dropped my deposit into the slot. Taking a deep breath, I said to myself, "Relax, her condition won't take but a few minutes to correct."

Little Bit, a fleecy white powder-puff, with short legs and huge blue eyes, had been gnawing gingerly on the tip of my finger with her baby teeth while I examined her earlier that morning. She would run back and forth to the toy box, bringing Telia one tennis ball after the other. Telia, a soft-spoken secretary for one of the large oil companies downtown, was clearly a worried owner. "What is it?"

"It's 'cherry eye', I told her. Considered a common ocular lesion in young dogs, cherry eye is a red tonsil-shaped node that swells and protrudes from the third eyelid on the inside corner of the eye. "I see them often. It's a simple procedure, needing minor surgery. But it does require some anesthesia."

Mrs. Beck nodded her head as we discussed the complications and risks associated with any type of anesthesia. And I tended to dwell on the brevity and simplicity of the excision. "There is little after-care," I stressed. "And any 'dry-eye' occurrence after surgery is rare."

"I understand," said Telia. Looking over my shoulder, Tracy added, "Ah, that's nothin', one small snip."

"Just leave Little Bit with us for a short while, and we'll get 'er fixed up in no time at all." Again, Telia nodded her understanding. The dignified young woman accepted the situation and asked no more questions. "Since she's so small," I added, "I think the best route will be to 'mask' her with a little gas. That way she'll be down for a short time. And, her recovery time will be much shorter, too." Telia agreed, and surgery was scheduled for early afternoon.

Tracy brought in the four-pound patient as soon as she heard me coming back from the bank. The thirteen-week-old Maltese handled the masking-anesthesia perfectly. Her induction into a sleep state went smoothly, and she stabilized on the vapors without the slightest bobble. Slick and fast, the surgery took one snip—and it was over. Her recovery seemed instantaneous.

Little Bit came up barking in less than two minutes. When Telia came in at 4:30, Rachel was enthusiastic, "She's ready to go home! Just put these drops in her eye for a few days. And watch for any involvement of the other eye. It's not unusual for the other side to flare up at some point in time. If another 'cherry eye' occurs, just bring her back for the same treatment." Clipping the leash on her fluffy pup, the congenial owner simply said, "I understand and I will. Tell Doc, thanks…"

Sure enough, two months later, Little Bit came back again through the same door, wagging her tail non-stop. This time, she had a 'cherry' in her left eye, almost identical to the first. Telia, brief as usual, said, "Well, she's got it, just like you predicted."

We all agreed this was a repeat performance, and she'd be ready to go home about the same time as before. Now a veteran to the procedure, Telia didn't hesitate, "Of course, I'll see y'all about 4:30." Handing Little Bit to Tracy, she was particularly warm, "Give her a few extra hugs and kisses for me when she wakes up." I thought to myself that Little Bit must be working her joyful magic on the lady. Tracy snuggled with the vivacious pup for a moment, before Little Bit squirmed free, making a bee-line for the toy box.

This surgery took even less time than the first operation. Snip...and, it was done. "There," I said. Then my heart skipped a beat...Little Bit quit breathing! Her mucous membranes turned blue from oxygen loss, and her body went limp. "She's crashed!" I yelled. Cardiac arrest was imminent. "Code Red! What tha hell happened? Damn it!" I immediately started CPR, but Little Bit didn't respond. I massaged her chest while administering respiratory and cardiac stimulants. She lay still. I frantically tried to jolt her vital signs—yet nothing worked.

"C'mon girl...breathe!" Little Bit's heart began to beat, faintly. She responded slightly. But I was still terrified. "Breathe," I coaxed, "Breathe. Okay, Little Bit...breathe now." Tracy looked bewildered. The pup began to breathe. She was alive...but comatose. Her heart, however, now beat rhythmically. I remained in shock. "Okay, now, don't die on me." Reaching for the phone to inform Telia of our crisis, I tried to explain the sudden turn of events. Trying to talk through her confusion, this time Telia just said, "I don't understand."

"Me, neither," I admitted. "Telia, she just crashed, right before my eyes. We did everything exactly as before. Now...only time will tell." I really didn't know what else to say. Everything had unraveled so quickly. All I could do was assure Telia that we'd continue intensive critical therapy for as long as necessary.

Neither Tracy nor I took our eyes off Little Bit for the rest of the night. There was no reason found for the pup's dramatic turn. We went over our steps a thousand times.

The next morning, Little Bit's condition was about the same. She remained in a coma, and her head and body were limp. Rachel and Tracy rolled her over every few hours, manually exercising her leg muscles. She showed no response to any stimulation. I pinched between her toes for a reflex...but nothing. When Little Bit was lifted by one of us, her paws and tail hung limp, swaying from her still body. Praying for a miracle, I fed her with intravenous drips, but feared for her chances of recovery. Over and over, I asked myself, "What happened?"

At dusk on the second day, there was some movement. Her feet moved a little. First, one toe twitched. Her leg bent. Then, her paws began to pedal. However, she didn't recognize any outside stimulus. We kept on trying. I raised Little Bit's eyelids to test the flash of a bright light. Nothing—her pupils remained fixed. My sense of hope went down the drain. Little Bit stopped moving. Again, I pinched between her toes...again, nothing.

On the third day, Little Bit's somnambulism had increased. Every so often, she would make a guttural sound. The slits of her eyes would crack open, but she saw nothing. We recorded every tiny mark of improvement. She couldn't focus, but her eyelids raised and lowered. Her pupillary response to the bright light began to constrict slightly, yet this, too, was considered a positive sign. My hope rose. Then, the little dog slipped back into her coma for a few more hours.

Tracy often leaned in close to Little Bit's ear to whisper, "C'mon, girl." My staff and I worked diligently—rubbing Little Bit's body with warm towels and constantly adjusting the supportive flow of the IV fluids. Several times we jumped up at false starts, trying to assume the best. By the fourth day, when hours seemed like months, Little Bit's swallow reflex slowly returned. Offering her some baby food on the tip of my finger, she awkwardly lapped at the nourishment with her tongue. Her head didn't raise up, and her eyes didn't open—but she seemed more aware of my presence.

The fifth day passed. As we continued to feed her by hand, her oral dexterity increased. Little Bit batted her eyes with pleasure, but locked her jaws when she'd had enough. The little creature was obviously trying to hang on. Tracy manipulated her head and legs, until Little Bit became more communicative as the seventh day approached. I wanted to be optimistic, but doubts persisted. On the ninth day, Tracy noticed that when she pulled or pushed on Little Bit's rear legs, the dog resisted. I pinched her toes, and she yelped. This was great! Then her eyes began to focus, and she barked, pawing Tracy's hand like she wanted something. She began smacking her lips to show she was hungry, and her ears would cock when we spoke. I held her in my arms for hours at a time, wondering if she would fully recover.

Telia and I were in constant contact. All the signs were encouraging, but I couldn't give her any promises and was careful to guard the words I used. Little Bit still couldn't left her head or control her bodily functions. But her spirit, I felt, had returned. I didn't know if there would be any permanent brain damage.

Each of us was touched by Little Bit's courage. Tracy, on the eleventh day, was finger-feeding her with baby food, when she yelled, "Come here, Doc, watch 'er." Until now, Little Bit's head mobility had been limited. But, this time, her head reached for the food, and the pup sniffed the air as if to say, "Wait a minute, bring that back." Tracy moved her hand back and forth.

Little Bit's nose followed the aroma, and her muzzle lifted. "What d'ya think, Doc?"

"I don't know what to think anymore." Feeling the elation of a father watching his child take the first baby steps, I was also fearful that she may fall. Little Bit was weak. "But that's the best sign...so far." Her limited body movements became more controlled, yet sometimes her general condition would fail. We'd raise our hopes, only to have them crumble. There were days that we took turns sitting and gently stroking Little Bit's fur. That's all we could do for her. Then, there were other days when she seemed to make huge strides.

Early on the morning of the fifteenth day, Karen answered our home phone, "Little Bit's up?" she said in a tone of awe. "Are you sure?" I bounded out of bed and raced to the clinic. As I drove, my heart pounded, and I wondered if she was really better this time.

Little Bit was sitting in her cage. Her back legs weren't working properly, but she'd managed to straighten her front legs into a sawhorse position. She wrestled to maintain her balance, and won. Tracy and I encouraged her efforts—and she barked with excitement. Vibrations from her vocal cords almost knocked her off her feet. I could hardly wait to give Telia the good news. "She's wobbly, and her hindquarters are partially paralyzed," I said, "...but she's mobile!" My voice cracked. "Telia, I guess anything is possible." Mrs. Beck softly said what she always said, "I understand."

This time, I smiled and said, "Good, because I don't."

On the twentieth day of her rehabilitation, Little Bit scrambled to follow me around the clinic, dragging her rear legs across the floor, like a dust mop. Her urination and bowel movements became more controlled, and we no longer had to bathe here soiled haircoat and treat her chapped skin. She was becoming more and more playful, but seemed confused by the reluctance of her hindquarters to cooperate. Even as we marveled at her progress, she'd growl in frustration. Time and time again, she'd stretch to retrieve another stuffed animal or ball from the toy box, until the treatment area floor was covered. I'd pick up the toys, and she'd drag them back out. To her, it was a constant game; to me, her physical therapy.

The pup was seldom idle. She'd get angry when we needed to put her in her cage. And her eyes would drill a hole in your heart as you closed the door. I began taking her into my carpeted office, where she would grip the fabric with her hind paws and push with all her might, again and again, trying to stand. She'd almost make it, then fall. But the brave little mutt wouldn't quit. She never let up trying, until fatigue would overcome her determination. We were all amazed. Sleep was the only thing that prevented her from chewing on the bars of her cage, or shredding the newspaper lining. A towel was simply something to destroy during her days of excess energy, while she waited for her rear legs to gain more strength. The stronger she got…the more determined she became.

Twenty-two more days passed—a total of almost six weeks from the beginning—and Little Bit walked normally for the first time. Coordinated and sure-footed, she stood and paced a few steps in a single direction, each paw placed where it should be. And, the look on her funny face was worth all the time and effort we'd ever thought of spending. Little Bit barked with glee, then darted off to get her favorite toy.

"What did she fetch?" asked Telia, when I called her with the fantastic news.

"The whole damn basket," I laughed. "She dragged the entire toy box into my office,"

A milestone had been reached. So Rachel and Tracy planned a party and, of course, Telia was invited to Little Bit's return-to-health celebration. Treats and milkbones were bought, and Telia brought in a basket of fruit. We all sat on the floor watching Little Bit jump and romp around the room. By this time, we'd changed the pup's name to "Little Bit of Miracle." My mood shifted from ecstatic to melancholy—because Little Bit's discharge date was fast approaching. After so many clinic visits, Telia was elated to swoop the pup into her arms and finally take her home. We knew we'd see her regularly, but her feisty spirit had become so much a part of our daily lives, that we felt an emptiness on the day she left.

* * * * *

That was then, fourteen years ago. I looked at my watch—noon. Telia came into the clinic, and I couldn't hide a heavy heart.

"Little Bit's time has come," said Telia. The tiny Maltese, with the giant spirit, had survived a coma, birthed three litters, one by cesarean section—and enjoyed years of her family's loving companionship. Telia now held Brandy, Little Bit's daughter, in her arms—as I lifted Little Bit, the sweet white ball of fur with the big blue eyes, into my arms. She was barely conscious, and my hands trembled when I stared down into her tired, unseeing eyes. Somberly, I carried her into the treatment area, gently placing her small body on the table—talking to her the whole time—then set a tiny gauge needle into one of her veins. I was unable to escape the feelings as I pressed on the syringe. We all knew this was for the best. But my vision blurred—and Rachel and Tracy stood there silently. Telia wanted to wait in the reception room until it was over. Then, as if to help us all through this moment, she turned Brandy toward us so we might see her cute little face, and how much she looked like Little Bit.

"Doc, can I pick her up at the usual time?" asked Telia.

Brandy had 'cherry eye', just like her mother. In a strange way, we were right back where we started. "Sure," I answered, "I'll snip that off this afternoon."

Time seemed to roll back—as we watched Brandy awaken from surgery. And, then, as if I were standing in front of her mother's cage, I found myself saying, "Little Bit...c'mon girl, stand." Brandy popped to her feet. Her big blue eyes drilled a new hole in my heart. Telia walked through the door to retrieve her pup...at 4:30.

"Put these drops in her eye. And watch the other one," I heard Rachel say.

Giving Brandy a big hug, Telia said, "I understand."

20

Blue Norther

I f the moon could talk, it would spin a tale about Texas 'Blue Northers'—and how quickly they can whip through a city of a million people, paralyzing man and beast. As generations of Texans have said, "Son, if you don't like the weather here…just wait a minute…'cause it'll change."

Startled by a loud crashing noise, I jumped from bed and dashed to our living room window. A huge limb from our oak tree had ripped from its base and was now lying across the hood of Ol' Blue. "Karen, come look at this. We were scorching in the hot sun yesterday, going barefoot in the garden…and now look." Karen, yawning, was never surprised by whatever changes met each dawn. "That was yesterday…" Then she hollered to our young son, "No school today, K.C."

Together, the three of us peered out from our bay window at nature's phenomena. A blinding-white, frozen landscape of ice smothered what had been our lush, green horse pasture on the north side of the house. Oddly, overhead, crystal blue skies stretched forever. I had the eerie feeling that the only thing blocking us from the North Pole was a single strand of barbed wire.

"It's blue, all right, and it gives the word 'blue' a whole different meaning. Dang, I've got to work in that stuff today," I complained.

Although K.C. had been through these Blue Northers before, this one, we all knew, was extreme. "Look!" he excitedly pointed in every direction, "…there, and over there." Our Polish-bred Arabian horses, more accustomed to arid surroundings, were standing with several inches of caked ice on their backs. Cone-shaped icicles hung in strips from the porch-top all the way to the ground. A couple of beetles were petrified on the outside windowsill. And two unfortunate squirrels had been instantly mummified in their tracks. "Wow, look at that!" To the right of the water trough resembling a miniature glacier, several birds lay dead below the skin-tight bark covering the elm trees' shivering trunks. "And, there." The Brangus cows in the next pasture snuggled tightly, surrounding their calves to keep them warm.

I should have seen the signs—an unseasonably warm day, horses standing in paddocks with their rears pointing to the north, a blue haze on the horizon, ants going crazy trying to pick up every crumb, and cattle lying down against the warmth of the soil. Somehow the animals knew, but I didn't pay attention. The only thing I noticed was the sight of flags at K.C.'s school abruptly flipping direction. Feeling the temperature drop a bit, I still didn't figure it would plunge seventy degrees in a matter of hours!

Our outside thermometer read…12 degrees. "Migod, I've got to get to the clinic." The chill factor was sub-zero.

Ol' Blue looked like an igloo with portholes. With Karen and K.C. helping, we managed to roll the downed limb off the hood—and the engine fired after only a few starts. The short four-mile drive to the clinic took forty minutes. "Whew, I made it," I sighed, trying not to slip at the entrance to Twin Oaks. Tracy was sitting behind Rachel's desk.

"I feel like a switchboard operator this morning," she said, "…and I just heard on the news that eight people have died so far in this freakish weather."

"I know you're worried," she added, "there's no water in the kennels. Pipes must have froze. But the dogs and cats are warm."

I was afraid to ask the next question. "And, the barn? How is Mr. Cameron's Paint stallion, the one with the twisted intestine that we operated on yesterday. Is he…?"

Tracy answered in her very direct manner, "Dead…frozen. But all the others out there are okay."

"Damn! Did you get a chance to call Duke Cameron—and where is Dr. Vest?"

"Iced in," Tracy replied, as the phone lines blinked. "Yes, I called Duke as soon as I checked the barn this morning. He said he didn't think his horse could have survived…that we can't fight the weather."

Handing me an earlier message, she said, "Here, you call Steve Jacobs. I'll catch the rest of these calls. Then I'll fill the animals' bowls with our bottled water, 'cause there's no tellin' how long this will last."

Reaching Steve on the first ring, I listened to him explain, "Doc, my son's mare, Snowflake, has a fence post—a T-post—stuck in her side."

I about choked, already picturing it—a lethal lance embedded through Snowflake's tissues. A six-foot barbed, metal stake with T-shaped shaft and flat plate was either dangling or wedged inside the young mare—Gary's pet.

Normally, the trip to Steve's place in Garland would take thirty minutes. This wasn't a normal day. Though Steve knew I was on my way, he also knew there was no telling how long it would take me. Tracy tried to head me off, "Have you lost your mind? Mr. Jacobs doesn't pay his bills, and you're liable to get killed out there in this mess. It'll take ya forever to even get there…and you won't have help when you do."

She was right, as usual. Steve was divorced, and had spent fourteen years raising four kids in an oil-field shack After striking 'pay dirt', he seldom parted with a dollar except for lavish toys. Money wasn't the issue here, though, and Tracy knew it. Though living an opulent lifestyle, Steve was still a sarcastic 'wildcatter'. But his son's horse was hurt, and our opinion of his dad didn't matter.

I chose to ignore Tracy's common sense, and she knew better than to question my bullheadedness. "You're goin', anyway. But I hope your damn life insurance is paid up, 'cause I'm not workin' for a dead man."

Quickly scrounging for the heater knob, I blessed Ol' Blue's surge of warmth. It was a slow, tricky drive, with power lines haphazardly draping down from the weight of ice, just waiting to entangle clumsy prey. I'd never seen the city so still.

Wrecks by the dozen lined the sides of the road. More than once, I got a mite nervous when Ol' Blue's tailgate weaved like a snake's tail…but I kept creeping along at five to ten miles per hour. Two hours later, arriving at the one-acre lot, I almost slid on a sheet of ice into Steve's parked car.

With all his money, I thought, you'd think he'd have a fancy, high-tech barn. But Snowflake stood outside, with her hindquarters backed against the tin of a three-sided windbreak. Half of the loafing-shed's roof was gone, and one corner sagged.

The old rough-scuff ran over to me, "God, I'm glad you're finally here." Fumbling with my coat buttons, I shivered, "Me, too…I think."

Dressed in Aspen's finest sable jacket and alligator boots, Steve seemed genuinely worried, "She musta done it…this morn'."

Whispering, "Whoa," to Snowflake, I reached for the lead rope that hung from the stiffened halter. "I'll be in the car," Steve called out over his shoulder. Vigorously rubbing my hands together, I said, "No, no you won't…that ol' dog won't hunt…I need you to hold Snowflake." He stopped in his tracks, breathing in short huffs. "But, it's freezin' cold out here. That wet wind will cutcha to the bone." I rolled my eyes, and he kept on arguing. "Besides, I called you."

"Yeah," I laughed, "…and that's why you're the one who's goin' to hold this horse."

Snowflake's wound was much worse than imagined. Her left side didn't have a scratch—but her right side was another matter. The T-post had entered her flesh behind her elbow. I figured she must have been on a dead run. The blunt point, apparently ricocheting, had bounced off her rib bones—and the barbed steel rod rammed with great force between the muscle layers of her thorax and abdomen. The flat, anchoring plate was resting against the outside of her forearm, while the other end had ripped a hole through the skin in her flank…just two inches in front of her hip bone. I was puzzled as to how she could have done this, and doubted if I could ever get it out. Long, thin bloody icicles were hanging from the pole's tips, but only small drops of red were able to fall without freezing to Snowflake's sorrel haircoat. I was glad Gary didn't have to see this. Thankfully, the nine-year-old lad was visiting his aunt up north.

Steve grimaced at the sight of the stabbing lance. How it kept from perforating her chest and belly was beyond me. "Geeze, he groaned, "how in the world could…"

Snowflake did not move a muscle. She seemed to sense her own desperate state, and stood there quivering with her hooves firmly placed. She did flinch, however, when I reached toward the pole. "It's locked in position," I said. "The rounded barbs on the shaft will not let the stake move." The cold steel ran deeper than I originally thought. Feeling along the borders to see if anything vital might get in my way, I prepared myself for a whole lot of cutting and sewing.

"I'm gonna hav't cut the damn thing out. The incision will stretch from stem to stern, about four feet. And it's liable to be a bloody mess—but it's gotta come out." Steve nodded, jumping in place to stay warm.

When he asked a foolish question like, "Is she in pain?" …at least I knew he cared. The temperature had dropped to 5 degrees. Winds whipped the falling sleet sideways. Snowflake bled and trembled. "Nope, she's numb," I answered, turning to gather my supplies. With my own hands and feet numb, I wondered how I'd be able to stay warm enough to work. Waiting for Snowflake's tranquilizer to take effect, I thought of a quick strategy. My fingers turned blue when I injected a local anesthetic in and around the lengthy shaft. And I didn't think I'd manage well with thick leather gloves, so decided that latex surgical gloves might act like a swimmer's wet suit. If one pair can prevent contamination, then three on at once should keep my hands warm enough to stitch.

Steve closed his eyes. I made one sharp, long—very long—incision through the skin and muscles on Snowflake's side. "Ough," he groaned, as blood oozed from every vessel. We were relieved to see smaller capillary channels being sealed by the frigid winds. I clamped the larger veins and ligated, as bloody popsicles formed in my palms. When a couple of puddles clumped and solidified into red ice cubes around my feet, Steve sputtered, "Holy Geeze, Doc!"

Dissecting gently, I lifted the T-post from the mare's raw flesh. She never moved. Then, like the sound of metal on metal, the freed lance rattled when the flat plate struck the icy turf. Figuring there'd be serious complications if I had to search for a million wooden splinters, I was exalted to see that the lance was all steel.

"Let's put 'er back together, and get out of this friggin' cold." Steve kept yards and yards of suture material coming to me, as I sewed and sewed. Snowflake finally shifted her weight after two muscle layers were matched and closed. This was an amazing horse. Her head even raised in cooperation as I sutured the last few inches of skin. Steve crooned to her in soft tones through his chattering teeth. "Boy, Doc," he said, "I'll bet you never thought you'd spend half your life sewin' one mare. Should we worry about infection?"

After cleaning the closed incision, and explaining that Snowflake had more than 300 hundred stitches, I told him that I had flushed the wound with antibiotics, and given her a tetanus shot. "Besides, no self-respecting bacteria would live in these conditions."

"I'm done," I said, walking toward Ol' Blue with my hands and feet throbbing. Then, yelping in pain myself, I realized how stupid I'd been. The perspiration from my palms had collected and frozen the rubber gloves to my skin. My fingers were on fire, and I couldn't flex my grip. While asking Steve what frostbite looked like, I chipped adhered latex from my raw palms and bleeding fingertips.

"I don't know, but look on the bright side, Doc."

I paused to plunge each hand into a jar of soothing antibiotic ointment. "What bright side?"

"Maybe Snowflake's cut will freeze together, like your fingers did. And maybe she won't have a scar. And maybe, since you've got sore hands, you can just wait and send me the bill."

Again, I was stupid. I knew better than to let him charge, but I did. Temperatures rose to 70 degrees three days later, and bills went out. But six weeks later, Steve Jacobs still hadn't paid. "No wonder he's so damn rich," I swore to myself.

I'd been checking on Snowflake regularly, but Steve was never around during my follow-up visits. On my final examination, there was just a thin scratch of a scar remaining on her left side. She had come through her ordeal beautifully—in no small measure due, I was sure, to Gary's constant attention.

I drove directly to Steve's Turtle Creek penthouse and knocked on the door. He seemed surprised when I said, "Steve, I'm not here for coffee and donuts." He knew why I was there, and didn't hesitate to say he should get a 'Blue Norther' discount for helping me.

"When heaven freezes," I grinned.

"But, it did," he argued.

"Yeah, but Dallas and I have thawed, and we're goin' to be burnin' up in no time at all."

Reluctantly counting out bills, "Ten, twenty, thirty, forty…" he stopped, "Can I write you a check for the rest?" With no response from me, he knew to keep going. "Fifty, sixty, seventy…" It was killing him to let go of each dollar, but he continued counting, saying, "Boy, it's hot in here."

"Don't fret, Steve," I laughed. "Haven't you seen the hazy blue skies? It'll be 10 degrees again…at this time tomorrow."

Winding my way home, I couldn't help but think, "Tracy's goin' to be proud of me." But I'll still have to promise her, on a stack of bibles, to never again let this slick gent pull one over on me…until the next time, that is.

Can a Pill Fix It?

F resh, fragrant pipe tobacco smoke filtered through the open, sliding-glass window that separated the treatment rooms from our reception area. Recognizing the scent that hung in the air like incense, I knew Cleave Greeley puffed such a distinctive aromatic blend.

Cleave was sitting in the lobby with the long, curved pipe stem hanging from the corner of his mouth. Rings of grey smoke floated from the big, hand-carved bowl as he slumped his bald head and smacked his lips before taking another draw. His constant sidekick, Patton, lay snoozing at his feet, with his muzzle resting on his crossed front paws. Loosely tied around the Boston terrier's neck was a red and green plaid bandanna, in the same plaid as the flannel shirt his owner had on. Both had their eyes closed. They look so much alike...I thought. Round, domed brows...drooping jowls, and matching clothes. Patton's white forearms were dusty and blended with the cuffs on Cleave's tan corduroy trousers. A felt hat on the widow man's lap was the same size and color as the black splotches in his pet's fur. Cleave had a slight double chin and a paunch of a belly, and, Patton, except for his short tail, had a similar physique. At one time or another, every vet has been amused at the similarities between owners and their pets. And, without the gold-rimmed bifocals tipping on the end of Cleave's nose, these two topped my personal list, and could have won a prize for 'looking like brothers'.

Intruding on their reverie with, "Howdy," Cleave's and Patton's eyelids popped open simultaneously, as they wrestled to attention. "Hey, Doc…" the sixty-four-year-old man mumbled as he stretched. "That sun's warm and I must've gotten a mite sleepy." Patton stretched, too, and sat up. Since they were the only ones in the lobby, I thought it best to visit informally, and talk about the two-year-old's affliction. Sitting down on the floor tiles alongside Patton, and crossing my legs, I began scratching him between his ears. Cleave used a hushed tone, "Doc, he had another spell last night. What does he have?"

"I believe it's epilepsy," and quickly added "…a common, treatable neurological dysfunction."

Cleave sat back heavily in his chair, as if I'd slapped him. I wanted him to understand that his companion's condition was serious, but not fatal. He didn't need another loss in his life. The whole town liked Margaret, his wife of forty years. She'd been a popular high school teacher before losing her life to breast cancer last year. And it was no secret that this whimsical pup was helping the quiet man cope with his grief.

The vivacious terrier squirmed up into my lap, wiggling. His hindquarters moved with such energy that his stump of a tail seemed to spin. Seeing him like this made me forget he was even ill. Patton kept licking my cheeks, as I stroked his back—and I couldn't help but laugh at his antics. Our romping broke Cleave's silence.

"Patton, sit," his soft-spoken owner said…but the pup kept bouncing, slurping, and rolling on his back, so I could pat his belly. "I was doin' just that last night, scratchin' his belly…when he began jerkin' and shiverin'," Cleave said, "…must've gone on for two or three minutes." Patton finally relaxed, stretching out his back legs and front paws.

"Doc, his eyes went into a glassy stare, and his mouth muscles constricted into a strange, quivering snarl. When his neck stiffened and his legs began to tremble, he began salivating, urinating, and moaning." Cleave paused and looked over at Patton, "My boy, I thought you were a goner. Doc, he was fine one minute, thrashing the next—then playing like a puppy an hour later. He staggered in a daze for a few minutes after the spell, but, soon enough he was back to normal." Taking the pipe from his mouth, Cleave's words became more precise, "Doc, what makes you think he has epilepsy?"

The worried man had described a typical seizure. It was Patton's third spell in four months. Cleave had made the diagnosis with his clear observations, but didn't realize it. And it was apparent that this gentle man had a thousand questions.

A smoke ring floated to the ceiling. Looking down at Patton, I explained that I'd ruled out every other cause and effect. "He's a young dog, so it's probably inherited. The spells are occurring without regard to time, place or reason, and there doesn't appear to be any permanent damage—no paralysis, or lasting effects."

Tightly gripping the bowl of his pipe and nodding in agreement, Cleave listened intently as I went on, "Patton's blood chemistry profiles are normal. There's no hypoglycemia, low blood sugar, or organ dysfunction causing these sporadic episodes." Another perfect smoke ring spiraled upward. Patton was now snoring.

Cleave fidgeted with his hat, as I started to explain the three phases of an epileptic seizure, and how they can vary in time and severity. The terrier's ears sagged as he sighed, and rolled over on his right side with an even deeper sigh. Then, after a snort, he was content and quiet.

"Cleave, the first is *aura*, a helpless, isolating phase when there's a sudden change in behavior. If normally aloof, he's underfoot. If attentive, he may go hide in…" Pretending to concentrate, Cleave pushed his hat onto the back of his head, and began tugging on the brim. I realized, then, that he didn't really want to cope with my medical lecture. Feeling he should at least understand the basics, I briefly let him know what to expect in the phases of *aura, seizure,* and *exhaustion,* so he'd be aware of the symptoms.

Cleave's eyebrows went up. Nodding his head with each puff, he said I had described Patton to a T. Then furrowing his brows with concern, he had one simple question, "Isn't there a pill or something to fix 'im?"

"Yes." But at that moment, the eighteen-pound pooch started making unusual whimpers. "Patton," I called out to no avail. Before my eyes, the black and white dog was going into seizure. He rolled back onto his side, and his eyes were wide open, fixed in a stare. I called to him again, but there was no response.

From his nose to his tail, Patton was stiffening. His lips curled, his jaw chattered, and his neck curved back as his spine became arched and rigid. I hollered to Tracy to fetch an injection of a central nervous system tranquilizer. "Hurry!"

Patton's legs were paddling with aimless strides and jerks, until an involuntary convulsion jolted his body like a high-voltage shock. Threading his cephalic vein and asking Tracy to hold his leg still, I pushed the plunger on the syringe to alter the path of the seizure—then waited to administer more of the calming medicine if needed.

Almost whispering, Cleave said, "That's exactly what he did last night...but I'm sure glad you saw it for yourself, Doc."

The terrier's muscles relaxed and his eyes blinked. In less than a minute, he was licking his lips and rolling upright—but, still, a little too disoriented to stand. "There, now...just lay there and rest," we kept telling the pup, who could sense for himself that something had happened.

When the caring owner asked what could have caused the sudden spell, I had to admit that, unfortunately, medicine didn't have an answer to that yet. So, in a tone of reluctant acceptance, Cleave finally said, "Well, Doc, I guess he really does have epilepsy."

Monitoring the terrier's strengthening vital signs, while explaining the kind of treatment regime needed to control his condition, I said, "We've got to use a mild barbiturate to stop the seizures. Phenobarbital or Primidone are the drugs of choice, and Patton will need the medicines daily."

At this, Cleave winced, "For how long...won't that make him dopey?"

Trying to give him as much reassurance as possible, I let him know that Patton would need to be on this medication for the rest of his life, but that the dosage will be adjusted until the seizures stop.

A big puff of smoke circled us both. Cleave smiled with relief. "So, Doc, my boy will live a normal life…like you and me?"

I thought this to be an interesting comment and comparison. But, after what he'd been through the past few years, he needed some security right now. "Yes," I said. "Just like yours and mine." Patton jumped for his owner's lap, but was about to miss—so I caught him mid-air. "Cleave…his life, yours and mine will always be catch-as-catch-can, with or without the epilepsy complication."

Only twice did Patton's dosage have to be revised. One pill morning and night made him act sluggish. And when a once-a-day treatment was tried, he had another spell. Cleave remained patient.

Now, day after day, Cleave administers a half tablet three times each day to his lovable friend. Month after month, I renew the prescription at the prescribed dosage. And year after year, the playful Boston terrier continues to keep the gentle man's life happy and active.

Seven-Star Ranching

Aren't you suppos't be at Seven-Star ranch in Dickens?" asked Dr. Vest. Like me, he, too, loved the people and simple, easygoing ways of West Texas. Since I hadn't had a day off in several months, this trip out to Uncle Grump's was also a good excuse for my dad and me to go quail hunting.

"Well," Rich asked again, "...shouldn't you be on the road already?"

My mind wandered off to a few things both Karen and K.C. had been admonishing me about. My son was frank, "Dad, you need an checkup from the neck up." And Karen said something about "an attitude adjustment." I didn't get out to my family's home often enough these days. Since our practice had no boundaries, it seemed a good idea to get back there and sort out the city stresses.

"Yeah, I'm going...after seeing the rest of my appointments." A raccoon neuter, a few more dog and cat vaccinations, and I was ready to head out to the not-so-scenic part of the Great State.

Both of us running late, as usual, my dad suggested we fly up in Lizzie. He taxied us down the small, private runway that stretched between the barbed wire fence line of the Rosemeadow Ranch and the S&L Polo Club. Clearing the buffalo pens on the south end of the McKemmy spread, we barely dodged a small flock of geese circling to land in a nearby pond. Then, the plane was aimed into the sun.

"Nice day for flyin'," my dad yelled through the mike. "Maybe we can hunt at dusk." Taking a snooze while he did the flying, an hour later I woke with a start when he yelled, "I'm taking 'er down." He dropped Lizzie's nose and swooped across the roofline of my aunt and uncle's stone house, then climbed again so we could view the screened-in porch that encircled the home. Dipping our wings back and forth, and making a second pass, he said, "I don't see anyone."

"Me neither… I know they're expecting us—maybe they're both over by the windsock."

From the plane, we could see most of the ranch and the nearby canyon walls reflecting amber lights of the setting sun. We shot over the Seven-Star entrance sign, and followed the lone, dirt road that cut a path between the lands where jackrabbits often died of dehydration, and buzzards sucked milk from rattlesnakes to survive. My father yelled again, "It always looks so dry."

There wasn't anyone who didn't describe this place as rugged. Uncle Grump would always laugh, trying to dismiss the myths of living in drought-like conditions, "Hell, son, we get a total of eighteen inches of rain a year. How much more do ya want? It ain't much, but you oughta be here on the night it comes!"

He'd never admit his lifestyle was hard and unchanging. He and my dad chose different paths, but were still alike in many ways. Though a few years older, my uncle always appeared younger. Grump was taller than most in our family. And the daily, rigorous ranch life kept him lean and muscular. With the sensitivity of a cactus leaf on the surface, he was pure mush at heart—just like my dad. The most obvious similarity was their shared talent for complaining about everything—and, this, they made into an art.

My uncle spouted off about the same things on every visit, "It ain't natural," he'd say, lecturing us about the plane we flew, and the helicopters used to run cattle from the underbrush so cowboys could catch them. "Cowpokes ain't suppos't drive whirlybirds. Damn ol' Republicans probably invented those funnylookin' contraptions while I was scratchin' out a livin' from the dust. Ain't right…I'ma tellin' ya! They ain't got no place on my ranch." I never did ask if he meant the plane, a Republican, or the helicopter.

"I'm going down to the strip," my dad said, as he banked toward the area where the earth was flatter than a beaver's tail. I wondered why he came out today, since he seemed so disgruntled, "Some things will never change…your uncle and this place are as predictable as dirt."

Seven-Star passed beneath our wings. The name and cattle brand, 7✫, originally came from my great-grandfather who, supposedly, won the ranch in a poker game. The story goes that he played seven-card stud and called the suit of diamonds 'stars'. We always heard his winning hand was a seven-high flush—and

Uncle Grump swore it to be true. After that, anything and every-thing on the ranch revolved around the number seven, reaching a point of either fun or obsession—depending on who you were.

The cattle brand made sense. But all gates—and there were a whole lot of them—were seven pipes tall. Every sign had to have seven boards. And the miles of fences across the ranch were maintained with seven strands of barbed wire. Even the house had seven doors. There were exactly 70,000 acres, verified by the land title. And though it sounds like an old western song, these acres corralled seven dogs, seven donkeys, 70 horses, seven bulls, 777 cows, and seven water tanks with seven windmills. This whole thing, of course, made gift-giving easy. Last Christmas, Uncle Grump got handmade, porcelain doorknobs for the out-house shaped into the classic '7' shape. Superstitious folks thought this to be the luckiest place on earth—and maybe it was.

After asking my dad if he thought Uncle Grump would have the runway plowed, he just grumbled again, "If that trac-tor of his ain't broke, as usual."

Circling our landing site, I thought of Uncle Grump's mes-sage just before we left Big D. "Get out here quick, son, calves are droppin' like flies from Bang's disease. And, even Jessie, our best Watusi cow, is havin' calvin' problems." After his urgent com-ments, I pictured our fun-time slipping away. Trying to be pre-pared for anything, I rang my brother-in-law, Frank, asking him to drive Ol' Blue to the ranch.

My father hollered again over the mike, "Son, what's this disease he's got out here?"

"Hell, pa, it's a quarantine nightmare, *Brucella abortis* is a bacteria that causes infected blood, spontaneous abortions in cows, and sterility in bulls. The aborted fetus and discharges are contagious, easily transmitted from animal to animal to man. Bulls shed the bacteria in their semen, and cows in their milk. Water supplies and feedstuffs can harbor and spread the disease, too. So carriers or reactors who test positive in blood testing need to be destroyed. There's no effective treatment in a herd situation."

"Damn, that's bad news all the way around…hey, is that Grump's tractor?"

In the middle of the runway, next to the scraggly pumpkin crop, was my uncle's favorite toy…and his huge plowing machine now blocked our path. He waved up to us, cussing and kicking at the tractor tires, while ranch hands struggled to tow the rusty John Deere out of our way. We ended up landing in a cotton patch.

But before we could go on to the ranch, Dad got hoodwinked into helping fix the tractor. When he noticed blood on the back hitch, he asked if anyone was hurt. Uncle Grump tentatively answered, kicking his boots in the dust, "That's cow blood." Then he nudged me with his elbow. "Don't tell anyone, but that's Jessie's blood. Remember I told ya she was havin' calvin' problems? At first, I tried to pull the calf by hand, but it was too stuck. Then I tried to crank it out with that calfjack you left me, but that didn't work, neither. So, then…I used the tractor."

A lump formed in my throat. After all, Jessie's been around a long time. She was a pet. Seeing my worried look, Uncle Grump went on to explain, "She bellared a mite, but she's fine. I still didn't get all of the calf out. Your aunt Sadie made me stop. So I called Maggie's boys from the neighborin' ranch to come help us. They'll meet us at the bunkhouse." I had to ask, "Where's Jessie now?" He said she was resting up in the north corral, by the old barn.

As we rounded the bend to the ranch, two cowboys I've know since grade school, Roper and Scram, were sitting on the porch of the bunkhouse. From the road, I couldn't see Scram's round, stubble-bearded face, or Roper's long, thin legs stretched over the railing of the hitching post. But it was easy to recognize Scram's distinctive garb—a short-brimmed, black derby hat, and wide leather suspenders. Both waved to me, as Scram rocked up against the wall in his straw-seated chair.

Top ranch hands, these two were experts at what they did, and could brand the hide on a gnat without ruffling a hair. But, amiable as they were, neither one seemed to exercise a whole lot of common sense. My uncle was always giving them explicit directions for their work. Or, maybe, the truth of it was they just knew he liked being the boss. Roper tipped his high-crowned, Montana-creased hat toward me, then lazily slipped one leg, then the other, from the post. When I asked, "Have y'all seen Jessie?" Scram said he thought he saw her up by the front gate when they came in.

My uncle snapped at that, "No, I left 'er in the pens." Roper and Scram asked if they needed their horses. "I told ya, no, I've done got 'er penned up."

This was turning out to be a comedy of errors, I could feel it.

The wranglers jumped into the back of the truck with my father and his brother, just as another pickup pulled in with a horse trailer. Maggie's foreman, Rex, had already put in a long day. His long-sleeved, snap-button shirt was soaked with sweat, but he asked if we needed a hand. The numbed thumb on his roping hand told me he could lasso most any steer. "Well, do ya?"

"Have you seen Jessie?" I asked. Pointing in the opposite direction from my uncle's pens, the parched wrangler said, "Sure, over yonder."

What followed next strained what little patience I had left. My uncle insisted we follow him to the barn and the pens. Hundreds of quail were feasting on scattered grain around the empty corral. Of course, Jessie was nowhere in sight because the gate-latch had been left open. This was a typical ranch episode.

When Scram found the partial remains of a calf's forequarters, the decayed fetus had been dead for days. My uncle admitted this, saying he figured she'd been carrying the dead baby for more than a day. After asking Maggie's boys to burn the remains, I urged Rex to find Jessie as quickly as possible.

Rex cinched his blue bandanna over his bushy mustache and sun-baked face, to block the sharp thorns of the mesquite scrubs. With a tug on his grey felt hat, he prodded his beefy horse into a fetching lope. Scram, Roper and I were following the dust of his galloping horse when Rex got a lariat around Jessie's horns. She dragged him through the briars, before stopping by the edge of a pond. There, he dallied his slack around the nearest tree trunk while Scram swung a loop around the furious Watusi's hind-legs. Jessie fought, lunged, bellowed, and kicked as Roper and I watched Rex and Scram cling to their ropes. "We got 'er, Doc," Rex yelled. "But I smelled 'er before I found 'er."

Jessie stopped, flaring her nostrils. And falling on her side, she 'sulled' as dust clouds puffed from her muzzle with the exhale of each angry hot breath. Grabbing a pair of Aunt Sadie's rubber washing gloves from the dashboard, I approached the brindle-colored, 1400-pound, possibly diseased bovine. Rex was right. A foul odor was coming from the discharge of Jessie's vulva. This could be undulant fever, I thought, and Bang's causes undulant fever in man. I didn't know if Jessie had been exposed to Bang's disease, or whether she simply suffered the aftermath of a fetal death and subsequent abortion. It really didn't matter. The Mexican cross-bred cow would die if we didn't extract the remainder of the calf from her womb. "Hold 'er tail, Roper," I said. Then, piece by piece, I methodically removed the remnants from her uterus. Time after time, I reached inside her reproductive tract as far as I could to blindly clutch, scoop, and take out another part of the calf's body. I held my breath to avoid the offensive stench, but Jessie's tail repeatedly slapped me across the face. Her secretions soaked my clothes, as I grunted. "I'm almost done, boys." Scram and Roper held tight, even though sweat hampered their grip, too. I had to make use of my uncle's antibiotic uterine tablets until my own medicines arrived. "That'll do for now. Let's take 'er to the barn. I'll flush 'er out better tomorrow. Cut 'er loose, boys."

We thought Jessie would stand quietly when the rope restraints were released. But her first kick caught Rex on the shin, and the second got Roper in the arm. When her horns swung around, I found myself waist deep in the pond water. "Gimme a'hand," I yelled, trying to scramble up the bank...as my dad and uncle arrive with the cattle trailer.

"Ough wee...you smell bad!" my dad laughed, "Sadie's goin' to make you strip down on the back porch before y'all can come inside." He was right.

Aunt Sadie's cooking gave us time to organize our plans and sit for a spell. After debating on the illness afflicting the herd, we figured that only one-third of the cattle could have been exposed to Bang's disease. Luckily, Jessie wasn't one of them. I also felt better when Frank arrived with my equipment and medicines. It was after midnight, but we were now prepared. Forty or more wranglers would assemble from neighboring ranches, and the roundup would begin at first light.

It had been a long time since I slept in the bunkhouse, and it was already quiet when I bedded down. The cowboys' gear, worn into permanent shapes through years of use in all kinds of weather, lay strewn about. In the moonlight, I could see their veteran horses standing, already saddled and tied to the fence. Every steed was groomed, grained, and watered. Out here, I thought, a cowboy's horse was his livelihood—and the only real priority.

At 5 A.M., the sound of rumbling hooves jarred me awake. From the window, I could see the boys already brushing down their horses. Then, as if time had reversed twenty years, there was sassy ol' Jessie, grazing, as usual, alongside Aunt Sadie's garden. Swirling clouds of dust blew up next to the corral, as a car sped to a stop. Good, I thought, he's here—Dr. Gary Franklin, the Texas State Veterinarian, had been called in to help me blood-test the herd. Uncle Grump and my dad were shaking his hand, as I grabbed my boots, limping out to the porch with one boot halfway on, and one still in my hand. "I'ma comin', y'all," I hollered to the gathering clan.

My uncle yelled out, "Okay, let's run 'em through the chutes." Amid the noise of clashing horns and bellows, cowboys rode in an out of camp pushing the first few hundred cows into the pens.

While the cattle were settling down, an indelible part of ranch life for me—breakfast—was being served on metal plates, and the heady aroma of high-octane coffee filled the air. Charred biscuits popped from the Dutch oven as Dr. Franklin and I took our positions.

Gates slammed, and two different chutes squeezed the first few heifers through in unison. "Git'up thar," wranglers yodeled. One by one, each cow was tested for brucellosis. I drew blood samples from the tail vein, while Dr. Franklin logged and identified each bovine from branded numbers and ear tags.

By noon, we only had two more batches to work. At three o'clock, Casper's black and grey horse tripped in a hole while trying to run down an escaping calf. It was serious. Snake couldn't bear any weight on his injured limb that dangled from the ankle. Dr. Franklin and I felt the fracture. With even the slightest rotation, Snake's fetlock and pastern bones ground together like gravel. We immediately took radiographs with my portable x-ray unit.

The most responsible of the cowpokes, having been with my uncle longer than any of the other hands, Casper sensed the worst and became unusually quiet. His stern, expressionless demeanor revealed the impact this was having on him. No one said a word. Casper and Snake had been partners for eight years, having worked as one. With support and faith in each other, day by day, they had endured the *vaquero* way of life. Casper's dark eyes reflected words each of us left unsaid. Giving Snake pain relievers, we waited for my uncle to come back from the local hospital with the developed pictures.

One look confirmed our diagnosis. Snake's ankle was shattered beyond sound repair. "Casper," I said slowly, "I can cast his leg…but, he'll always be crippled." Each of the men standing there knew what that meant—a chronically lame horse was worthless to a cowboy. "I'm truly sorry," I said, "but there's nothing else I can do."

Casper's eyes lowered beneath his hat brim. Nodding his understanding, he mumbled something as I turned to look for the euthanasia solution in my medicine bag. "No, Doc, I appreciate your concern…but this is 'our way'." With that, he unsaddled Snake, slid his rifle from its sheath, and slowly led his four-legged companion down the rutted canyon path.

This was not a small moment…the horse had been his family, and part of the entire ranch family. As Casper walked passed, with Snake hobbling beside him, each cowhand removed his hat. After a while, from the distance, a single shot was heard.

I knew this was "our way." But my uncle seemed to mourn only for as long as the echo lasted, "Okay, boys, let's get these cattle done…and Casper's goin' to need a new mount." At first I thought him cold and indifferent, until my dad pulled me aside, saying, "He's got an ace in the hole, I'll betcha, son."

When Casper returned, his hat covering his face, my uncle said, "I want you to have one of Silk's colts, if you can catch 'im." Silk Tie was my uncle's favorite Paint stallion. Retired, and still beautiful, he lived with a harem of Quarter Horse mares, and had several wild colts roaming the range. I'd seen their eyes peeping over the lip of the canyon's crest, and knew they'd never been touched by human hands.

At four o'clock, we finished drawing the blood samples and my uncle yelled, "Boys, y'all get goin' after those colts."

As each man rode off into the bright sun, I looked over at Dr. Franklin. "They're tired and they're insane...chasin' colts in that rough canyon terrain is hopeless." But, at the same time, I knew this is what they needed to do for Casper and Snake. This was an abiding ritual of respect.

"We'll see," my uncle said, smiling, then added, "Doc, in the morning, you can castrate whatever colts are brought in. Casper will pick the one he wants, then we'll turn the rest loose." I still couldn't shake the image of Snake's demise, and didn't want to think about the next day's plan.

At dawn, several saddle-weary cowboys and ten untouched two-year-old colts greeted me. The castrations were routine, but administering the anesthetic to rank and resistant wild broncs made me more than a little nervous. Going through this might have been tough, if it were not for the rare ability of the cowhands. The horses fought as they were roped and snubbed against the fence. But the whole process took less than ten minutes for each colt.

Casper's eyes never left one of the black colts. Particularly calm, while the others whinnied and pranced around him, this one had the most promise—and Casper knew it. Making his choice, and calling his new partner 'Gambler'...the longtime wrangler finally smiled for the first time in two days. And, by nightfall, Gambler was under saddle.

When the results were in, sixty-three head of cattle tested positive for Bang's, not as bad as anticipated. Still, we had to separate the 'reactors'. Negative cows were put in holding pens, while positive cows were loaded on a cattle truck destined for humane slaughter. Ear tags and tattoo numbers were used to confirm each animal's status. Not until two negative checks of the entire herd were made could Seven-Star Ranch be released from quarantine.

That evening, I was tired and weary when I said, "Dad, let's go home." The clinic in Dallas would look like a sanctuary after this. My father flew the plane, and, again, I slept most of the way. A lot had been worked out—including, for better or worse, my "attitude adjustment."

It took three months for the restrictions on Seven-Star to be lifted. And my dad called to say that he, Sadie, Grump, Rex, Slim, Scram, and Casper celebrated by playing seven hands of seven-card stud.

Thieving Jack

ooking at his watch, Dr. Vest said, "Hey, let's go to Gerrado's for supper. Call Karen and ask her and K.C. to meet us there. If you and I help Tracy walk the dogs, we can take everyone out to celebrate the end of the week—and Seven-Star's quarantine release. And, Doc…you're buyin'."

When it came to my favorite Italian restaurant, he knew I'd be a pushover. But the large smiles from Tracy and Rachel cinched the deal. I could already taste the honey-mustard dressing on my salad, and smell the hint of garlic in the creamy pesto sauce smothering the succulent shrimp and steaming angel-hair pasta. My real downfall, though, was the bread—warm, long, pull-apart rolls of goodness—the chef's famous golden brown loaf filled with melting Mozzarella cheese. "Okay, let's hurry to beat the crowd."

Karen was elated, too, since she wouldn't have to cook. For once, we could all enjoy a real 'sit-down' dinner. "It doesn't have a drive-through window, so it'll be a change of pace for K.C. We'll meetcha there in thirty minutes," she said.

In anticipation of our gathering, we all moved into high gear to complete the day's tasks. On his way to the kennel, Dr. Vest had to gingerly step over Jack, his ninety-pound golden retriever, who was sprawled out and sleeping in the middle of the hallway. Originally, he brought Jack in to the clinic to serve as a blood donor for a litter of five poodles suffering from hookworm anemia. Only a smidgen of his blood supply was needed to save the tiny puppies from the parasitic blood loss. And he has since remained available for other emergency transfusions. Still, he never takes kindly to the procedures, acting as though they interfere with his naps.

The huge, flop-eared pet was lying with his chin resting on the corner of our wicker toy basket, and his back paws extended out so his pink tummy could lie flat against the cool flooring. When his legs and feathered tail were spread out like this, there wasn't room for anyone to walk by. We should all have it so rough, I thought. Nothing fazed this husky fellow.

"I'll take him with us, too," commented Rich.

I liked giving my partner a bad time about Jack, "Why not just put a DO NOT DISTURB sign on his back. He looks plum tuckered."

Jack knew we were talking about him, but didn't move. With a wide yawn and sigh, he rolled on his side, smacking his lips…and ignoring us.

We all grabbed a leash to walk the kennel dogs. "Doc, you take the Irish setter and I'll walk the beagle," said Tracy. "And Dr. Vest can take the two grey littermates, the weimaraners."

Trekking into the darkening paddock next to the barn, we exercised the boarding dogs, then brought them back to their separate kennel runs. "Let's go. I'm starving," said Rachel, as she locked up.

"Go, Jack, get in the truck," Dr. Vest coaxed. Taking his time, Jack stood up, slowly stretched, and ambled toward the back door, as if to say he wasn't thrilled to be going along. "Hell, don't get yourself rushed," my partner laughed. Then, straining to lift the lazy pooch into the seat, he turned to me, "You'd think we were inconveniencing him. I'd like to drive, if I can ever push this lug out from behind the steering wheel." This was, of course, their ongoing game.

When he was just a pup, my partner's canine companion accompanied him every day. He was either riding in the truck to farm calls or bounding around our Twin Oaks clinic in play. In fact, Jack was better known in town than any of us. He'd go inside or outside the clinic at his own leisure, taking care of his business, or visiting with several owners of neighboring establishments. Patricia Joplin at Russell's Cleaners kept a box of dog biscuits under the counter for him, and Jack knew where they were. If Patty was too busy in the back of the store to talk with him, he'd just help himself—which he seemed to prefer. There were some folks who just wanted to pet his silky, groomed coat, but had no goodies to offer—and our fickle Jack seldom visited them twice. But his best buddy was the manager of the corner movie house. Greg never failed to provide him with a variety of snacks…buttered popcorn being Jack's favorite. And he often took a notion to nap in one of the aisles during a film. But whenever his snoring got too loud, an usher would have to send him home.

This retriever had a lot of character, all right, but I figured his attention wasn't always real. He was, after all, cunning, and knew how to play the game, cultivating friends who had what he wanted. It wasn't unusual to see him trotting through our back door several times a day with a mouthful of treats that he'd leave with Rachel, or to see him taking a post on the school grounds pretending to watch the kids play kickball…then using his abilities to con them into giving him their lunch tidbits. After a while, he'd mosey back to the clinic—mainly to rest up after a day of eating and socializing. If the back door was closed, he'd come around to the front porch and bark until Rachel let him in. I had to admire the big guy's style. He had everyone trained.

Ol' Blue led the caravan of four vehicles to Gerrado's, which was only about a mile down the road, on the same side of the street as Twin Oaks. From my rearview mirror, I could see Jack with his huge paws on the dashboard of my partner's truck, barking recognition whenever he saw people he knew. "Hey, Jack, howya' doin'?" they'd wave back. This was really his town, I thought.

As soon as we stopped, Jack jumped to the ground, sniffing the night air. Then he joyfully dashed off with his tail wagging a mile a minute.

Karen and K.C. were saving us a table next to the open-style, brick kitchen. My son's voice was easy to hear over the clatter of plates. "Look, dad, we can watch the chef cookin'." The maitre d' directed us past the hearth-shaped ovens with sizzling pizzas and other Italian delights. As Anthony Gerrado, the owner, approached our table in his madras tuxedo, my young son slumped in his chair and whispered, "He looks like Mafia." I didn't respond, figuring his imagination would conjure up its own story...and, besides, maybe this thought would keep the restless K.C. on his best behavior.

The short, olive-skinned man greeted us in his broken English, "Good evening, good doctors, what is'a your pleasure?" Spreading his arms apart, and raising his chin in pride, it looked as though he might break into a song. Gerrado's hands moved faster than his lips, and K.C. giggled at the dramatic gestures. Swinging his arms high in the air, this happy-faced, hospitable man said, "You already know we hav'a tha best'a food in town."

"We'll start with your house wine and many Italian loaves," I said.

At this, Gerrado's head bowed, and, cupping his palms together in front of his lips, he mumbled in embarrassment. Shaking his fingers to the heavens, he said, I'ma sorry, but our bakerman...he not'a deliver." He couldn't apologize enough. "He said'a that he come, but there was'a no bread at my door. I'ma sorry...I'ma sorry."

I was, too, since my mouth watered for this treat. "I thought you baked your bread right here," I said.

"No...no...," Gerrado explained. "We hav'a bakerman— he deliver just'a before we open for evening business. When'a I call him, he say bread come, but I say, we hav'a no bread."

Anxious to eat, K.C. said he'd just have the spaghetti. "And I'll have the shrimp ravioli," said Karen. Everyone chimed in with their favorite dish. Gerrado put his fingers to his lips, saying "Excellente!" as he clapped for more waiters to serve us. We were always treated well here, especially tonight, since we'd been deprived of the house bread. The talkative waiters, with white linens draped over their forearms, brought on our simmering plates of tasty selections. After eating until I thought I'd pop, I asked everyone else how they liked their meal. Their silence and body language said it all.

Dr. Vest contentedly patted his stomach, and motioned the waiter with the check toward me, saying, "We forgot to leave Jack in the truck. I've got to go find him." Rachel interrupted, "He's probably back at the clinic, barking on the front porch."

Again, Ol' Blue led our mini-caravan back on down the street, while K.C. perched in my passenger seat. As soon as Twin Oaks came into view, my son hollered out, "There's ol' Jack!" Like everyone else in town, K.C. loved this dog. Sticking his head out the window, he called, "Jack...Jack!" My headlights illuminated the golden dog who calmly sat at our door next to a large brown sack. As soon as we pulled up, K.C. ran from the truck and threw his arms around him. A familiar scent hung in the air.

In addition to his other talents, Jack was, by instinct, a hunter and fetcher. And he liked bringing us the 'catch of the day'. His tail now wagged with the same excitement as he had on the day he brought us his first field mouse—then, the sparrow, and, then...a grass nest of baby bunnies. Of course, they were never harmed. He was just sharing his daily bounty of gifts.

Stepping from their cars, Karen and Tracy almost sang in unison, "Boy, something sure smells good."

After looking inside Jack's sack, my partner said, "It should!"

K.C. smiled broadly when Jack jumped up to lick his cheek. "Oh, dad, he's got cheese on his whiskers, and his breath smells like garlic."

Seeing what was left of Anthony Gerrado's bread delivery, I patted Jack on the head, saying "Good dog, Jack," then passed around the few remaining untouched loaves of culinary perfection.

We decided we didn't wish to be 'accessories' to Jack's crime, nor did we want to deprive future diners of this special delicacy. The truth was always the best course of action, so Dr. Vest was elected to 'spill the beans' the next morning.

Not surprisingly, the big-hearted Gerrado loved the story, saying he was, "…just'a happy Jack hav'a such'a good taste." And he refused to let us pay him for the sack that our hunter had so stealthily whisked away. We heard, too, that the famous restaurateur even enjoyed this story about his 'bread thief', and added the gossip to his regular, animated conversations with patrons.

Now, like Patricia, Greg, and his other fans, Gerrado has fallen under Jack's spell. In a wise move, though, to guarantee the safety of future bread deliveries, he has his chef bake a 'daily special'—one small loaf just for Jack—so it'll be there whenever he's in the mood for Italian.

Racing Mules

My wife's relatives are known to be educated and cultured. My side of the family tree, however, held a different story. When it comes to family characters, my distant cousin Nybil tops the charts, even surpassing our legendary Uncle Grump, in a style as personal and unique as anyone could imagine.

A seventy-year-old single lady, Nybil has always jumped from one interest to another. Her given name was Bethany Elizabeth, but, as a child, she never stopped eating—a nibble here and a nibble there. So my grandpa called her Nybil, and the name stuck.

Fatter than she should be, and as gritty as they come, she never has a problem speaking her mind. The woman is sassy, cantankerous—and, always happy.

When Rachel said she called, I wondered what she could be up to now. Two years back, her passion was exotic goats and cheese making. Last year, miniature horses and potbellied pigs were the rage. And, now…I heard from my dad that racing mules thrilled her. The one mule she already has kicks, bites, and tears up everything in sight.

Rachel heard me grumbling, "God musta recognized his mistake with mules…at least he made them sterile and unable to reproduce." Stopping by the sink to scrub off my hands, I procrastinated about returning Nybil's call. The lingering chemical odors on my hands even reminded me of the scented aerosols that Nybil used to spray on the compost pile next to her garden.

Rachel didn't know what she was in for when she asked, "If mules can't have babies, then where do they come from?" Rich grinned, and I waved him the go-ahead to explain it all…as briefly as he could.

"Let me see," he began, "I'll start at the beginning. A donkey is an ass. A male donkey is called a jack. Thus, a male ass can be called a jackass." Since Rachel was still waiting for more explanation, he didn't disappoint her.

"The female donkey is termed a jenny. Although jacks and jennies are fertile, mules are not. Now, a filly is a sexually immature female horse or donkey. A mare is a sexually mature female horse or jenny, while a stallion is a sexually mature male horse or jack…and, may be referred to as a stud when breeding. A colt is a young stallion, horse, or ass…and a gelding is a castrated horse or jack."

He paused, wondering if Rachel was getting all this—and she nodded her head, so he went on, " A jack bred to a mare horse produces a mule. A female mule is called a molly, and a male mule is a john. But, if a stallion horse is crossbred to a jenny, then the female progeny is called a henny."

At this point, Rachel asked him to forget the long lesson. Dr. Vest's run-through was correct. However, thinking I'd like to add to her confusion, I said, "Okay, then follow this. A henny is sterile and usually crazy, so isn't desired. But, remember, a john can't breed a henny because both are sterile. A molly can't breed a stallion horse because she's sterile. Yet, a horse, mare or stallion, can breed an ass, jenny or jack, and produce a mule. See? It's simple."

Pretending to pull out her hair, Rachel asked what was so special, then, about racing mules. Dr. Vest took up the gauntlet again. "Racing mules are a breed within themselves. They're similar to the racing Quarter Horse—what we call appendix bred —or, part Thoroughbred. They are taller, longer, and leaner than the true breed. Racing mules are narrow-chested and broad-butted, yet their ears give their heritage away. Quarter Horse starting-gates are used, but the mules' ears must adapt."

Then I finished, "They make the 'hee haw' sound rather than the 'neigh' sound. Sometimes their ears extend through the bars on the gates, like they're listening to the crowd. But once the race begins, they'll fold 'em backwards like a jackrabbit's in full stride."

Rachel had had enough, and asked Tracy if we were joking.

Tracy said, "Nope, it's astonishing to see them flying down the track. Mules are extremely fast, especially when you consider they're runnin' on bush-tracks or scrub-dirt surfaces of non-sanctioned raceways. They're a hoot to watch!"

"And who in blazes would race 'em?" asked Rachel.

"Doc's cousin, Nybil," Tracy laughed.

I never knew why it always took Nybil so long to get to the phone. Answering my call on the tenth ring, as usual, she shouted, "Sonny…is that you?" Nybil never called me by my name. "Junior, speak up. Y'know I'm deaf in my left ear. Are ya there?"

"Switch the receiver to the other side," I shouted back.

"Damn phone company oughta know I'm left-handed. I can hear ya, now. Darlin', I need for ya to come out to my place. I buy'd me a prize."

She didn't know that I'd already heard, and that two of her neighbors even called Twin Oaks to complain. So, I listened.

"Yep, Sugar…I went to the mule sale." She sounded more pleased than a peach-orchard sow. "Bubba, I bought me some mules…racin' mules."

That's Nybil for you, I thought. She's worth a bloody fortune, but prefers to drive her '52 Ford pickup to the grocery store, rather than her Mercedes. Every day, she dresses in the same railroad-type, navy coveralls. I'd never seen her in anything else, except for one time, years ago, when she wore a black dress to a family wedding.

The front of Nybil's home on White Rock Lake was immaculate, with a groundskeeper tending to the landscape. But her barn out back was a hovel of decaying boards. She didn't care that this was the most exclusive part of Dallas. Priceless, antique furniture decorated the inside of her enormous abode, but each piece was carefully covered with sheets and bedspreads —so her two dozen cats could roam free throughout the entire house. During my last visit, I did checkups on eight potbellied piglets being cared for in her den, as well as a quarrelsome yellow parrot in the kitchen.

Nybil had purchased an entire ghost town in Colorado because of the "good trout fishin' nearby." She didn't have a high opinion about some of her wealthy neighbors, and accused them of being eccentric. Yet, Nybil used her swimming pool to raise catfish.

"Oh, Buddy, you shoulda been at the sale," she crowed. "The deal was so good—I had to buy two. Named 'em Too High and Too Low. Ya see, I paid too much for one, and too little for the other." Then, laughing, she asked, "When can you see 'em? Honey, speak up."

Beginning to enjoy this, in spite of myself, I said, "Two. TWO O'CLOCK. Two P.M. Put the phone on your right ear."

"Dear, you don't hav't yell. We'll be waitin'."

When I arrived, Nybil had her lanky mules tied to a new, green and white horse trailer parked alongside her pool's cabana. Too High and Too Low were identical: sorrel, sixteen hands tall, four white socks, long eared, and matching stars on their foreheads. "Ain't they gorgeous, Bud," she bragged. "When I grow up, I'm gonna be their jockey."

I pictured her hefty, 250-pound frame sitting on a poor mule's back, her stubby round legs reaching for the stirrups, and the tiny leather saddle pushed by weight into the animal's U-shaped sway. "Yeah, they're purdy…but what's all this regalia?"

Too High and Too Low were harnessed in saddlebred show bridles and silver bits. Their withers sagged with a horse-shoe-array of roses, but Nybil thought them stylish. I was there to check them for soundness, and it was obvious they were healthy and had patient dispositions. She then displayed the gold satin 'coolers' she had special-ordered from Kentucky's premier maker of fine blankets.

After jogging the mules as part of their examination, I stopped to rest a moment. Patting each mule on the rump, Nybil said, "Well, Buckwheat, you'll see 'em run again on race-day, plenty fast. Next Sunday, I'll come a callin' 'bout ten. Ten o'clock. Now, you be ready, ya hear?" She gave me no choice. As I climbed back into Ol' Blue, she had the last word, "And you be sure to wear what I send ya."

Her package came to Twin Oaks on Friday. And Tracy and Dr. Vest made strange faces when I lifted a luminous, lime-green sport coat from the white box. Reluctantly, I had to admire the detailing and embroidered stitching of a mule's head on the jacket's pocket. "Damn, this is ugly," I muttered…then tried to imagine what Sunday might bring.

* * * * *

Bounding from the back seat of a white stretch limousine, Nybil was raring to go, flapping her arms like a sparrow in a headwind, and yelling, "Hey, Docterie…let's fly." Her excitement was infectious. Though I still felt like a fool, sitting on our front porch swing, dressed in calfskin boots, denim jeans, white shirt, black felt hat—and the fluorescent green 'mule-head' coat.

"Let's go," she hollered. "We're gonna be late." I took a double-take at Nybil, short and round, dressed in a pink antebellum gown with matching floppy-brimmed lace hat, and elbow-length velvet gloves. This sweet character looked like a melon in a sunflower patch. "Sport, are ya ready?" I nodded, and Cleo, her driver, dropped a red carpet-like floor mat on the ground as I quickly ducked into the sedan.

Maybe nobody will see me behind the dark-tinted glass, I thought, but I should have known better than to underestimate my cousin. She had friends in high places. And, to my surprise, we stopped to pick up two state senators, in their 'mule-head' coats, along with their wives decked out in southern-belle costumes. They gave me an enthusiastic greeting, saying, "You must be Doc…we've heard so much about you."

Now I really felt foolish. "Howdy," I replied. "Are y'all ready for the race?"

As the two couples settled into the car, Nybil pointed to a small brown keg between the seats, "Hand me that jug of moonshine." After taking a big sip from the spout, she squeezed her hoop skirt through the door, commanding, "Drive on, Cleo. Turn right on the highway and left on Old Settlers Road. Hurry, we've only got a few minutes."

As we rumbled across the cattle guard leading down to the track, Cleo asked where he should park. "In the shade, son. Lord knows, us fat women don't want to sweat," said Nybil as she slapped Senator J.P. Powers on the back, offering him a sip from her jug. Then, as we all stepped out of the cool vehicle, Nybil ordered, "Now, y'all follow me, but watch your step, 'cause there's fire ants and buffalo chips along the way."

We had special 'Reserved Seating'. Temporary bleachers at the finish line had been pulled by tractor from the Little League baseball park across the pasture. For luck, Nybil tossed a fistful of salt on the ground in front of Too High's and Too Low's starting positions. Then, she dashed off a pinch over her own shoulder.

The track, muddy and wet, was a wide strip cut evenly around the edge of the grass field, with cone-shaped pylons outlining the racing turf boundary. Most of the people in attendance watched either from the infield, or from the hoods of their cars and trucks.

Too High and Too Low weren't predicted to win, since both had lost in their previous qualifying heats. But, since Nybil had money to spend, her mules were allowed to race in the finals.

Excitement began swelling from the crowd as twelve mules strolled toward the paddocks. Nybil cheered, almost hysterically, when her two mules strutted past the grandstand. And, at the same time, she waved and cursed the jockeys on the other mounts.

The owners thoroughly enjoyed heckling one another. As we dusted dead crickets off our seats, Nybil yelled, "Ned, you might as well take your 'ass' home. And, Benny, your mule couldn't out-run a chicken. Hey, you, Bobby Jo, your mule has cement hooves." She had them where she wanted them. When a long-haired trainer, whom I didn't know, asked her to "…put up or shut up," she was ready.

"Come and get it," was her retort, as she began spreading a fistful of hundred-dollar bills across the empty seat in front of us. I'd seen bundles of bills before, but never a stack of C-notes that would match this. Cleo, now doubling as Nybil's bookmaker, collected the wagers. My mouth fell open. He began dropping wads of cash into a paper bag, like I'd drop pennies into a piggy bank. One handful…then, another. Just a nod and a handshake sealed a bet. Cleo, very calm and apparently a pro at this, did not write anything down.

The signaling for the 'Call to Post' was sounded by a pickup's horn. Too Low drew the number nine spot, while Too High slipped into the fourth starting gate. Nybil doubled the odds. Every mule, except Too High, was ready to run. The flow of cash tripled.

Too High's ears twisted between the bars on the head-gate

when he heard Nybil's voice. He seemed to be listening to her as she argued with another owner who wanted ten-to-one odds. "I'll betcha," he said, "your two motley mules won't rank even 'place' or 'show'. My mule will win."

"I'll take that bet," Nybil hustled, "and raise ya…another thousand," This one bet stood at $20,000. I began to wonder what could be in that moonshine. Pawing the ground, Too Low packed the salt into the soles of his hooves. And Nybil, now on a roll, said, "Teddy, make that another ten grand." The amount, $30,000, was more than a country vet makes in a year. Cleo nodded, and they all shook hands. "Let 'em run," Nybil hollered, clearly in control, "Let 'em go!"

Too Low heard the hammer cock on the starter's pistol. Slamming his ears down flat, he anticipated the loud gunshot. POP! When the gate flew open, he bolted from the steel cage, slid to the inside rail, and muscled his way to the lead. Too High cautiously ducked at the sound of the bullet, then his ears sprang straight up when he realized the race had begun. He began slipping and sliding. I gasped when Too High nudged and bumped his way into last place. I found myself yelling, "Run!" as hooves slapped the splashing puddles, blinding his chances. "Let him through," I urged, when the rumps of the other mules formed a wall of showering muck in front of him. I hope he's a sleeper, I thought, looking at Cleo's bag filled with cash, and figuring that Nybil would lose. "Run," I choked.

My cousin leaned over to me. "Now, don't you fret, Junior. He hates gettin' mud in his face," she said, as Too High darted from the outside and fell even further behind. Nybil's senator-friends groaned.

"Watch his ears," Nybil said. "Watch!" Too Low was still leading, and his ears were flat. Too High was last, and his ears were erect. On the back stretch, I noticed that every mule, except Too High, had its ears pinned back. I couldn't figure this out.

Suddenly, Nybil stood up, took off her gloves…and said, "Watch this." With two fingers stuck in the corners of her mouth, she whistled in a piercing pitch. One blast…then, two. On the third whistle, Too High dropped to the inside. And Two Low's jockey log-jammed the pack with a slowing pace. Immediately, Too High's ears flattened down as he snorted mud and shot the gap, in the last turn, to head for home at full-out speed.

Teddy screamed, "Foul! Foul!" as Too High and Too Low crossed the finish line—first and second.

Nybil bellowed, "All's fair in love and mule racin'. Besides, your mule ran seventh." Teddy had no comeback. After losing both the race and his bet, he must have figured there was no way to debate a woman who was kissing senators in celebration, and patting every other cowpoke's rear.

"Cleo, get the camera," instructed Nybil, as she draped the winner's wreath over the limousine's hood. "Wait just a minute, here," she said, climbing into the long chariot and emerging from the sunroof to show off her robust cleavage stuffed with hundred-dollar bills. "Okay, I'm ready now…snap this," she dared, as cameras went off all around her.

I thought—only Nybil. Only she could take mules' ears, politicians, and costumes…and turn a Sunday morning into a day of Mardi Gras adventure. I wondered, then, what she'd do with her winnings, what her next passion would be—and what would I do with this abominable coat.

A few months later, I called cousin Nybil. Again, she answered her phone on the tenth ring. "Nybil, wear what I sentcha," I said, "and K.C. and I will pick you up at one o'clock on Saturday for the Little League baseball game."

"That'll be fine," she said, "and you don't hav't shout. Where's the game?"

"Next to the mule track." I shouted.

Driving the same route as we did on her Sunday race, we again went across the cattle guard leading down to the diamond-shaped turf.

Taking her seat of honor in the reserved bleachers, Nybil couldn't resist, "I hope you spent my money wisely, Junior. After all, you know baseball's my latest love. How do the boys look?"

"See for yourself," I said, pointing to the nine revved-up young men with bats and gloves, jogging on to the field in their brand new, green and white uniforms...with a large, mono-grammed, iridescent 'M' reflecting from their caps.

It did my heart good to see Nybil so ecstatic. Snubbing down the cap I'd sent her, she yelled, "Play ball!" Her smile said it all. "This is the best idea I ever had, Honey. We're going to win. Watch!" Then, with her arms stretched to the sky, she hollered to everyone, "Let's do the wave." Bounding up and down, her broad frame shook the grandstands. And her stomping feet struck the wooden planks with loud, reverberating rumbles.

As the game progressed, Nybil became hoarse hollering, "Strike him out, Baby." Throwing a kiss from her bright red lips to K.C., who stood at second base, then waving to the team's coach, she asked, "Who's that?" She didn't recognize Rich in the green 'mule-head' jacket. "Who's the coach of my new team?"

"That's Dr. Vest," I said. "Doesn't he look grand?" Unable to control herself, she giggled, "He looks more like a jackass, if you're askin' me."

Her new team of 'two-legged' mules won their first game with a final score of 23 to 2. With Nybil's brand of magic always working, what else could we have expected?

Foaling a New Year

oc…Doc…are you okay?" Rachel was calling from the barn door. "I was on my way home from the party, and saw the lights on…then, your truck. It's three o'clock in the morning, New Year's day… what are you doin'?"

Sitting in the corner of a stall, gently stroking the six-hour-old filly's neck, I motioned for Rachel to be quiet, and tried not to move myself. I slipped the newborn's pink muzzle away from where it nestled in the crook of my arm. The small head was now resting on my lap as her eyes half-opened from the exhaustion of the night's events. I laid her cheek on the soft, wooden shavings, and tried crooning her to sleep, "Whoa, little girl. You don't hav't worry. Whoa." Her eyelids closed, then quickly opened. Her head began to snuggle, then rose up again. "Whoa, I'm not goin' to let anything happen to ya, little gal…rest now." While I stroked her mane, she nudged into the velvety pine chips with her small rump, and sighed deeply like a fawn napping in the warmth of the sun. Her eyes blinked as moist droplets trickled down her nose.

Rachel stood there perplexed, as I gingerly slid the stall door open, then tried to explain why this had been an unusual night. "Sleep, baby...sleep," I cooed over my shoulder. Walking Rachel down the aisle, I said, "Let's talk softly, she's had a rough start."

Rachel still looked befuddled, although she wasn't surprised to see me at the clinic, even at this time of morning. She didn't understand what had happened, since, only a few hours earlier, all was normal. She and Tracy had left to get dressed for the New Year's party we'd all been invited to. And she'd seen me in a tuxedo, ready to go on ahead of them.

Her long, sleeveless silver-sequined gown blew in the warm morning breeze. Noticing that I wasn't myself, she also saw the aftermath of an emergency with its array of medical supplies strewn about. Looking at my blood-spattered coveralls over my white shirt and black bow tie, she asked again, "What happened?"

In my pocket was a paper requesting the filly's euthanasia. But I didn't have the heart to tell everything to Rachel... especially on New Year's day. I simply said that I was called away from the party, and that the sorrel baby was an orphan, but, "...at least she's alive."

I needed time to think...and the foal needed time to grow stronger. Walking back to the stall, I said, "Shrimp...I've nicknamed her Shrimp, but her real name is Cool Act."

The foal wiggled into the corner covered with shavings, where she and I had spent these past few hours together. Then Shrimp snorted and her eyes opened.

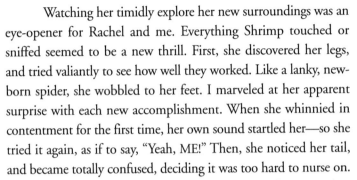

Watching her timidly explore her new surroundings was an eye-opener for Rachel and me. Everything Shrimp touched or sniffed seemed to be a new thrill. First, she discovered her legs, and tried valiantly to see how well they worked. Like a lanky, newborn spider, she wobbled to her feet. I marveled at her apparent surprise with each new accomplishment. When she whinnied in contentment for the first time, her own sound startled her—so she tried it again, as if to say, "Yeah, ME!" Then, she noticed her tail, and became totally confused, deciding it was too hard to nurse on.

I'd birthed a thousand foals, yet never really stopped to watch them 'imprint' their senses. She cuddled to me so much, that I must have smelled like the mare. Studying her reflection in the water trough, her tongue darted in and out at the cool liquid. But watching her learn to nurse from a formula bottle was the most engaging sight. Shrimp tried to suckle my finger, the toes of my boots, and my sleeve before she found the flavor of milk escaping from the end of the rubber nipple that I'd coated with honey. Her first urination scared her to death, and she bucked and ran from the gushing noise. Of course, yawning, stretching, and nursing soon became favorite things—whenever she wasn't nuzzling me, her mother.

This was a serious dilemma, I thought. How could I put her to sleep? Rachel whispered, "Doc, she looks so healthy. What are you *not* tellin' me?"

With both of us now sitting in the shavings, cuddling Shrimp, I took a deep breath and related the night's adventure. "Cooper Naples called me from Rock Bottom Stables on his cell phone." Rachel ran her fingers through Shrimp's forelock while she listened. "Moonbeam Lady, Alison Mercer's Quarter Horse

mare was suffering from colic. So, I left the party in a hurry."
Shrimp licked the back of Rachel's hand, and she tickled the foal's
tiny ears.

"At the farm, I found Moonbeam 'down' in the pasture.
Mrs. Mercer was worried sick, and Cooper had just arrived with
his horse trailer. Pain relievers were of little use. When I rectally
palpated Moonbeam, I found two potentially fatal problems.
First, there was an obstructive mass blocking her small intestine.
And as I examined the structures of the pregnant uterus, I felt
a torsion in the uterine horn."

Pausing to pick up a towel to be more graphic, I put the
stall's salt-block in the center of the cloth. Holding each end of
the fabric, I twirled and spun the block like a mixer, until the
churning action twisted the towel. Rachel gasped, "The baby was
trapped?"

I'd assumed that Moonbeam, in the process of rolling on
the ground to fight off the pains of the impaction, had flipped
the fetus and twisted the uterine horn—entrapping her foal.
"There was no way out of the womb."

Rachel, truly concerned, asked, "What did you do then?"
I told her that I gave Moonbeam a massive amount of IV fluids and pain relievers to stabilize her condition. "I also knew full
well that surgery was her only hope, so I asked Cooper to drive
her to the clinic right away. Then, the rest of the night was something of a blur."

Rachel filled the foal's bottle with milk, waiting for her
to nurse. Snickering as Shrimp noisily slurped, she also cringed
a little when the filly drooled on her sequin gown. Then, smiling over at me with a maternal wink, she said, "Go on…"

"Anyway, from then on, I've felt torn between a rock and a hard place. Prolonged surgery on the ailing mare would abort or kill the baby, and possibly both could die. And to sacrifice the mare for the foal would result in the same. Maybe, I thought, I could do a C-section—but that would take too long."

It was now early dawn, and Rachel laid her head down next to Shrimp, imprinting her soothing sounds on the newborn…as I continued.

"Cooper pulled to a screeching halt out front, here. When I opened the trailer door, Moonbeam fell to the ground with her last breath. All we could do was watch her crater and die. For a split second, I thought a good vet and a good doctor were the same. I had no control over death, but could fight for life. It was too late to move her the last few yards into the clinic. So, with my scalpel at hand, I quickly cut the mare's lead rope loose from the trailer wall, sliced through Moonbeam's belly muscles, and incised into the uterus. Rachel…I plunged into the depths of her abdominal cavity with bare hands…and grasped the lifeless body inside with every ounce of my being."

"When Cooper and Alison asked, 'Won't the baby be dead?' I didn't even take the time to answer 'em. I ran into the clinic with Shrimp clutched in my arms and, wrappin' her in a blanket, vigorously tried to massage the warmth of life into her bones. Cupping my hands over her nostrils, I dilated her lungs with what breath I had. 'C'mon, girl,' I begged, running an endotracheal tube down her windpipe. And, in the focus of the moment, I paid no mind to Cooper and Alison. With one hand, I turned on the oxygen—and with the other, stripped away placental tissues."

Rachel held the filly close. Then they both snoozed…as I went on talking. Shrimp opened one eye, listening to me babble. And I wondered, who's nurturing whom? "Shrimp, you stopped breathing twice. Your heart skipped more beats than mine, then, stopped."

When I revived the foal for the third time, Mrs. Mercer said, "Doc, let 'er go."

And Cooper Naples agreed, "She'll never be no good, Doc…she'll be a 'dumby'. Give it up…"

With one last thump on the foal's chest, I pleaded, "Gimme a chance."

As if Shrimp understood my words, she pawed a little at the straw. Looking down at her, I whispered, "About that time, you coughed…and spit my trach-tube clear across the room. And, then, you tried to stand, as if to defy their very words."

Raising an orphan would take countless hours, and frequent feedings. Alison Mercer worked full-time, and had two young children. Cooper had no interest in staying up night after night. I understood their positions, but…money was also a factor. A 'nurse-mare' would be expensive, and Alison didn't have the coin to spare. Besides, they both knew there were no guarantees. We'd all seen orphaned foals live a short time, then die—even after the best of care.

Alison was a kind, gentle woman—but, practical. She had to be. Moonbeam had no pedigree, and Cool Act would never be able to replace the cost of her upbringing. Fairness was not the question. We were down to the nitty-gritty of dollars and cents. As sad as Alison felt at her decision, I had to respect her wishes. In a tightened voice, she said, "Doc, I'm in a real jam.

I've got to cut my losses." Then, she left me alone—with the permission slip in my pocket, signed and dated.

Empty oxygen tanks, used IV bags, heating pads, feeding tubes, and bottles of medications dotted the barn aisle. For hours, I'd worked toward this end. I thought about the Olympic athlete who trains for years, then loses the race. For personal reasons, I compared my 'practice' career and this New Year's morning to such an event. I was a 'vet' running a race. I'd be a 'good doctor' when the race was done.

Rachel opened her eyes when I reached in my pocket to take out the euthanasia permit. "What's that?" she asked, as Shrimp pushed her muzzle into Rachel's neck. I finally showed her the form, but she couldn't believe it. "Oh, no…Doc, no…"

Leaving her and Shrimp in the stall, I said I'd be back in a minute. I was preparing myself for business, but each step I took toward the clinic seemed to echo the 'lub-dub' of my pounding heart. In our pharmacy, I reached for the solution—but my palms turned clammy. Instead, I reached for the phone…

When Alison Mercer answered, I paused to catch my breath. "Alison, if I can save the filly…can I have 'er?"

My steps and my heartbeats sounded different when I walked back to the barn. Rachel stared at me, hugging Shrimp's neck so tight that the foal whinnied. "Well?" she asked.

"Will you turn *my* horse loose?" I said.

"*Your* horse?" gulped Rachel.

"Hey," I said, now feeling great…and patting my new filly on her brow. "I've been through just about everything in this profession, Rachel, but, ya know…this filly got to me in ways I never expected. Happy New Year!"

A week later, Rachel had a bunch of messages. "Don't you dare sit down, Doc. Uncle Grump is on line 1, A.J.'s on line 2, and Pete's on line 3. Have y'all spayed Caitlin Jasper's cat yet? Is Bogart ready to go home? And are Dr. Vest and Tracy in the barn?"

"And what is Shrimp doin' outside? Did you feed her?"

"Yes, I fed Shrimp. She's outside runnin' the fence. You'd think that filly was practicin' for the race of a lifetime." I loved watching her prance across the paddock...and I couldn't help thinking, again, how this spirited creature really did bring new meaning into my life and work.

Answering each phone call, while simultaneously packing my medicine bag, I heard Rachel's voice ring out, "Aren't you?"

"Ain't I what?"

She asked, "...going to practice for a lifetime?"

The answer was simple. "Yep!"